Canyoneering the Northern San Rafael Swell

CANYONEERING

THE NORTHERN SAN RAFAEL SWELL

STEVE ALLEN AND JOE MITCHELL

THE UNIVERSITY OF UTAH PRESS
Salt Lake City

The Defiance House Man colophon is a registered trademark
of the University of Utah Press. It is based on a four-foot-tall Ancient
Puebloan pictograph (late PIII) near Glen Canyon, Utah.

Library of Congress Cataloging-in-Publication Data
Allen, Steve, 1951-
  Canyoneering the northern San Rafael Swell / Steve Allen and Joe Mitchell.
    p. cm.
  Includes bibliographical references.
  ISBN 978-1-60781-238-8 (pbk. : alk. paper)
  ISBN 978-1-60781-239-5 (ebook)
1. Canyoneering—Utah—San Rafael Swell—Guidebooks. 2. San Rafael Swell
(Utah)—Guidebooks. I. Mitchell, Joe, 1969- II. Title.
  GV199.42.U82S264 2013
  796.52'409792—dc23

                                        2012047313

Cover photo courtesy of Ryan Choi.

Frontispiece: A nameless squeeze in the northern San Rafael Swell.

Printed and bound by Sheridan Books, Inc., Ann Arbor, Michigan.

Contents

FOREWORD

It became apparent several years ago that the first edition of *Canyoneering: The San Rafael Swell* was woefully out of date. Much of the original research for the book had been done in the 1970s and '80s and so much had changed in the San Rafael Swell. In the early days we were out there on those bumpy and dusty back roads all by ourselves. There were few signs, there were actually not that many roads, and, in reality, there were not that many people who were interested in the area.

The completion of Interstate 70 made the traveling public aware of this mostly unheard of area. Who could not be affected by what one saw from the rest stops and overlooks along the interstate, and how many wondered what was just out of sight? My twin brother, Ace, and I definitely wondered and that began our love affair with the Swell. And so, too, was it the start for many. Years of hiking in the San Rafael Swell culminated with the publication of the first edition of this book.

But, the changes on the land were happening way faster than I would have thought. Old and barely noticeable roads were upgraded, and with the final completion of the Interstate, the mileposts were rearranged. The biggest change was the influx of off-road vehicles (ORVs). Cattle trails became ORV highways (the Devils Racetrack); once quiet areas became ORV play areas (Coal Wash, Factory Butte, Temple Mountain); and once remote areas became accessible to ORVS (the Eastern Reef, lower Muddy Creek). I very much wanted to do an update, but work on a large history research and writing project (*Utah's Canyon Country Place Names: Stories of the cowboys, miners, pioneers, and river runners who put names on the land*) was taking all of my time. Bruce Roberts (1949–2010) at the University of Utah Press suggested that I meet Joe Mitchell and talk to him about doing the update.

Photo courtesy Ryan Choi.

I knew Joe by reputation and through his work coauthoring the book *The Hayduke Trail* (University of Utah Press, 2005), which I had been very impressed with. Joe agreed to do the update.

A couple of years later, when I received Joe's manuscript for my approval, I was astounded. It was so much more detailed than the original, and, I daresay, so much more accurate. Joe not only hiked all of the original routes, he also developed many of his own. Unfortunately some of the old hikes had to be left out of this second edition—even such great ones as my hikes #29: The Best Views in the Swell and #30: The Devils Racetrack, Bullock Draw, and the Golden Gate—because the area is now an ORV playground. Joe has an interesting eye for country, and though some old hikes had to be dropped, his new hikes add new and welcome dimensions to the book. Joe has done a yeoman's job with the second edition. I hope you, the reader, will enjoy it as much as I do. Happy hiking in the San Rafael Swell.

—STEVE ALLEN

ACKNOWLEDGMENTS

When I started doing the field research for the guide, I knew no one in Southern Utah. After a year in the San Rafael Swell, I found I had made dozens of friends.

To the store owners in Price, Green River, and Hanksville who always had a word of encouragement and a moment to chat, thank you.

To the Bureau of Land Management personnel in Price and Hanksville, thank you for sharing your love of the San Rafael Swell with me, offering advice, and taking time out from a busy schedule to discuss routes and canyons.

To Wendy Chase, an extraordinary adventure partner, I have to thank you a hundred times over for hiking several of the routes, helping edit the manuscript (for the original guide), providing untiring support above and beyond the call of duty, and otherwise being instrumental in seeing this project to fruition.

To Ann Perius-Parker, thank you for providing several of the pictures, printing all the black-and-white photographs (for the original guide), and joining me for several weeks in the Swell.

To Trish Lindaman, thank you for your unflagging support and for drawing the maps (for the original guide).

To Jan Fenner, thank you for proofreading the manuscript (for the original guide).

To Lynn Jackson of the Moab Area BLM office, thank you for allowing me to include your geology cross-section chart.

To the many hikers who shared routes with me, thank you. My brother Ace was in on the project from the beginning and hiked several of the routes. Lou, my father, joined me on several occasions. It is due to him that many of the routes suitable for seniors are included in the guide. My young friends Jessica and Adrian Upham and Erin and Andy Sobick added a new dimension to the way I look at canyon country. They are responsible for the inclusion of many of the routes that youthful adventurers will enjoy. Mike Enos, Jonathan Rapp, Doug Sundling, Bill and Lynn Booker, and Bert Fingerhut joined me on backcountry excursions and offered criticism and advice.

Joe Bauman, author of *Stone House Lands*, added panache to the hikes we did together and introduced me to the University of Utah Press.

A cast of characters helped in essential ways. They include Ron and Sue Russel, Jim and Deborah Nickelson, Rick and Beverly Upham, Kris Patrick, Bob Wetzel, Tom Weinreich, and Wayne Ludington.

Special thanks goes to my mother, Ruth (1919–2011), a desert rat for fifty years, who encouraged me every step of the way.

—STEVE ALLEN

My first exposure to the glorious canyon country of Southern Utah was through the rear window of the family station wagon. I was just a young kid at the time, but I was paying close attention. This was while on one of the many unforgettable road trips that my parents hauled my five siblings and me on during the 1970s. It was also on one of these great family adventures that I first donned a backpack as we hit the trail for an overnight trip into the High Uintas Wilderness in Northern Utah. I was four years old and I was instantly hooked. To my parents, Col. Corless and Linda Mitchell, my undying gratitude for introducing us to the art of travel and for making us feel at home in the natural world. Thank you for encouraging me to explore the Great Outdoors and for instilling in me the confidence to create and embark on my own adventures.

When I moved to Utah more than twenty years ago it was with my cousin, Scott Nielsen, that I began to explore the redrock wilderness. Thank you, Scott, for showing me around some of your favorite places and for all of the hilarity that only you could provide.

One of the first guidebooks I bought upon my arrival to Utah was Steve Allen's *Canyoneering: The San Rafael Swell*. I have used this book well over the many years and it is my own tattered and dog-eared copy that I used for reference to write this revision. Thank you, Steve, for creating this wonderful work and for the tremendous amount of effort it took to unlock the mysteries of the Swell and present them to the public. I am honored and humbled that you chose me to undertake this project.

To Peter DeLafosse, acquisitions editor at the University of Utah Press, thank you for allowing me to juggle this work around my guiding schedule and for your patience as this project dragged on.

To Mark Silver of iGage Mapping Corporation, maker of All Topo Maps Software, thank you for all of your help in producing the map plates and elevation profiles for this guide. I couldn't have done it without you. To me you are the Yoda of cartography.

To Ryan Choi, thank you for allowing me to use some of your incredible photographs in this guide. I've enjoyed traipsing around the Swell with you and look forward to many more adventures to come.

To Mike Pfotenhauer of Osprey Packs, Inc., thank you for supplying me with the best packs on the planet. I am grateful for your support on this project as well as on my previous endeavors. (Steve Allen's note: My thanks, too, to Osprey Packs for supporting not only me, but Utah Wilderness as well.)

Thank you to my precious daughters, Lily and Iris, for allowing your daddy to be gone so much and for always showering me with so much affection when I return home.

Most importantly, thank you to my best friend and wife, Rachel, for your unselfish support during this and other projects. Thank you for holding all of the pieces together while I have been away for so many months. I could have never done it without you.

—Joe Mitchell

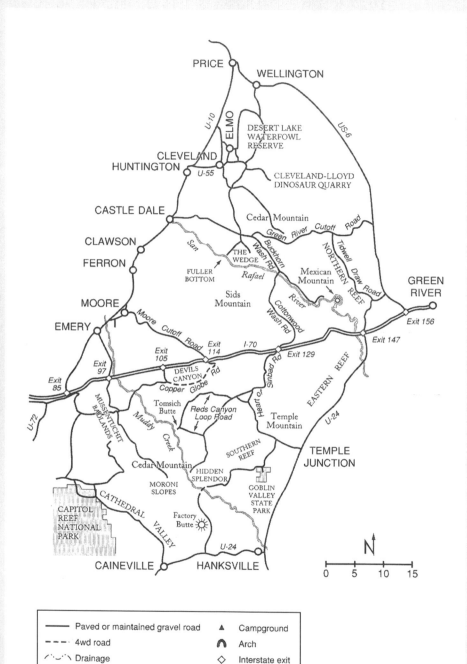

PRICE

WELLINGTON

U-10

ELMO

DESERT LAKE
WATERFOWL
RESERVE

US-6

CLEVELAND
HUNTINGTON

U-55

CLEVELAND-LLOYD
DINOSAUR QUARRY

CASTLE DALE

Cedar Mountain

Green River Cutoff Road

CLAWSON

San

THE
WEDGE

Buckhorn Wash Rd

NORTHERN REEF

Tidwell Draw Road

FERRON

FULLER
BOTTOM

Rafael

Mexican
Mountain

GREEN
RIVER

MOORE

Sids
Mountain

River

Cottonwood Wash Rd

Exit 156

EMERY

Moore Cutoff Road

Exit
114

I-70

Exit 147

Exit
105

Exit 129

Exit
97

DEVILS
CANYON Rd

Heart of Sinbad Rd

EASTERN REEF

Exit
85

Copper Globe

Tomsich
Butte

Reds Canyon
Loop Road

Temple
Mountain

U-24

U-72

MISSENTUCHIT BADLANDS

Muddy Creek

SOUTHERN
REEF

TEMPLE
JUNCTION

Cedar Mountain

HIDDEN
SPLENDOR

MORONI
SLOPES

GOBLIN
VALLEY
STATE
PARK

CAPITOL
REEF
NATIONAL
PARK

CATHEDRAL VALLEY

Factory
Butte

U-24

N

CAINEVILLE

HANKSVILLE

0   5   10   15

—— Paved or maintained gravel road   ▲ Campground

---- 4wd road   ∩ Arch

⌒⌒ Drainage   ◇ Interstate exit

☼ Peak, knoll or high point   ⑰ Start of hike

⊙ Point of interest   — Air strip

■ Building

INTRODUCTION

I love wild canyons—dry, fragrant, stone-walled, with their green-chocked niches and gold-tipped ramparts.

—Zane Grey

The San Rafael Swell is located in the northern part of what is commonly referred to as Utah's canyon country. Its neighbors are Canyonlands National Park to the southeast and Capitol Reef National Park to the southwest. The area is further bounded on the east by the San Rafael Desert, on the northeast by the West Tavaputs Plateau, and by the Wasatch Plateau to the west. It is a varied and complex 1.2 million acres of seemingly endless expanses of slickrock, stunning vistas, deep canyons, high walls, arches, pinnacles, towers, mesas, and mountains. Several small rivers and seasonal streams, welcome ribbons of lively green, also run through the Swell. It is the wilderness home of coyotes, eagles, mountain lions, and bighorn sheep.

During the first part of the twentieth century conservationists recommended that three canyon areas in Utah be designated as national parks. The San Rafael Swell was one of them. Economic pressures removed the Swell from the list, but Arches National Park and Natural Bridges National Monument were acquired. The San Rafael Swell was left open for mineral development. The decades passed. Other areas in canyon country—Box-Death Hollow Wilderness, Canyonlands and Capitol Reef National Parks, Grand Staircase-Escalante and Vermilion Cliffs National Monuments, Glen Canyon National Recreation Area, and Dead Horse Point State Park—came

Mountain lions still roam the canyons of the San Rafael Swell.

under federal or state protection. Again the San Rafael Swell was left open for development.

As the years passed the times changed. The public demand for more wilderness—areas suitable for nonmechanized recreation, relaxation, and solitude—has brought the canyon country of Utah and the San Rafael Swell into the limelight. Although it is true that miners have left their handiwork scattered here and there throughout the Swell, much of the area is still pristine. Many of the old mining tracks have fallen into disrepair and are now used to access some of the most wild and scenic lands in canyon country. The San Rafael Swell now contains seven BLM wilderness study areas (WSAs). These are being recommended for federal protection in America's Red Rock Wilderness Act. This act is seeking Wilderness designation not only for areas in the San Rafael Swell, but in many areas of southern Utah. The protection of the San Rafael Swell has become a national issue. Your support of the organizations that support Utah Wilderness will help protect the San Rafael Swell for all time.

The purpose of this guidebook is to provide accurate information to visitors of the San Rafael Swell. It is designed to be used by sightseers, photographers, hikers, backpackers, canyoneers, rock-climbers, and mountain bikers. People of all ages and skill levels will find adventures that will fulfill their objectives.

Canyoneering (called *canyoning* in other parts of the world) is the act of traveling in canyons using a variety of techniques that may include walking, scrambling, climbing, rappelling (abseiling), wading, and swimming. Canyoneers generally differentiate between technical and nontechnical canyoneering. Nontechnical canyoneering refers to simple canyon hiking and technical canyoneering requires the use of specialized equipment and techniques. The hikes described in this guide fall into both categories.

In comparison to many hiking guides, the material presented in this guide may, to some, seem exhaustive. Unlike some of the nation's more heavily traveled natural areas, however, there are very few established trails in the San Rafael Swell. The routes described herein often traverse very rugged terrain or bare rock and are void of any trails at all. Some of the routes require competent navigational skills and all of them demand at least some basic orienteering knowledge.

Even if you are using a Global Positioning System (GPS) unit in conjunction with the coordinates listed throughout the guide, you must still carry a compass and the recommended maps and know how to use them. One thing about electronic gadgets that you can always count on is that at some point in time they will cease to work. If a GPS was your only means of navigation, this would be the last place you'd want to be when that happened. In this extremely harsh and unforgiving landscape, getting lost or off-route can have dire consequences. Some of the terrain you will cover has never been thoroughly explored. There are still arches, bridges, pinnacles, and towers hidden in unknown canyons to be discovered and savored. This is the essence of adventure.

Because of the enormity of the area, and the wealth of information and maps provided, the guide has been divided into two parts. The first covers the area north of Interstate 70, which neatly separates the Swell in half. The area south of the interstate will be covered in a second book. There are hikes that will satisfy any canyon explorer, from the novice to the expert. Day hikers can choose routes from an hour to a long day in length. Backpackers will find many multiday trips. With the use of the guide, longer routes, taking days or weeks, will be possible to design.

The San Rafael Swell has been largely ignored by rock climbers, though there are many pinnacles, towers and miles of walls up to three hundred feet high that have never been touched or described in the literature. Although this is by no means a rock-climbing guide, there are several easy climbs described in the guide. More valuable to the climber are the notes on the pinnacles, towers, and walls that have potential routes.

Mountain bikers will also find a joyful home in the San Rafael Swell. While most of the single-track trails are within the WSAs, which are thereby closed to bicycles, there are dozens of quiet double tracks heading off of the main roads that lead to amazing places. Many of the tracks can be linked up to create loop rides of varying lengths. Mountain bikes can also prove useful in setting up shuttles or accessing hikes. You will want a long cable or chain to lock your bike to trees. All of the Road Sections in the guide mention how suitable the roads are for mountain bikes.

Dozens of main dirt roads and many side roads are described in detail. These lead into nearly every corner of the San Rafael Swell. With the maze of dirt roads and tracks running through some areas, the Road Sections will eliminate the confusion often endured by hikers trying to find a trailhead.

An awareness of the physical world around you can greatly increase your appreciation for the land and your time spent in it. Though it is not in the scope of this guide to provide comprehensive details, there are short chapters that will give you general insight into the geology and natural history of the region and the Native Americans who lived there. Visits to the area's excellent museums (see Access and Information for details) are a great way to learn more. The bibliography at the end of the guide provides a list of books and articles for those wanting to dig deeper.

Like mountaineering, canyoneering often asks more of the traveler than just hiking skills. In a land with few trails, and many inherent dangers, route-finding and map-reading skills are imperative. On some routes, rock-climbing and rope-handling skills become paramount. For the more audacious, strong swimming skills will also be needed while descending some of the Swell's more challenging canyons.

As with any outdoor activity done far from medical help, basic first aid skills (hopefully never needed) are essential. Thinking and judgment become an integral part of any hike.

Nearly all of the mine sites in the San Rafael Swell are the remnants of the uranium mining that took place from the turn of the century to the mid-1960s. Though recent medical evidence has shown that there is little danger from short-term exposure to radon gas, which collects in the old mine shafts, the mine sites do contain other dangers. Stagnant, oxygenless air, caught in pockets in the mines, can cause asphyxiation. The old mine tunnels are also in imminent danger of collapsing and contain vertical shafts that are often difficult to see. Be safe. Stay out of the old mine shafts and tunnels.

Access and Information

On the San Rafael Swell's northern end, access is through Price, a large town on Highway 6/191 with all the amenities. It is the home of the College of Eastern Utah and its Prehistoric Museum in the center of town is a worthwhile stop. The Price BLM office, located at 125 South 600 West (435-636-3600), is a valuable resource. The personnel there can provide the most current information on road conditions, hiking, biking, climbing, and river-running opportunities.

Green River, several miles east of the Swell on Interstate 70, provides access to the heart of the Swell. Though not a large town, it does have motels, gas stations, markets, and garages with towing services. The John Wesley Powell River History Museum (435-564-3427), sitting on a hill overlooking the Green River, is a must for all canyoneers and river-runners. As well, it has a good and growing archive of local history. Call the museum to arrange access to the archives. Interstate 70 cuts through the middle of the San Rafael Swell, making access to many areas convenient.

Hanksville, on Highway 24, provides access to the southern areas of the Swell. It has few services, but it does have a motel, a market, several cafes, and gas stations. The personnel at the Hanksville BLM office, located at 380 South 100 West (435-542-3461), can give current information and offer advice on exploring the southern portions of the Swell.

Along the western side of the Swell, on Highway 10, are a number of small towns that have gas stations, cafes, and small markets. These include Huntington, Castle Dale, and Ferron. The Museum of the San Rafael, located at 96 North 100 East in Castle Dale (435-381-5252), is the ultimate place to learn about the natural and human history of the San Rafael Swell. This outstanding museum has interesting artifacts and displays describing the local dinosaurs, present plant and animal life, and prehistoric Native American occupation of the area. A visit to this museum will surely enhance anyone's experience exploring the Swell.

Emergency Information

Call 911 in case of emergencies! Cell phone service is limited but in many cases you can get a signal if you can get to higher, open ground.

Medical services are located in Price (Castleview Hospital), Castle Dale (Emery Medical Clinic), and Green River (Green River Clinic).

- Castleview Hospital (435) 637-4800
- Emery Medical Clinic (435) 381-2305
- Green River Clinic (435) 564-3434
- Emery County Sheriff (435) 381-2404
- Carbon County Sheriff (435) 636-3251
- There is a Park Ranger at Goblin Valley State Park (435) 564-3633.

PROTECTING THE SAN RAFAEL SWELL

*... an area where the earth and its community of life are untram-
meled by man, where man himself is a visitor who does not remain.*

—This definition of wilderness is from the Wilderness Act of 1964.

The desert from afar looks massive and solid. The towers, cliffs, mesas, and plateaus appear indestructible and unalterable. Up close though, the desert proves to be a fragile environment, one easily damaged. Wounds inflicted fester and rot. The scars remain.

By its beauty, the desert invites intrusion. The hiker, climber, biker, and river-runner are attracted, as are the photographer and picnicker.

By its potential for riches, the desert invites exploitation. The cattleman, the sheepherder, the horse packer, and the tour operator look to the desert to bring them a means to make a living, as do the miner and the gem hunter.

By its lack of defenses, with no way to retaliate, the desert invites destruction. Holes gouged in its cloak, marks left on its skin, its bowels ripped asunder, the desert can only stand stoically.

The settlers and cowboys came and used the desert harshly. The hills that we see today look nothing like what the first pioneers saw. The plains of soil-holding grasses have been reduced to barren plains spotted with sage, pinyon, and juniper by the over-grazing of cattle. The scars remain.

The miners came with their bulldozers and graders, dynamite and drills. To explore Temple Mountain is to discover that it is a hollow shell, its innards removed to make atomic weapons. The Pasture Track above Muddy

Tread lightly.

Creek, Tomsich Butte, Calf Mesa, and many other areas have been mutilated in the search for wealth. The scars remain.

Today it is the off-road vehicle (ORV) that is ravaging the San Rafael Swell. These two- and four-wheeled vehicles can, and do, go just about anywhere. In the Wilderness Study Areas (WSAs), areas set aside until Congress can decide exactly how they should be used, it is illegal to take ORVs off of designated roads. As with many sports, it is the few bad apples that are ruining it for the masses. The ORV riders who illegally enter Wilderness Study Areas are the scourge of the San Rafael Swell.

In former years little notice was taken of the destruction. The times have changed. Though cattle still graze the canyon bottoms of the Swell, their days may be numbered. Many question whether the damage done by cattle is worth the environmental cost. Many cattlemen realize this. They have full-time city jobs. Cattle are a sideline, a clinging to the past. As canyon country attracts more visitors, economic forces may dictate their removal.

It is time to let the San Rafael Swell recover. The rotted parts, over time, will heal. The grasses will reassert themselves. The mining tracks will wash away or be covered by rockfall. The tunnels will collapse. The convalescence will take a long time, certainly longer than our lives or the lives of our grandchildren. It will recover, though some scars will remain.

In 1964 Congress passed the Wilderness Act. That act defined wilderness as "an area where the earth and its community of life are untrammeled by man, where man himself is a visitor who does not remain." The Wilderness Act further stated that wilderness is an area where one can find solitude and where there is an opportunity for primitive and unconfined recreation.

Unfortunately, the Wilderness Act only applied to certain U.S. Forest Service, National Park Service, and Fish and Wildlife Service lands. These agencies were then required to inventory their holdings and recommend areas that met the criteria for wilderness. This led to the establishment of several small National Forest Service Wilderness Areas in Utah.

Fortunately, though, the Wilderness Act did provide the language and an implementation model that was incorporated into the 1976 Federal Land Policy and Management Act (FLPMA, pronounced flip-ma). That act required the Bureau of Land Management (BLM) to inventory its holdings and to recommend areas worthy of wilderness designation. By 1980 they had done this. Of the 22 million acres the BLM controls in Utah, 1.9 million acres were deemed suitable. These areas became WSAs. Of the 1.2 million acres of the San Rafael Swell, only 242,000 acres were found to have wilderness qualities.

It quickly became apparent that the BLM inventory was badly flawed. Instead of using the definition of wilderness provided by Congress, the BLM made up their own definition which reflected not Congressional will, but the wants of the extractive industries and local politicians.

It was at this point that environmental groups stepped in. They decided that Congress needed an accurate description of the wildlands of southern Utah to counter the inaccurate information presented by the BLM. In 1985 they formed the Utah Wilderness Coalition (UWC), now an association of more than two hundred conservation groups such as the Sierra Club, the National Parks and Conservation Association, Great Old Broads for Wilderness, and Southern Utah Wilderness Alliance.

Members of the UWC went out on the land and did their own inventory, using the definition of wilderness provided by Congress. Finding that the BLM inventory was, indeed, flawed, they proposed their own bill. In 1989 Utah Congressional Representative Wayne Owens (1937–2002) introduced a Utah BLM Wilderness Bill which would have set aside 5.1 million acres in Utah as Wilderness. This included 752,900 acres in the San Rafael Swell. These areas included the BLM Wilderness Study Areas as well as many other deserving parts of canyon country.

In the fall of 1996 Interior Secretary Bruce Babbitt and Utah Representative Jim Hansen, recognizing the inadequacies of the first wilderness inventory (Babbit said it wasn't enough—Hansen said it was too much), initiated a reinventory of the BLM lands of Utah by the BLM. The reinventory—this time a much more honest appraisal by the BLM—raised the number of acres that met the Congressional definition of wilderness to over six million acres.

Since the first edition of this book was written in 1992, the Utah Wilderness Bill has changed in acreage and in name. A more careful appraisal of the land, the use of better computer-aided mapping systems, and the addition of lands on Utah's West Desert, upped the number of acres to 9.1 million. These are included in America's Redrock Wilderness Act.

To bring this number into perspective, realize that the state of California has fourteen million acres of designated wilderness, Colorado has over three million acres, and Arizona has well over four million acres. Utah— even with its world class canyons—has less than one million acres of designated wilderness.

While 40 percent of Utah's lands are controlled by the BLM, America's Redrock Wilderness Act proposes that only about 35 percent of that be set aside as wilderness. This leaves about 60 percent of the BLM lands of Utah open to ORV use and to the extractive industries. Those who say that environmentalists want too much land just haven't looked at the statistics—or at the land.

A couple of years ago a sign near the start of the western end of the Green River Cutoff Road—on private land—welcomed visitors to the San Rafael Swell with this message:

Enjoy the Multiple Use of Public Lands
If Wilderness/Parks Come
You, Roads, and Vehicles
Will be Prohibited

Installed by an anti-wilderness group, the sign was a blatant lie meant to scare those who enjoy public lands. The truth is that with wilderness designation the changes that occur would have few negative impacts on the majority of people who now use and enjoy the San Rafael Swell. Current mining claims and cattle grazing are allowed. Hunting would continue, as would the use of pack animals. As with other Wilderness Areas, there may be some restrictions placed on where camping is allowed, whether dogs need to be leashed on some trails, or whether camp fires are allowed in some areas. Most of the roads now open to ORV use in the San Rafael Swell would remain open. Those roads that are closed would simply open up large areas to multiple use by those seeking quiet recreation: hikers, climbers, canyoneers, campers, picnickers, and horse packers.

It is just a reality that ORV use and those participating in quiet recreational pursuits are not compatible. One ORV enthusiast told me that his group only wanted "fifty-four inches in every canyon and you tree huggers can have the rest." Fifty-four inches is the width of an ORV. He just didn't understand that a lot of people are out to actually enjoy the landscape in a quiet way and that the noise and smells of their vehicles interfere with that goal.

It is disheartening to acknowledge that in the twenty years since the first edition of this book was written, the Wilderness battle has not been resolved. Over one hundred years ago H. L. A. Culmer wrote about the San Rafael Swell. Even back then he expressed what too many people do not recognize today—the intense beauty of the San Rafael Swell: "No adequate description has ever been given of the wonders of the San Rafael Swell. . . . Yet they are of a character so imposing and extraordinary that in any other state they would be exploited far and wide, bringing thousands to see them from every land and adding to the fame of Utah as one of the greatest scenic states in the Union."

Low-impact techniques are imperative in the backcountry.

Low-impact Camping Techniques

*To many of us, the wilderness truly unaltered by human interfer-
ence, the wilderness with its wealth of life rolling across it in great
surges, ebbing and flowing with the seasons of the years, is insepara-
ble from our innermost beings.*

—Ian McTaggert Cowan

While visiting the San Rafael Swell there are a number of things we as
individuals can do to minimize our impact and protect its natural beauty.
Because of the unique and fragile desert environment, there are some special considerations to take when traveling here in addition to the standard
principles of "Leave No Trace." None of them are difficult; none take much
effort. The goal is to leave the desert and its inhabitants as you found them,
or better. There is nothing worse than reaching the end of a spectacular canyon and finding a fire pit with aluminum foil and beer cans in it. The following guidelines are some of the ways that we can all reduce our impact in
canyon country.

Cryptobiotic soil. Made from a conglomeration of algae, fungi, moss,
and lichen, cryptobiotic soil, or crust, is the black-crusted soil that is spread
throughout the desert. It is invaluable in retaining moisture, holding the
soil together, and checking erosion. Other plants in the community rely on
it. While it withstands the natural forces of this extreme environment, it is
destroyed by crushing forces such as footsteps. Make great efforts to stay off
of it and try to go around it whenever possible.

Trails. Always hike on trails when present. Stay within the confines of the trail and don't shortcut switchbacks. There are very few designated trails in the Swell, but there are plentiful stock trails, use-trails, and game trails. When traveling in trail-less areas, always hike on durable surfaces. These include rock, sand, gravel, and snow. As a general rule stay off of vegetation whenever possible. Dry grasses, however, can be resistant to trampling and are sometimes useful when trying to avoid cryptobiotic soil.

Trash. The most obvious eyesore. Pack out *all* trash, not just your own. If you find garbage left by others, pack it out, too (this will make up for the sandwich bag that blew off of the top of Pinnacle #1). Not just in the back-country, but in the front-country at trailheads and campsites, too. "Finders, keepers." If you find it, you own it. Leftover food should also be packed out, not buried or burned. Burning leftover food and garbage in fire-pits leaves a mess and a potentially hazardous situation for wildlife. Scavenging animals and small mammals may be lured into a seemingly extinguished fire-pit by the odors and then be burned by hidden embers or they may ingest pieces of paper or foil.

Bodily waste. Since the moisture and organisms that help decompose human waste are usually not present in arid lands, it is best to pack out human waste when possible. Slot canyoneers *must* carry out their waste. Except for trying to skinny by a dead cow floating in a pothole, there is nothing worse than finding crap in a slot canyon. It is easy to carry out your waste by using either specially designed bags (Wag Bags) or Poo Tubes. These are home-made PVC or ABS tubes of an appropriate size with removable ends. They are easy to empty out and clean at home.

For those that are car camping in the San Rafael Swell, unless you are staying at one of the campgrounds with toilets, it is imperative that you carry out your own effluent. This is easy using commercially available Port-a-Potties that are made just for camping. After all, by law you must carry out your waste at Lake Powell. It should now be done in the San Rafael Swell as well.

If you are backpacking, you will not be able to carry out your waste. Do dispose of it properly. Dig a shallow (six inches deep), cat-hole in organic soil if present. Because cat-holes in the desert rely partly on heat to break down the waste, try to locate them in sunny, south-facing places, preferably near trees or as close to vegetation as you can. The limited microorganisms they provide will help to speed up the process. Always go well away from established campsites, trails, and water sources (even if dry). Three hundred feet is the minimum. In narrower canyons this can sometimes be difficult. Scramble up a rubble heap or find a high ledge. Be especially sure not to do it in a wash bottom or sand bar.

In the past it was okay to burn your toilet paper. This is no longer appropriate. The new ethic is to always carry out your toilet paper. This is easy to do and it is now a regulation in the Grand Canyon and in the canyons of the Escalante. Carry sandwich-sized plastic bags and dispose of them at home. We do this on thirty-day expeditions. It just isn't as bad as you think.

Campsites. It is always best to *find* your campsite and not *create* one by altering the landscape. Always use an established campsite if available. If there are multiple established sites to choose from, select the most heavily impacted one that is big enough for your group. Be sure to camp on durable surfaces. Because sand, gravel and bare rock are so plentiful in canyon country, there should never be a need to camp on vegetation. Don't clear away pine needles or leaf litter, camp on top of them. They reduce erosion, retain moisture, and return nutrients to the soil and are important to surrounding plants. Camp at least 200 feet from springs, seeps, and potholes or you may be keeping wildlife away from vital water sources.

Water. Wash dishes and bathe at least 200 feet from any water sources, especially nonmoving ones like potholes or tanks. Use only small amounts of biodegradable soap, if any. You don't need soap to sterilize your dishes. Metal utensils and cooking gear can be held over the flame of a stove for several seconds or dipped in a pot of boiling water. Or carry rubbing alcohol and swab your dishes out with it. A tiny, two ounce container of alcohol will last a week or more. Strain wastewater through a fine screen and pack out the particles with your trash. Then disperse the water rather than pouring it in a single spot.

Scarce water is especially important to desert wildlife and other hikers. Treat it with care. Save your swimming for abundant moving water like streams and rivers. Stay out of still water, especially potholes. Things like sun-screen, detergents, and your body's oils will taint the water. Potholes rarely, if ever, "flush out" so whatever you put in them is likely to stay there forever. This may be the only water available to local wildlife and their survival might depend on it. Carelessly polluting it or wasting it could have dire consequences. If you must use this precious water for anything other than drinking, carry it away from the source (200 feet) and use it there. Gather your water during the day and avoid these water sources at night. Many desert animals are nocturnal or come to drink under the cover of darkness. Try to eliminate your effect on their critical night-time activities.

Fires. Campfires are a thing of the past. The warmth is rarely needed in the Swell and the scars they leave remain for years. If you are going to have a campfire at an established or designated campsite, always use an existing fire ring. Because water is so precious here, people often extinguish their camp-fires with sand. Fire pits at heavily used sites sometimes turn into piles of sand. Do not make a new one. Excavate the old one (make sure it's not smol-dering) and scatter the blackened sand. With the scarcity of firewood, bring your own to front-country sites. Although it is legal to gather dead and fallen wood in the San Rafael Swell, it is scarce. Most campers will want to bring their own wood. Light-weight backpacking stoves eliminate the need for cooking fires, especially in the back-country. If you must have a fire in the back-country—stove broken or in an emergency—do not build a fire ring. This only blackens the rocks and leaves permanent evidence of your visit. Build your fire in a wash and on the sand, never bare rock. Let all fires burn out completely so you don't leave behind half-charred wood and a potential wildfire hazard.

Fire restrictions are now a part of our modern world. These may not be posted anywhere so it is your responsibility to know if there are restrictions in place and what they are. Sometimes they are limited to campfires, but in extreme cases may be restricted to all fires (including charcoal or even smok-ing outside of a vehicle). Contact or visit one of the BLM offices (see Access and Information) for current fire restrictions and fire hazard conditions.

Archaeological site etiquette. (Adapted from the blm.gov website). The San Rafael Swell and surrounding areas have many fine examples of Native American rock art, and a rich archaeological heritage. Our past, however, is being threatened by people who collect artifacts and dig sites as well as by those who vandalize rock art panels. Many visitors do not realize that collecting artifacts, digging sites, and defacing rock art have several harm-ful results. These actions destroy important data, attack Native American cultural heritage, and rob other people of the opportunity to appreciate and understand other cultures and human history. If you see people vandalizing sites, please report it as soon as possible by calling 1-800-VANDALS. Obtain as much information as possible without putting yourself in danger. If you find something that appears particularly interesting or possibly valuable, contact the BLM (801-539-4001 in Salt Lake City). This applies especially to human remains which have occasionally weathered out.

The Archaeological Resources Protection Act of 1979 (P.L. 96-95; 93 Stat. 721; 16 U.S.C. 47Oaa et seq.), as amended, has felony-level penalties for excavating, removing, damaging, altering, or defacing any archaeological resource more than 100 years of age, on public lands or tribal lands, unless authorized by a permit. It prohibits the sale, purchase, exchange, transportation, receipt, or offering of any archaeological resource obtained in violation of any regulation or permit under the act *or* under any federal, state, or local law. Its definitions, permit requirements, and criminal and civil penalties augment the Antiquities Act of 1906, which it partially supersedes. People go to jail or pay huge fines for not following the rules!

Do your part to help preserve archaeological sites!

1. Touching rock art will leave oils from your fingers that may speed the rock's natural deterioration process.
2. Making paper rubbings or tracings may crumble rock art.
3. Making latex molds of rock art should only be done by professionals if the rock art is going to be destroyed by construction or development.
4. Building fires nearby can cause serious damage from smoke and high temperature.
5. Do NOT take it home. Collecting is illegal and punishable by law.
6. Chalking (once a common practice) is harmful to rock art, and makes it impossible to use new methods of dating the figures.
7. Re-pecking or re-painting a difficult-to-see image doesn't restore it, but rather destroys the original.
8. Defacement. Insensitive people often paint or scratch their names over rock art, or shoot bullets at it. Defacement is a sign of disrespect for other cultures.

Dogs. At the present time there are no restrictions in the Swell. Be realistic about the quality of your animal. If it is loud, aggressive toward other hikers or wildlife, chases cattle, defecates on the trails, doesn't respond to your commands, or is in other ways obnoxious, leave it behind. In some areas water sources are infrequent. They become very valuable. Don't let your dog muddy up an isolated water source. If you don't have enough control of your dog to keep it out of potholes, don't bring it.

Off-road vehicle use. Throughout most of the San Rafael Swell ORVs must stay on established roads, or in designated areas. There are several designated areas in the Swell that permit off-trail riding. None are within Wilderness Study Areas. In contradiction to the purpose of Wilderness Study

Areas, there are three motorized routes that go through the Sids Mountain WSA: TR638, TR639, and TR641. This may change in the future. Ask at the BLM offices for maps, details, and current closures. Nonriders must realize that ORVs in some areas are legal. Report any illegal riding to the BLM office in Price.

THE GEOLOGY OF THE SAN RAFAEL SWELL

*When speaking of these rocks, we must not conceive of piles of boul-
ders, or heaps of fragments, but a whole land of naked rock, with
giant forms carved on it; cathedral-shaped buttes, towering hundreds or thousands of feet; cliffs that cannot be scaled, and canyon
walls that shrink the river into insignificance, with vast, hollow
domes, and tall pinnacles, and shafts set on the verge overhead,
and all highly colored—buff, gray, red, brown, and chocolate; never
lichened; never moss-covered; but bare, and often polished.*

—John Wesley Powell

The geology of the Colorado Plateau and the San Rafael Swell, in particular,
is complicated. For the canyoneer it is not necessary to know the technical details. A basic understanding of how the canyon country was created
and knowledge of the characteristics of the common formations will prove
valuable. It will add insight and increase your sensitivity while hiking in
the area.

The San Rafael Swell is part of a larger area, the Colorado Plateau, which
comprises a vast area that contains most of what we now call canyon country. It is an area bounded by the Aquarius Plateau to the west, the San Juan
and Colorado Rivers to the south, the San Juan Mountains to the east, and
the Book Cliffs to the north. The San Rafael Swell is in the northwest part of
the Colorado Plateau in an area geologists call the Canyon Lands section.

The canyon country is composed primarily of sedimentary rock. The
sedimentary rock is made of grains of minerals (geologists call these clastic

particles), mainly silica, which were broken and weathered from igneous rock on the Uncompahgre Uplift, an area to the east of canyon country.

Several hundred million years ago the Uncompahgre Uplift and several lesser uplifts formed a partial ring around the eastern edge of the Colorado Plateau, much like the rim of a broken bowl. The area was the western boundary of the North American continent. Much of it was at times under the ocean. The sea level varied as forces under the earth's crust either pushed the area higher or let it sink back into the sea. The forces were induced by plate tectonics, the shifting of huge subsurface plates bumping into each other.

Also affecting the sea level were temperature variations which caused glaciers to advance and recede. With cooler temperatures large volumes of water were locked in the glaciers making the oceans shallower. Higher temperatures released the water from the glaciers making the oceans deeper, often inundating otherwise dry land.

From the uplifts a variety of forces brought the mineral grains down into the bottom of the bowl, separating them by size. Gravity, helped by the freeze-thaw cycle and the force of running water, brought down a mix of

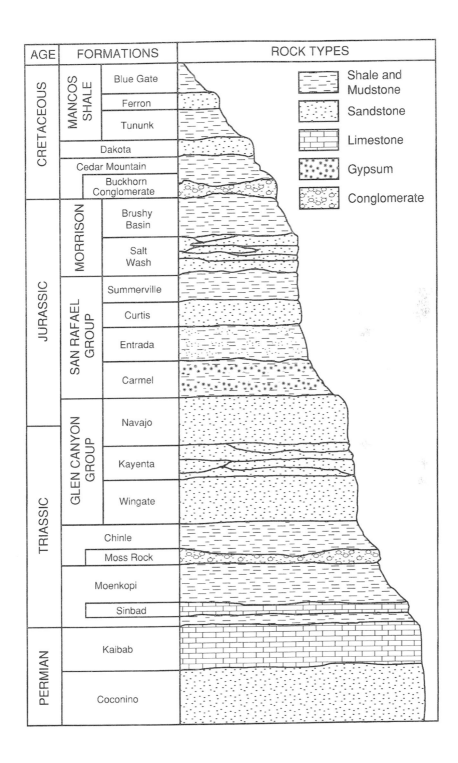

sizes from boulders to sand grains. The wind carried even smaller material, often just dust particles or volcanic ash from active volcanoes to the west and southwest.

As the material worked its way down from the high country other forces came into play. Not only were the mineral grains separated by size but the depositional environment, the bottom of the bowl, changed. The layers, or strata, that were formed by the accumulation of silica grains in the bottom of the bowl were deposited in two ways: parallel stratification (this is also called parallel-bedding and deposits of this type are referred to as a formation); and cross stratification (this is also called cross-bedding and deposits of this type are referred to as a sandstone).

Parallel-stratified formations were formed when the silica grains were deposited in layers. This indicates that deposition occurred in quiet water—the ocean bottom, tidal flats, or fresh water lakes. Layers of different thicknesses were formed. This was dependent on the nature of the forces bringing the material down from the heights, the amount of material, and the stability and length of the period of deposition. Thin, uniform layers are thought to have been deposited in concert with natural rhythms—the rise and fall of the tides or the change of the seasons. These thin layers are called varves.

The Moenkopi Formation is a classic example of a varved rock. This stratum was deposited in tidal pools and mud flats. Due to tidal variations different colored layers were formed. Lighter-colored layers were deposited while underwater and when there was little motion in the water. This allowed the buildup of salts and the accumulation of marine fossils. The darker layers were deposited while above water and do not contain salts and fossils. The Moenkopi, Chinle, and Summerville Formations are examples of parallel-stratified deposition.

Cross-stratified sandstone is a deep, homogeneous layer that was deposited by the turbulent flow of wind or water. A large amount of material was deposited over a geologically short span of time. The climate and environment during the period of deposition was similar to that of the present day Sahara Desert, hot and dry. Huge sand dunes drifted across the landscape. Once the material was deposited, either groundwater or the sea level rose, dampening the sand and holding it in place until it could harden. Coconino, Wingate, and Navajo Sandstones are examples of cross-stratified deposition.

While the various layers were being laid down, external forces were at work. Individual layers in a plastic state were bent and folded. The forces acting on the layers came from the unequal weight of the material above, volcanic pressures, and movement in the crust of the earth. The bending of the strata is called folding.

There are three basic types of folds. Anticlines are arched or upfolded layers of rock. Synclines are downfolded or trough-shaped layers of rock. Monoclines are steplike bends in otherwise horizontal layers of rock. All of these folds can range from hundreds of miles long to just several yards across. The San Rafael Swell itself is an asymmetrical anticline. Smaller folds can be seen along the Southern Reef near Ding and Dang Canyons and in lower Devils Canyon where they are particularly convoluted and spectacular.

The plastic rock, now formed into its final configuration, hardened. This was caused by two forces. First, the weight of the material above compressed and aligned the silica grains, increasing its density. Second, chemical reactions between the rock particles, water, and the atmosphere bonded the rock together.

Ten to fifteen million years ago the deposition of the silica particles stopped. The Colorado Plateau started to rise. Areas that had once been at sea level were lifted ten to fifteen thousand feet. Instead of being an area of deposition, the Colorado Plateau started to erode.

Softer layers and weaknesses in harder layers of sandstone were eroded by moving water. Sheet erosion acted on the rock when rain fell and the water moved over the rock in broad sheets. Stream erosion was the concentrated effect of the water while running in confined areas. While the land lifted around it, the canyons became deeper. Slit canyons developed in layers of harder sandstone, those formed by cross-stratified deposition. They are uniform in width and height and typical of most of the canyons in the San Rafael Swell.

Stair-step canyons were formed when water cut through alternating soft and hard layers of sandstone. These are formed in canyons containing both parallel-stratified formations and cross-stratified sandstone. The Grand Canyon is a classic example of a stair-step canyon. V-shaped canyons were formed in uniformly softer rock. Many canyons are a combination of all three types: slit, stair-step, and V-shaped.

The San Rafael Swell started to form between fifty million and sixty million years ago. Pressures from deep beneath the earth's crust pushed the strata upward like an expanding balloon, forming a dome-shaped anticline eighty miles long and forty miles wide. The strata on the periphery of the anticline were tilted back forming the near vertical walls that we see today along the Northern, Eastern, and Southern Reefs. The area in the middle of the Reef, the Swell (Sinbad Country), was higher than the Reef itself. Higher elevations invited more rainfall making the area more susceptible to the forces of sheet and stream erosion. The rounded dome, or swell, slowly eroded forming the deep canyons that now cut through the area.

About a million years ago there was a period of volcanic activity to the south and west of the Swell. Two things happened during this time. First, molten rock forced its way into cracks in the sandstone forming dikes, sills, volcanic plugs, and more massive igneous intrusions. These can be seen throughout the Cathedral Valley, Mussentuchit Badlands, and Cedar Mountain areas. Second, after the period of volcanic activity, a time of global cooling brought glaciers to Thousand Lakes Mountain, an area to the west of the Swell. The glaciers carried an immense amount of volcanic rock into Cathedral Valley and the Mussentuchit Badlands, leaving a layer of volcanic boulders sitting on top of the sandstone.

THE STRATA

The sole actuality of nature resides in change.

—Heraclitus

The sandstones and formations detailed below are listed in order of age, from the oldest or lowest stratum to the youngest or highest stratum. Only the dominant sandstones and formations found in the San Rafael Swell are described.

Coconino Sandstone is a part of the Cutler Formation. It is cross stratified and is up to 400 feet thick. Coconino Sandstone is the petrified remains of huge sand dunes that once covered the area. Coconino Sandstone is fine grained, white to light brown in color, and its surface is soft. It forms vertical walls that are often coated with black varnish. One distinctive feature of Coconino Sandstone is that it is topped by a band of limestone that varies from 10–50 feet in thickness. The band is called the Sinbad Member.

The Moenkopi Formation is one of the most common and easily recognized strata in the Swell. It is parallel stratified and is up to 400 feet thick. It was formed by stream-born silt and mud being deposited in tidal pools and mud flats. The layers vary considerably in color, ranging from near white to red, brown, and dark brown. The Moenkopi Formation has been characterized as looking like a chocolate torte. It forms either vertical walls, or at times, steep slopes.

The Chinle Formation is parallel stratified and is up to 150 feet thick. It was formed by streams depositing mud, silt, and volcanic ash in alluvial plains. It contains a rainbow of colors—red, brown, purple, gray, and green—and forms steep and often shaley slopes. The gray to buff, finely grained layer in the Chinle Formation is ash from volcanoes that were active to the west and south. The Chinle Formation often contains petrified wood.

A substratum of the Chinle Formation, the Moss Back Member, contains uranium. Uranium particles in solution, which for some unexplained reason were absorbed onto decomposed plant material, were able to leach along the porous sandstone of the Moss Back Member. The plant material had been washed down streams and had collected in pockets and seams. Later, uranium miners looked for these pockets and seams. The presence of petrified wood was an indicator that uranium deposits were near.

Wingate Sandstone is a part of what is called the Glen Canyon group. It is cross stratified and is up to 400 feet thick. It was formed during a period of high winds that carried an immense amount of material down from the highlands to the east and covered most of the Colorado Plateau in sand. Its usual colors range from a light red to a near brown. This varies considerably and it is not unusual to see near-white Wingate Sandstone. This can make it hard to differentiate from Navajo Sandstone. Often the context it is in, immediately above the Moenkopi and Chinle Formations, is the clue to whether it is Wingate or Navajo. It forms vertical walls that have vertical cracks. It is the densest of the sandstones.

The Kayenta Formation is also a part of the Glen Canyon group. It is parallel stratified and is up to 100 feet thick. It was formed by stream-deposited sand or the shuffling of the Wingate sands. It is red to brown in color and forms broken ledges and steep slopes. The Kayenta Formation is the friend of the backpacker as it can provide wide benches that are easy to negotiate. It often contains dinosaur bones and dinosaur footprints. It is interesting that in some places in the San Rafael Swell, the Kayenta Formation does not exist between the Navajo and Wingate Sandstones.

Navajo Sandstone, another member of the Glen Canyon group, is cross stratified and is up to 500 feet thick. It was formed in the same environment as Wingate Sandstone. It is usually lighter in color than Wingate Sandstone, varying from dirty white to red. Navajo Sandstone forms vertical walls, but the tops of the cliffs tend to be more rounded than Wingate cliffs.

The Carmel Formation is parallel stratified and is up to 100 feet thick, though it is commonly no more than 25 feet thick. It was formed by a combination of wind and stream deposition in a marine environment. Red to brown siltstone layers are intermixed with limestone layers that often contain marine fossils. It forms sloping ledges that are often unstable to walk on.

Entrada Sandstone is a bit of a puzzle. It is cross stratified and is up to 500 feet thick, although it is more normal to see it in the 150 foot range. Though it usually presents itself as a homogeneous formation, it sometimes shows distinct parallel bedding. It was formed in two ways: by windblown silt and sand settling into quiet waters, and in other locations by the same forces that formed Wingate and Navajo Sandstones. It is off-white to a rich red in color and usually forms steep, rounded walls and domes. The goblins in Goblin Valley State Park are formed from Entrada Sandstone.

The Curtis Formation is parallel stratified and is up to 150 feet thick in the northern parts of the Swell. It was formed by silt deposition in a shallow marine environment. It has thin layers that contain microfossils and mollusks. It is brown to faded green in color and weathers into sandy benches or shaley walls.

The Summerville Formation is parallel stratified and is up to 325 feet thick. It was formed as the sea retreated leaving tidal and mud flats into which deposition could occur. It is a fine-grained, chocolate-colored stratum that has thin layers that sometimes contain marine fossils. It forms either shaley walls or gradual slopes. The Summerville Formation often contains agates.

Note: Throughout the guide the geologic descriptions of the various formations have been shortened; e.g., Wingate-walled instead of a wall of Wingate Sandstone, and a Navajo dome instead of a dome of Navajo Sandstone, etc.

Humans in the San Rafael Swell

If one is inclined to wonder at first how so many dwellers came to be in the loneliest land that ever came out of God's hands, what they do there and why stay, one does not wonder so much after having lived there. None other than this long brown land lays such a hold on affections. The rainbow hills, the tender bluish mists, the luminous radiance of the spring, have the lotus chosen.

—Mary Austin

The story of man in the San Rafael Swell starts with the antecedents of the American Indians, the Mongoloids, in China. They were a Stone Age people, possessing crude stone tools and living in caves and other natural shelters. They were the big game hunters, following the migration of the animals—mastodons, mammoths, bison, sloths, and tapirs—as they slowly worked their way north into Siberia.

Eighteen thousand years ago—during what geologists called the late Pleistocene—earth was locked in an ice age. As much of earth's water was tied up in glaciers, the level of the sea was lower. The area between Siberia and Alaska, called Beringia, was above water. Ocean currents, originating in equatorial waters near Japan, brought warm water up to Beringia which kept the temperatures reasonable. By 12,500 BP (before the present) a small number of Stone Age people crossed Beringia from Siberia to North America. Archaeologists call these early migrants Paleo-Indians. It is doubtful they realized they were crossing onto a new continent. They were simply following sources of food and their instinct for survival.

Once in North America they migrated south. Though tongues of glacial ice pushed south, migrants found ice-free corridors. Two documented corridors were along the McKenzie River and along the eastern edge of the Rocky Mountains. These led the Paleo-Indians into the Great Plains area. They were big game hunters who utilized crude stone tools and sharp sticks. There was some social organization. There is a site in Wyoming where a mammoth was driven into a bog and killed with rocks. Bison were stampeded off cliffs and the meat retrieved. Activities such as these could have only been perpetrated by groups who could work together toward a common goal.

From 12,500 BP to 7,500 BP the Paleo-Indian Culture changed. The most important advance was the proliferation of the projectile point, thin sharp slivers chipped from larger rocks. These points, tied to the end of a stick and used as a spear, were employed to kill game that had formerly been unobtainable. Man was better able to exploit the land. More food meant that the population could increase. Hunger became less of a worry.

There are a dozen recognized types of projectile points The oldest of these, the Clovis point, has been found in association with mammoth, bison, horse, and camel kill sites. Folsom points, the most common of the Paleo-Indian period, were found only in bison kill sites.

On the Colorado Plateau there are few Paleo-Indian sites. A Clovis point was found in Emery County. A Plano point, slightly younger than a Clovis point, was discovered near Ferron. Both of these sites are on the west edge of the San Rafael Swell. Other signs of habitation were discovered to the south of Vernal, Utah, and many sites have been found along the Flaming Gorge in Wyoming.

Approximately eight thousand years ago the largest of the Pleistocene megafauna died out. Two reasons are cited. First, the climate was getting hotter. The Great Plains were turning into the Great American Desert. Second, the Paleo-Indians may have precipitated the first man-made environmental crisis. Over-hunting may have eradicated such large numbers of animals that there was no longer a breeding population. With the decline or decimation of the chief food source, man was again on the move looking for a hospitable environment. A new home was found in the Great Basin, the area to the west of the Colorado Plateau.

This leads to the Desert Culture which flourished from 7,500 BP to AD 500. (The Desert Culture has also been called the Western or Desert Archaic Culture. To differentiate a general Desert Culture from the people living in the San Rafael Swell area, some authors have called it the Barrier

Head of Sinbad area.

Canyon Culture.) They were the first to inhabit the Colorado Plateau and the Great Basin. The Desert Culture evolved from the Paleo-Indians with a big game hunting tradition to a people of cultural diversity. A hunter-gatherer tradition was born. Instead of meat being the main food staple, the gathering of nuts, roots, and berries predominated. A supply of these could be stored and saved for less prosperous times. Their diet diversified as new food sources were recognized and exploited. Manos and metates, or grinding stones, were used to grind the products of their foraging. Baskets, crudely woven at first, became more sophisticated. Pottery was introduced. The baskets and pots were needed to store the new foods.

Atlatls, or spear throwers, increased the distance and velocity a spear could be thrown, multiplying its effectiveness. Later, the bow and arrow replaced the atlatl, another step up the cultural ladder. Antelope and bighorn sheep were added to the diet. Bone awls were used to pierce leather, making clothes easier to produce. Woven sandals and blankets also made life easier. The principal sources of shelter were caves, though simple lean-tos were also utilized.

The Desert Culture left behind ample evidence of their passing. Danger Cave and Hogup Cave near the Great Salt Lake in Utah and Lovelock

Cave in Nevada, among many sites, provide definitive information about the Desert Culture. These caves show evidence of continual use from about 10,000 BP to AD 1. The Cowboy Cave site in Horseshoe Canyon, which is a part of Canyonlands National Park twenty-five miles east of the San Rafael Swell, was one of the few prolific sites on the Colorado Plateau. It was occupied from 8,300 BP to the modern era.

Evidence of the Desert Culture is also apparent in the extensive pictograph panels they left behind. Pictographs are paintings drawn on a rock surface. They used colored minerals mixed with animal fat or vegetable oil which they brushed onto rock walls with twigs, branch ends, or bits of fur. Different colors were obtained from whatever was handy. Reds were produced from hematite, an iron oxide. Yellow was made from limonite, another type of iron oxide. Black was obtained from coal deposits. Other colors were procured from beds of clay.

In the San Rafael Swell the pictographs left behind by the Desert Culture are of the Barrier Canyon style. They have been dated from about 7000 BP to AD 500, though archaeologists have not been able to agree on either date. The pictographs are generally anthropomorphic (having a human form) figures; ghostlike and supernatural in appearance. The bodies are tapered and have elaborate head gear. Barrier Canyon style pictographs are found throughout the San Rafael Swell: Buckhorn Draw, Wild Horse Canyon, Old Woman Wash, and South Temple Wash, among others. Barrier Canyon style pictographs are also found outside the San Rafael Swell. The most famous panel is the Great Gallery in Horseshoe Canyon in Canyonlands National Park. There are other panels in Capitol Reef and Arches National Parks, and in scattered locations throughout the Colorado Plateau.

To the south of the Colorado Plateau, in Mexico and Central America, prehistoric peoples developed a cultural identity of their own, one substantially more advanced than that of the Desert Culture. They developed a complex agricultural society. The significance of this was profound. No longer did primitive people have to constantly follow the herds of animals. They could plant and harvest corn, beans, and squash, which could be stored and used at a later time.

A stratified society evolved. As with other developing societies there was a hierarchy. Those at the top controlled the society, telling others what to do. In this way larger and more sophisticated projects were possible. Complex irrigation systems were built, opening up more land to cultivation. Fewer people produced more food, leaving others time to devote to such diverse projects as building cities and temples. More time was available to develop religions. The arts flourished.

From AD 1 to AD 500 these developments were introduced into the Desert Cultures of the Colorado Plateau. Archaeologists call this period the Basketmaker Stage. By AD 500 the Basketmakers had divided into several distinct cultures. Among these were the Ancestral Puebloans. They are thought to have been descendants of a Basketmaker Culture who developed along the banks of the Colorado River and occupied the Four Corners Region in an area east of the Colorado River and south of the Escalante River. The Ancestral Puebloans were quick to assimilate the new innovations that originated in the south, introducing horticulture, irrigation, and domesticated animals to the southwest.

Another group some archaeologists think were descendants of the Basketmakers is the Fremont Culture. Other archaeologists think the Fremont Culture started with the remnants of a Desert Culture from the Great Basin, though there isn't conclusive proof. The Fremonts also may have been a group who broke away from the Ancestral Puebloans, or the Mogollon, a group to the southwest of the Ancestral Puebloans. Regardless of their origin, the Fremonts did become a distinct cultural group who occupied the territory to the north of the Ancestral Puebloans. This area was to the west of the Colorado River and north of the Escalante River, an area that included the San Rafael Swell. Except for the Ancestral Puebloans to the south, they dominated what is now the state of Utah.

The Fremont Culture developed somewhat differently from that of their Ancestral Puebloans neighbors. The Fremonts had communities of up to several hundred people, though they did not build the walled cities so typical of the Ancestral Puebloans. Instead, they built clusters of pit houses and utilized caves which were improved with crude masonry walls. Like the Ancestral Puebloans, the Fremonts cultivated their food and built irrigation systems that stretched for miles. They became proficient fishermen, and made feather and hide blankets, finely tailored leather clothes, leather moccasins, and jewelry. In addition to simple, unpainted pots and finely woven baskets, many small clay figurines have been found, as have round rock balls that were apparently used in games.

Evidence of the Fremont Culture is found throughout the region. There are Fremont sites in Nine Mile Canyon near Price, in Arches, Canyonlands, and Capitol Reef National Parks, and along the Escalante, Green, and Dirty Devil Rivers. Small granaries are common. These, often found in small caves high above the floor of a canyon, were used to store corn and to keep it away from rodents. Pit-house towns, chipping beds, and grinding surfaces for corn have also been found.

Except for pictographs and petroglyphs, evidence of the Fremont Culture is relatively scarce in the San Rafael Swell. Caves in Black Dragon Wash and at the head of Cane Wash were certainly used. There is a cliff dwelling with masonry walls in a cave high on a cliff behind the Sid and Charley pinnacle near the Moore Cutoff Road. The cultural detritus left by most Native Americans—chipping grounds, the remains of pit houses and areas of communal use, and burial sites—are nearly absent in the Swell.

In the San Rafael Swell the principal remnants left behind by the Fremonts are the many rock art panels we see today. Often extensive in nature, these are usually found associated with cultures that had enough free time to spend on activities that were not essential to their immediate existence.

Pictographs, so dominant in the Desert Culture, were secondary to petroglyphs in the Fremont Culture. Petroglyphs are shapes that were pecked onto rock walls. Petroglyphs are generally younger than the pictographs, ranging in age from AD 500 to historic times. In the San Rafael Swell the petroglyphs are predominately of the Southern San Rafael style. The figures have an outline formed by solid pecking. Like the Barrier Canyon style pictographs, the human shapes tend to be tapered and have elaborate head gear. Facial features and jewelry are often shown. Fingers are splayed and the feet point out. The figures often hold shields. Later petroglyphs tended to be more realistic. Although there are petroglyphs scattered throughout the Swell, some of the best panels are at Rochester Creek, Cottonwood Wash, and Three Finger Canyon.

By AD 1300 the Fremonts had left the canyon country. As with the Ancestral Puebloans to the south, the reasons for this are not clear. Drought, disease, population pressures, or war-loving intruders are all possibilities.

The next inhabitants of the Swell were Utes and Piutes who migrated from the west and north. These Shoshoni-related peoples had not advanced culturally during the Basketmaker Stage as did the Fremont and Ancestral Puebloans cultures. They retained the old Desert Culture tradition of hunting and gathering. There is little evidence of their inhabitation of the Swell.

The first time the San Rafael River name showed up in today's Utah was on the Don Bernardo de Miera map of 1776. Miera, the cartographer for the Domínguez-Escalante Expedition, used three names for today's Colorado River: the *Rio Colorado*, the *Rio de Zaguagana*, and the *Rio de S. Rafael*.

While not in the same place as today's San Rafael River, at least the San Rafael name was in use in Utah.

The next time the name was used was on the Alexander von Humboldt map of 1809. Unfortunately, the river he assigned the name to was an indeterminate eastern tributary of the *R. Zaguananas* (now called the Colorado River). Zebulon Montgomery Pike made the same mistake on his 1810 map, as did John Pinkerton on his 1811 map. Most likely both of them were copying the Humboldt map.

By the early 1800s a slow push started from today's New Mexico into the San Rafael Swell and the Book Cliff areas by Spanish explorers, traders, and trappers. The Old Spanish Trail cut through the northern part of the San Rafael Swell starting in the early 1800s. The trail crossed the San Rafael River in Castle Valley, but the names the early explorers used for the river have been lost in history.

That changed with the first John C. Fremont Expedition in 1843–44. Although the expedition did not get near the San Rafael River, they were apparently told about it as it showed up on their map of 1845, and in approximately the right location. The John C. Fremont Expedition of 1853–54 followed the San Rafael River upriver from its junction with the Green River as far as Mexican Bend. That story is told in the Lower Black Box hike.

The Mormons arrived en masse in Salt Lake City in 1846 and 1847. It didn't take long for a few hearty Mormon pioneers to travel south and settle in the San Rafael Swell. They used the canyon bottoms in the winter and the top of the Swell (Sinbad Country) in the summer to graze their livestock. Though the Mormons did not build large settlements in the San Rafael Swell, they are responsible for the development of the towns surrounding the area: Castle Dale, Emery, Ferron, Green River, Hanksville, Molen, Price, and Wellington.

THE OLD SPANISH TRAIL

This historic 1,120-mile pack trail went from Santa Fe, New Mexico to southern California. Along the way, it cut through the northern portion of the San Rafael Swell. Although pieces of the trail were used as early as the late 1600s, it was only used in its entirety from 1830 to 1850. The trail is not marked on the current USGS 1:24,000 scale maps, but is shown on the Huntington 1:100,000 scale map revised in 2006. The Huntington map shows the portion of the trail that crosses the Swell. Many references are made to the trail in this book.

From the historical perspective, the name "Old Spanish Trail" is misleading. It is true that starting in the mid-1700s there was documented trade between the Spanish in Santa Fe and the "Yuta" (Ute) Indians in the vicinity of Utah Lake (near today's Provo). Expeditions by Don Juan María Antonia de Rivera in 1765 and Domínguez and Escalante in 1776 helped develop sections of the trail. In 1813 Mauricio Arze and Lago García followed what was apparently an established route from Santa Fe to Utah Lake. They were the first to document their expedition along this section of the Old Spanish Trail.

But, there is only fragmentary evidence for an established trail continuing on to California. That was remedied by Jedediah Smith in 1826 when his expedition became the first to document a route from the Great Salt Lake to southern California along what is now termed the Old Spanish Trail. Smith repeated the route, with variations, in 1827. At that time, though, the Spanish no longer owned or controlled the states the trail went through. It had become Mexican territory in 1821, so Smith's routes could not be considered "Spanish."

Ewing Young of Tennessee led a company from New Mexico to California in 1829 along much of the Old Spanish Trail. Although he is credited with being the first to travel the whole route—the Old Spanish Trail from Santa Fe to western Utah and the Jedediah Smith route from Utah to southern California—he did not document his trip and few details are known.

In 1830–31 the William Wolfskill–George C. Yount Expedition became the first to document the whole route. The trail then became popular. The John C. Fremont Expedition of 1843–44 was the first to actually use the name "Spanish Trail."

In 1848 the Kit Carson Expedition along the Old Spanish Trail, documented by George Brewerton, marked the end of the trail's popularity; California gold seekers established faster and more direct routes. With the coming of the Mormons, the Old Spanish Trail was upgraded into the Mormon Road (also called the California Trail and the Utah Trail), which was used to help establish colonies not only in southern Utah but in Nevada and California as well.

The Pinney-Savage Party of 1849 is credited, along with the Jefferson Hunt Party, with being the first to take wagons over the western half of the Old Spanish Trail. William B. Lorton of the Pinney-Savage Party gave the most riveting description of the trail after the expedition, during which many died:

"Our route lay among fearful rocks and steeps, from which our animals fell and were dashed to pieces. We penetrated about two hundred miles into this vast region, and travelled [*sic*] five days without any water for ourselves or animals, except what we could get from the rains, and suck up through pipe stems from the crevices of the rocks. The sufferings of some were intense, a water fever seized the senses, they could not eat for want of water; every rustle of the wind was a bubbling brook to the imagination, and all the delicious drinks that the subject had taken for years arose before him to torture. . . . No pen can describe the sufferings and fatigue endured by those coming on the Spanish trail. Thousands of oxen and horses laid their bones upon the deserts. . . . Great has been the destruction of property, and all have suffered more or less, from travelling [*sic*] over a country blasted by nature."

Leroy Hafen succinctly described the trail: "The Old Spanish Trail was the longest, crookedest, most arduous pack mule route in the history of America." Ralph Moody wrote that: "[The Old Spanish Trail] was never

THE OLD SPANISH TRAIL THROUGH THE SAN RAFAEL SWELL

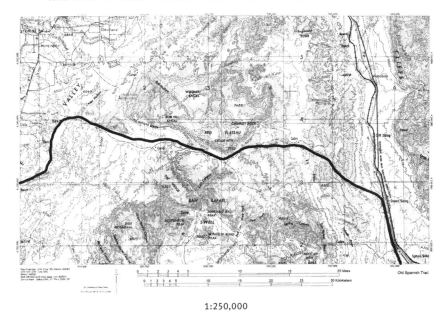

1:250,000

a single well-worn road but a series of trails that converged and separated. Much of it was blazed by Indians and wild animals."

A diarist from 1841 described the trail:

"Caravans travel once a year from New Mexico to Los Angeles. These consist of 200 men on horseback, accompanied by mules laden with fabrics and large woolen covers called *serapes*, *jerzas*, and *cobertones*, which are valued at 3 to 5 piasters each. This merchandise is exchanged for horses and mules, on a basis, usually, of two blankets for one animal. Caravans leave Santa Fe, New Mexico, in October, before the snows set in, travel west…and finally reach the outlying ranchos of California from where the trail leads into El Pueblo de Los Angeles. This trip consumes two and one-half months. Returning caravans leave California in April in order to cross the rivers before the snow melts, taking with them about 2,000 horses."

The main route of the Old Spanish Trail started in Santa Fe, entered Utah by way of East Canyon and Casa Colorado and then went up Spanish Valley, crossing the Colorado River at today's Moab. It then went north and west across Tenmile Country and crossed the Green River just north of Green River Town. After the crossing, the route went along Saleratus Creek to the east side of the San Rafael Reef. After following the Reef north via Cottonwood Wash, it went west (parallel to today's Green River Cutoff Road) to Big Hole, Little Holes, and Red Seeps. The trail then dropped off the San Rafael Swell into Castle Valley, which it followed south to Meadow Creek.

The trail went uphill for a short distance, through Emigrant Pass, down Salina Creek, and south to the head of Clear Creek Canyon (paralleling today's Interstate 70). Marysvale Canyon was traversed, as was Bear Valley. Now on the west side of the state, the trail went by present-day landmarks Enoch, Iron Springs, Antelope Spring, Newcastle, Enterprise, Mountain Meadows, and Central. The trail left the state near Utah Hill before dropping to Beaver Dam Wash and going on to Las Vegas.

There were many variations to the Old Spanish Trail. Group size and composition, water, feed for livestock, food for the expedition members, time of year, knowledge of the route, and current conditions all played a part in which specific trail was taken.

In 1994 the Old Spanish Trail Association (OSTA) tried to persuade Congress to include the Old Spanish Trail in the National Trails System as a National Historic Trail. Their first effort failed when the National Park Service failed to find that the trail was significant. In 2002 the Old Spanish Trail, after a lot of effort and lobbying by OSTA, was declared a National Historic Trail.

The major variations of the Old Spanish Trail, going east to west, include:

San Rafael Swell. Although the major route was to the north, under the south end of Cedar Mountain, two other routes have been documented. One went up Black Dragon Canyon, then down Coal Wash to Castle Valley. Another went up Temple Wash, over Sinbad, down Coal Wash, into Castle Valley.

Salina Canyon. The lower canyon was quite narrow and rugged. A major variation avoided this by way of Niotche Creek, Antone Hollow, Gooseberry Creek, and Soldier Canyon.

Fish Lake Route. This variation left the main Old Spanish Trail at the top of Ivie Creek and went up Red Creek, along UM Creek, and then along the west shore of Fish Lake. From there it went across the northern-most reach of the Awapa Plateau, and into Grass Valley, where it followed Otter Creek to today's Otter Creek Reservoir. It then went up East Fork Sevier River, joining the main Old Spanish Trail at what would become Junction.

How to Use the Guide

One thing that appears clear to me now is that the moments of adventure—for the most adventurous—are widely separated by long periods of hard work. Perhaps it's best that way.

—Kent Frost

The guide is set up in an orderly fashion. To get the most out of it and to help you understand some of the terminology, read this section carefully.

The guide is divided into chapters, each representing a cohesive and physically separate area. Each chapter is prefaced with a general description of the area, its main features, a short history, and an overview map. This is followed by a Road Section and 1:100,000 scale map that describes the roads used to access the hikes. Each Road Section is followed by descriptions and detailed maps of the individual hikes they provide access to.

Road Sections

The San Rafael Swell is crisscrossed by a maze of roads; a few are paved but the majority of them are not. Most of these are unmarked or have multiple names, making it confusing for the first-time visitor. The Road Sections are designed to help alleviate the confusion. The very useful "San Rafael Motorized Route Designations Map," available from the Price BLM office (see Access and Information), shows the names and numbers of the motorized routes in the Swell including Emery County roads, BLM roads, and BLM ORV trails. The map also shows the approximate distances between road junctions. This guide uses the names and numbers of these roads, as shown on the San Rafael Motorized Route Designations Map, whenever possible.

The Road Sections direct you to the trailheads for each hike. They are placed in the guide immediately before the hikes they refer to. In most cases these trailheads are undeveloped. Very few of them have any signs, trail registers, kiosks, parking lots, or anything else of the kind. Most will require diligent attention to the road descriptions to find. The hikes accessed by a particular Road Section are noted at the top of each road description. In a few instances you will have to use two Road Sections to get to the start of a hike.

Each Road Section starts with a list of which hikes are accessed, where the road originates, and the appropriate 1:100,000 scale maps that cover the area. Next is a description of how to get to the desired road from a major road, usually a highway or Interstate 70. The Road Section then informs you as to what type of vehicle is appropriate for that road. This is broken down into four categories: most vehicles, medium-clearance vehicles, high-clearance vehicles, and high-clearance four-wheel-drives (4WDs).

- Most vehicles: Means just that. Low-clearance cars, motor homes, vehicles towing trailers, etc.
- Medium-clearance vehicles: Includes a lot of small car models and most pickups.
- High-clearance vehicles: Includes SUVs, short wheelbase vans, and pickups. Make sure you have good tires, a jack, and a spare.
- High-clearance four-wheel-drive: These roads are rarely described in the guide. When they are mentioned, realize that these roads are for real 4WDs. Most SUVs will be okay. The smaller four-wheel-drive and all-wheel-drive cars do not have the ground clearance to make it over most of these roads. These roads are often very rocky. Make sure you have a shovel, good tires, a good jack, and a full-sized spare.

There is a difference between a dirt road and a track. An unpaved road, though also dirt or gravel, is one that is maintained by grading. Tracks are rarely, if ever, maintained. They can range from good, well-packed dirt roads to rough, high-clearance 4WD trails that have never seen a grader.

With rain or snow any of the roads can become impassable, even to 4WDs. If you are leaving ruts in a wet road, get to a firm spot quickly and stop! It usually doesn't take long for things to dry out around here. If you can wait until it does, you'll save the rest of us the headache of dealing with rock-hard, axle-deep ruts later on. On some roads short sections of deep sand can be encountered. Roads can suddenly change overnight. It is best to be wary. If in doubt, walk through suspect sections of road first. Roads may become washed out or have unexpected rocky sections. Most of these roads contain blind turns. Make sure you stay on your side of the road and slow down as you take these corners. You may not see an oncoming vehicle until it is too late. Try not to drive the roads at night. A black cow on a black road on a black night will not be seen. Deer, antelope, and two types of jackass will all also conspire against you. Play it safe.

The introductory paragraph also informs you whether there is camping in the area. This does not necessarily mean there is a campground, though. It simply means that there is free "at large" camping available off of short side roads or pullouts. These will have no facilities. You can camp anywhere on the Swell as long as you pack everything out and do not damage the environment. Do not make your own track to a campsite. There are plenty enough already. Some of the more popular areas now have designated camp-sites (Buckhorn Wash, Wedge Overlook, Temple Mountain, etc.), please use them. This guide will point them out whenever possible. There are only two "developed" campgrounds in the San Rafael Swell. There is a self-pay camp-ground at the San Rafael River bridge (see Buckhorn Draw or Cottonwood Wash Road Sections) with lots of sites, picnic tables, fire rings, and pit toilets, but no running water. If this is still too primitive, Goblin Valley State Park at the southern end of the Swell has a 21-site, full-service campground with culinary water, modern restrooms, hot showers, and a sanitary dump station for trailers and motor homes. This popular campground gets very busy and reservations are often necessary well in advance (1-800-322-3770). There are fees for camping and entrance to the state park.

Next is the road mileage list. It starts with a description of where the mileage begins. All mileage is cumulative and approximate. If you are traveling these roads in the opposite direction of how they are described here, you will need to do some math. There are several features within the mileage lists. Cumulative mileage is included so you can keep tabs on how things are going. This is meant to reassure. Though this may seem to be overkill at times, it will help you know whether you are at the right spot or not. Note that odometer readings can vary from vehicle to vehicle depending on a number of factors. Use these mileages to add your own finds or to backtrack without having to go to the start of the road. When important side roads are reached, the mileage list for that road is indented. If your vehicle doesn't have an odometer that you can zero, and you can't add and subtract in your head, bring a hand calculator.

Waypoints are shown with frequency throughout the road mileage list for those using GPS units. These UTM Zone 12 NAD 83 coordinates will provide an approximate location. For those navigating these roads with maps only, match the lines and waypoints from the maps in this guide with the appropriate 1:100,000 scale maps and/or the San Rafael Motorized Route Designations Map.

Throughout the road mileage list, at each trailhead the number of the hike is printed in bold type. Shorter hikes, those that don't warrant their own heading, are described in brief in the Road Sections. They are all worthwhile.

Historical notes are added throughout the manuscript and often appear in the Road Sections.

Points of interest are also noted in the Road Sections. These include exceptional overlooks, good campsites, and Native American rock art panels.

Some of the roads and tracks detailed in the guide may in the future be closed to vehicle use. Without definitive data it is impossible to provide accurate information on these possible closures. Please obey all signs.

The Road Sections may seem complicated at first, but they are infinitely less confusing than being lost in a maze of roads. Follow the Road Sections assiduously as you drive along.

At the beginning of each road section will be an overview map highlighting the road described, the trailhead locations, and general course of the hikes.

Description of the Hikes

The description of each hike is prefaced by a concise section that will tell you at a glance the pertinent parameters for that hike. These categories include:

Season

Any hike described can be done almost any time of year. Recommended seasons were partly chosen based on what would be best for most people. Consideration was given to how seasonal differences such as snow, ice, high water, or lack of water would affect a route. Also noted are which seasons are considered the off-season, seasons when you will likely find little traffic and few people.

Early Spring and Spring—March to June—is usually an idyllic time on the Swell. Snow melt ensures good water supplies. Occasional rain or snow-storms sweep the area. Flowers start budding and blooming. This is the time to do hikes with potential water shortages like Cottonwood Wash and Devils Canyon. By the end of spring you will start seeing bugs in quantity.

Summer—June through July—has temperatures that occasionally go over 100 degrees and road temperatures that approach 140 degrees. This type of heat can be unbearable to most. Summer is the time to hike narrow canyons like Little Wild Horse, Quandary, or Cable. Flash floods can occur in the narrower canyons. This becomes apparent when you see logs jammed well above the floor of a canyon. Stay out of narrow canyons when there is a threat of rain. They can flash flood even though it is not raining on you. An ominous rumble from up the canyon may signify a flash flood. Scramble to high ground. Hikes at higher elevations will be cooler. These include the San Rafael Knob and those on Sids Mountain. Bugs—gnats, mosquitoes, and deer flies—can be a real problem, especially along water courses. This is not the time to be on the San Rafael River or Muddy Creek.

Late Summer—August to mid-September—though still hot, has occa-sional rain storms and fewer bugs. This is the time to do the Black Boxes.

Fall—September through November—Off-season—has the most settled weather, with warm days and cool nights. This is the ideal time to be on the Swell. All hikes are doable, though a lack of water can be a problem on some of the backpack trips.

Winter—December to March—Off-season—has temperatures that can drop to -10 degrees at night. Periods of cold weather are usually inter-spersed with periods of warm weather, with daytime temperatures getting up to 50 degrees. You should be prepared for the colder temperatures. There are rarely more than a couple of inches of snow on the ground except at the higher elevations and on north slopes. With snow on the ground, plan trips as you would for a winter mountaineering excursion. It is a rare day, though, when there is enough snow to ski on. Winter is the time to do the nontech-nical hikes in Eagle Canyon or to explore the Eastern and Northern Reefs. Roads have to be a consideration in winter. When snow covered they can be dangerous. When the days warm up the roads turn into a slick clay, and even 4WDs will have problems.

Time and distance

For the most part, the time listed is the time it will take the average fit and moderately experienced person to do the described hike. A hike that is for youngsters and seniors and takes three to four hours will take that long for them. A hike that takes ten to twelve hours for advanced canyoneers might take twenty hours for a beginner. The time does include short lunch breaks when appropriate and rest stops.

After the time, total mileage is shown in parentheses ( ). Mileage was calculated using digital mapping software. Because maps are flat and don't take into account vertical rise, mileage is approximate. For instance, to cover a level mile on a map you would need to walk a mile. To cover a mile that goes up or down a slope on the same map, however, and you will need to walk more than a mile. The steeper the angle is, the longer the "mile" is.

Water

Water is most abundantly available during winter and early spring. After a good rain or snow, water can stay in potholes for days or weeks, even in the summer. Water is often the determining factor in deciding which hike to take. Many a desert agenda has changed due to a lack of or a plethora of water. In canyon country, water is usually found in two quantities: too much or not enough. Springs marked on the maps can be unreliable. Sometimes they are seasonal or change from year to year. Do not count on them to be where marked or to be producing. Bring all of your own water whenever possible. In hot weather water requirements go up. In midsummer, with temperatures near 100 degrees, two gallons over a 12-hour period might be realistic. Otherwise generally count on needing one gallon of drinking water per person per day. Consumption of alcohol promotes dehydration. Wait until the end of your hike to imbibe.

All water should be treated or filtered, without exception. Giardia and other pathogens are everywhere in the Swell. Giardia is a protozoa that can cause you no end of bowel distress if you should happen to "get the bug." For some, hospitalization becomes necessary due to massive fluid loss leading to dehydration. Because of the hard shell encasing the *Giardia protozoa* it is difficult to kill. Research has shown that there are several effective methods for eradicating these pests.

- Heat your water. Giardia and other pathogens are killed at temperatures of about 155 degrees. You just need to bring the water to a boil. You don't have to keep boiling it.
- Use Chlorine Dioxide Tablets or Liquid. These are the latest and the most effective water treatments available. Brand names include Aquamira (Water Treatment Drops), Potable Agua (Chlorine Dioxide Water Purification Tablets), and Katadyn Micropur MP1 Tablets.
- Use iodine. The 2% tincture of iodine liquid available at the grocery store works well. Add two drops per quart if the water is clear. Add four drops per quart if the water is cloudy. If the water is over 68 degrees let it sit for a half hour before drinking it. If it is cooler than that, you will have to let it sit for a longer period. Iodine pills (Potable Agua) work fine but are expensive. Always use fresh iodine liquid or pills. Iodine loses some of its effectiveness when exposed to air. Some people get a sore throat from using iodine for long periods of time.
- Chlorine and halazone. These are ineffective against giardia though they are effective against other pathogens.
- Filters. Though some of the older, charcoal-based filters did not remove giardia well, the new generation of filters, whether paper or ceramic, will all do the trick.
- Ultraviolet light purifiers. While they are the latest, lightest innovation in treating water, they only work reliably well in clear water. This is not always an option in canyon country.

Some of the water in the Swell comes from sulphur springs or is highly mineralized. The taste can be masked with powdered drink mixes. Some of the water may act as a laxative (such as the San Rafael River and Muddy Creek); water from other sources may cause constipation.

Maps

There are two types of maps listed. The maps listed first are USGS 7.5 minute series topographic maps. The scale is 1:24,000. These are the most current and accurate maps available and have replaced the notoriously inaccurate and out-of-date 15 minute series topographic maps. They are listed in the order of overall importance to the hike. All map references contained in the text refer to the 7.5 minute maps.

The maps listed second, in parentheses ( ), are the USGS metric series topographic maps. These are at a scale of 1:100,000. They cover a lot of territory but are not detailed enough to use for hiking. They do show most roads well and are included for that purpose as well as to provide a broad scope of an area. These maps are also noted at the top of each Road Section. Use the metric maps to get to the trailhead; then use the 7.5 minute maps on the hike itself. The metric maps are available at most BLM and Forest Service offices throughout the state. These offices generally do not have the 7.5 minute maps.

Both map types are available for sale at the Utah Natural Resources Map and Book Store; in person at 1594 West North Temple in Salt Lake City, or by phone at 1-888-882-4627. You can also view the "Index to Topographic and Other Map Coverage for Utah" and order from the United States Geological Survey in Denver online by visiting their website at www.usgs.gov or order by phone at 1-888-275-8747.

These days digital mapping products, such as iGage's *All Topo Maps* software, are available that provide complete state-by-state coverage of all topographic maps. You can view, manipulate, and print these maps from your home computer.

Loop hike

Describes whether the route is a loop or an out-and-back hike. Most of the hikes are designed to be loops.

Skill level

Don't kid yourself here. Have an idea of what you are capable of. Realize that if you are not prepared mentally and physically for some of the routes you could get yourself and your party into serious trouble. For those new to canyon country, start with the shorter, easier hikes. Get a feel for the terrain, your reaction to it, and the problems that off-trail hiking present.

Although the desert terrain can seem benign at times, realize that danger lurks around every corner. A young woman died in Quandary Canyon, an older woman died in Knotted Rope Canyon, and an older gentleman died in the Upper Black Box several years ago in separate accidents. All were preventable. Be prepared, be careful, and be thoughtful about the actions you take.

Difficulties in route finding can take several forms. Interpreting the guide and matching it with what you see on the ground could admittedly be confusing. Picking your way up or down steep ledges or in and out of canyon systems can be frustrating and time consuming. The 7.5 minute maps have contour intervals of 40 feet, which means a 35-foot cliff will not be shown on the map. After a 500-foot scramble up a steep, loose, and troublesome slope it is not fun to find a 20-foot cliff blocking progress. A hundred dead-end canyons were hiked while preparing this guide so you wouldn't have to.

Some of the routes in the guide are technical, requiring the use of climbing ropes and other specialized equipment. Unless you have extensive experience using this type of equipment, stay away from the technical routes. When ropes are mentioned, realize that old clothes line, ski ropes, or nylon parachute cord are not adequate. Suitable climbing equipment and the knowledge of how to use it properly is essential. Proper techniques can be learned by attending an accredited climbing or outdoors-skills school. Climbing gyms often offer classes for people of all abilities. The American Canyoneering Association teaches courses ranging from basic skills to advanced techniques and wilderness first aid. Many universities also offer such courses.

The two-part Canyon Rating System is used here to indicate the overall technicality of a hike's canyon sections and the type of rope work required (if any), followed by the degree of complication due to flowing or still water. The rating is shown in parentheses ( ) and is explained as follows:

Canyon Rating System

Technical Classification

1. Canyon Hiking: Nontechnical, no rope required. Hiking mostly on established routes. Involves some scrambling with the occasional use of hands.
2. Basic Canyoneering: Scrambling, easy vertical or near-vertical climbing and/or down-climbing. Rope recommended for handlines, belays, lowering packs, and possible emergency use. Exit and/or retreat possible without ascending fixed ropes. Scrambling requiring the use of hands and arms for pulling yourself up.
3. Intermediate Canyoneering: Technical canyoneering and climbing. Routes may involve any combination of the following: Problem-

solving. A basic knowledge of technical climbing. Rope and climbing hardware for single-pitch rappels and belays. Basic pothole escape techniques. Obvious natural anchors. Retreat up canyon will require ascending fixed ropes.

4. Advanced Canyoneering: In addition to intermediate canyoneering skills, you will require one or more of the following skills: Advanced free climbing. Difficult and/or exposed down-climbing. Climbing using direct aid. Multipitch rappels. Complex rope work (i.e. guided rappels, deviations, rebelays). Obscure or indistinct natural anchors. Advanced problem-solving and anchor-building. Advanced pothole escape techniques.

Water volume/current

A. Normally dry or very little water. Dry falls.
B. Normally has water with no current or light current, Still pools. Falls are dry or running at a trickle.
C. Normally has water with strong current. Waterfalls.

Yosemite Decimal System

The Yosemite Decimal System, shown in brackets [ ], is used to describe how difficult a section of terrain is at its hardest, most technical part. It is also used to describe the relative difficulty of individual climbs. This system has been used for years by hikers and climbers throughout the United States. The Yosemite Decimal System is broken down into 5 classes:

1. Trail or flat walking. No objective dangers.
2. Off-trail walking, some scrambling and boulder hopping. Steeper terrain.
3. Definite scrambling. Hands may be needed for balance. Exposure to heights possible.
4. Large hand and foot holds are used. A fall could have serious medical consequences. The use of a rope with beginners may be necessary. This is as hard as the average, experienced, and fit hiker can handle. If you get to a section that looks too hard, don't do it. A brave, dead canyoneer is remembered not as brave but as dead.
5. The 5th class category, which is the start of roped climbing, is broken down into smaller segments; 5.0–5.14.

The steep route into Pine Canyon. Photo courtesy Ryan Choi.

5.0–5.4:   Novice. A person of reasonable fitness can climb at this level with little or no rock climbing skills.

5.4–5.7:   Intermediate. Requires rock climbing skills or strength.

5.7–5.9:   Advanced. Good rock climbing skills and strength are generally needed to climb at this level.

5.10–5.14:   Expert. Excellent rock climbing skills are required to climb at this level.

In this guide no climbing problems are over 5.6 in difficulty. If you are not familiar with roped climbing techniques you should stay away from the 5th class routes. Experienced rock climbers may wish to forgo a rope on some routes. For them the exposure levels are influential. A 5.6 move on a 10-foot wall is not that dangerous while a 5.4 move 30 feet off the deck is a bit more serious. There should be at least one person in your party who can lead the hard parts of a route without protection and then belay others if necessary. Belay anchors are usually nonexistent. Exposure heights are given in the description of the hike when applicable. Example: [5.4, 30'] means there is a 30-foot-high wall, slab, or chimney that has a 5.4 move at its hardest part. All ratings are assuming hiking shoes or boots are to be worn. Specialized rock-climbing shoes could drastically lower the ratings.

There are other notes included under Skill level. Hikes that entail much wading or swimming are mentioned. Depending on the length of the swim, a life jacket or an inner tube may be needed. Hikes that involve wading or swimming will require the use of wading shoes. Although most shoes will be adequate for wading, hiking in wet, sandy shoes and socks is a quick way to develop blisters. Sport sandals (no flip-flops!), such as those made by Chaco or Teva, are a great way to go. You may not want to hike long distances in them, but they are easy to carry along in a pack and use when needed.

Each hike description starts with a brief summary of the route. Following that is a detailed mileage list and "play-by-play" account. All mileage is cumulative and approximate. Within the body of the description are several things to note. *Digressions* describe short side trips or note points of interest. *Rock climber's notes* describe short, difficult side trips or variations that will be of interest to rock climbers. Pinnacles with potential routes are also mentioned. The *Historical notes* bring a sense of history to the hikes.

Waypoints are shown with high frequency throughout the mileage list for those using GPS units. These UTM Zone 12 NAD 83 coordinates are equivalent to WGS84 for navigation purposes and will provide an approximate location. For those using GPS units, deep canyons and heavy cloud cover often block satellite reception, rendering them useless. For those using map and compass for navigation, match the lines and waypoints shown on the maps in this guide to the appropriate 7.5 minute (1:24,000 scale) sheet maps.

A compass is essential when using the guide. Compass bearings are used extensively. Don't count on your innate sense of direction to get you through. A couple of sharp turns in a sinuous canyon can be confusing. Inexpensive compasses work as well as expensive ones. Carry one and use it regularly. Don't count on your digital compass on your GPS to always work in canyon country. A weak signal or nonfunctioning unit could leave you in a dangerous situation.

Names for features are as historically accurate as possible. In several instances more than one name was found for a feature; e.g., Delicate Arch in Spring Canyon has at least three documented names. To complicate things, in some cases more than one feature has the same name. There are two Cedar Mountains, two Red Canyons, three Jackass Flats, and at least three Cottonwood Washes in the Swell. Names may differ locally. Sometimes the best sounding name was chosen for the guide. If no names were found, the liberty of putting a simple name on a feature was taken.

At the end of each hike description is an elevation profile and a detailed map or maps showing the exact course of the route with mileage. These invaluable, hill-shaded, 7.5 minute (1:24,000 scale) topographic maps also have a 1,000 meter UTM grid and an accurate map scale. These maps are to be used as a reference only and in most cases are too narrow in scope to be used solely for navigation.

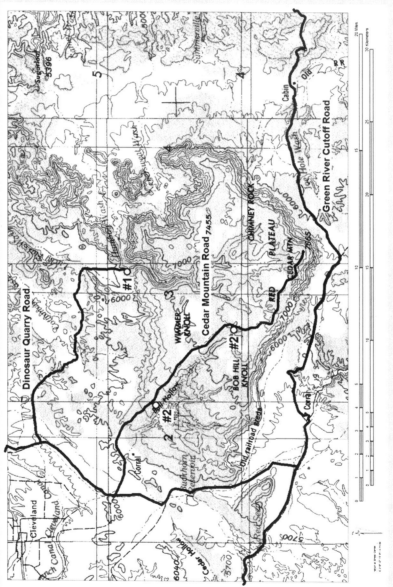

1:250,000

1 CEDAR MOUNTAIN AND THE CLEVELAND-LLOYD DINOSAUR QUARRY

Cedar Mountain and the Cleveland-Lloyd Dinosaur Quarry are at the northern end of the San Rafael Swell. Unlike the other areas in this guide, the Cedar Mountain area does not have many routes for the canyoneer, though it does offer two day hikes, great bouldering, excellent views, and good camping. The view area at the top of the mountain has picnic tables, grates for BBQs, a short nature trail, and plenty for children to do.

For rock climbers the conglomerate cap that sits atop Cedar Mountain offers good bouldering and top rope problems up to fifty feet in length. The rock consists of smooth river pebbles imbedded in a tough matrix. Pinch holds on near-vertical walls predominate. These walls are rarely ascended, so loose rock will be encountered.

The Cleveland-Lloyd Dinosaur Quarry boasts the densest concentration of dinosaur bones from the Jurassic Period ever discovered. It is part of what is known as the Colorado/Utah Dinosaur Triangle. The other corners of the triangle are Vernal, Utah, and Grand Junction, Colorado. All three areas are known for their fossilized dinosaur bones. At the Dinosaur Quarry there is a visitor center which has interpretive exhibits, sells books and souvenirs, and has picnic tables, and water. Three short hiking trails originate here. In the quarry buildings you will see dinosaur bones still imbedded in the sandstone. This is a great place for kids.

The Dinosaur Quarry has a limited season of operation. From late March through Memorial Day (end of May) it is open on Fridays, Saturdays, and Sundays only. From Memorial Day through Labor Day (early September) the quarry is open seven days a week. Labor Day through the end of October it is open only on Fridays, Saturdays, and Sundays again. Hours of operation are 10 a.m. to 5 p.m. except on Sundays when it is open from noon to 5 p.m.

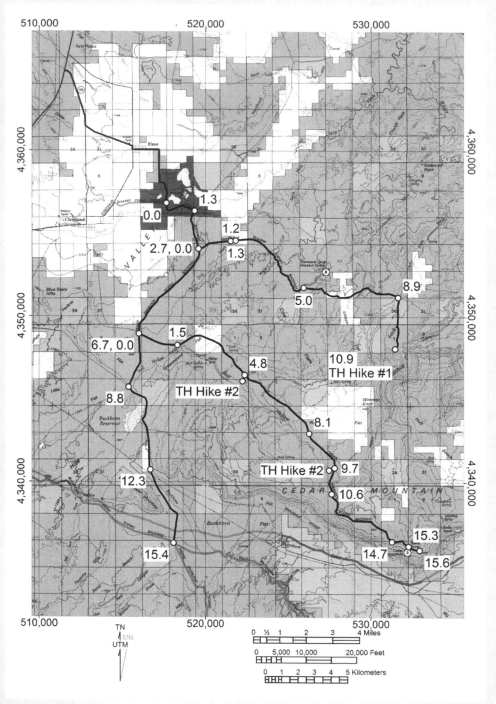

1:100,000

EM206/Cedar Mountain and
EM216/Dinosaur Quarry Road Section

Access to Hikes #1 and #2.

Access is from Highway 10.

1:100,000 map: Huntington.

The graded Cedar Mountain Road, also called the Cedar Overlook Scenic Backway, begins near the towns of Elmo and Cleveland and goes to the top of Cedar Mountain. The Dinosaur Quarry Road spurs off of it and leads to the Cleveland-Lloyd Dinosaur Quarry. Both of these roads are suitable for most vehicles unless wet or snowy. There is quite a network of dirt roads and shortcuts along the way. To reduce confusion, only the designated Scenic Backway routes will be described in detail. Numerous signs point the way. There is camping on the many side roads.

To get to Elmo go south from Price on Highway 10 for twelve miles and turn east onto Highway 155 between mile-markers 56 and 57. Go southeast on 155 for 2.2 miles to a signed intersection. (Continue south for another 3.5 miles to go to Cleveland.) Turn left (E) and follow this road (West Elmo Road) for 2 miles to Elmo and a 5-way intersection. Go right (S) on Center Street for one block then turn left (E) onto Main Street and follow it east for one mile. Turn right (S) onto EM110/Desert Lake Road and take this graded dirt road generally south. In 2.1 miles you will intersect EM211/Cedar Overlook Scenic Backway coming in on the right (W) from Cleveland. Reset your odometer here.

0.0   Mileage starts at the intersection. 0517602 E, 4356818 N Z12 NAD83.

1.3   Continue heading south on EM110/Desert Lake Road. You are now on the Cedar Overlook Scenic Backway. The road turns and starts heading generally east. You'll come to a sign at the junction with EM215 on the right (S). 0519259 E, 4356368 N Z12 NAD83.

2.7   Follow this road south. On the left will be the signed junction with EM216/Dinosaur Quarry Scenic Backway. 0519542 E, 4354041 N Z12 NAD83.

Dinosaur Quarry Scenic Backway

0.0   Mileage begins at the junction with EM215/Cedar Overlook Scenic Backway. 0519542 E, 4354041 N Z12 NAD83.

1.2   Head generally east on this well-groomed dirt road. The road goes down a long hill then crosses a wash. On the far side of the wash is a dirt road on the right (S). 0521533 E, 4354513 N Z12 NAD83.

Historical note: This medium-clearance double track leads to some nice petroglyph panels. Follow the track southwest. Soon it crosses a wash. Follow a high-clearance double track southeast up the wash a short way to some likely looking boulders on the left (E). There are several small panels scattered on various rock faces. It may take some searching to find them all. They can be found on both sides of the wash.

1.3   Keep heading east. You will immediately encounter another dirt road on the right. This high-clearance double track heads southeast to the climbing area known as "Land of a Thousand Boulders." 0521823 E, 4354546 N Z12 NAD83.

5.0   The road continues east then swings to the southeast. There are many small tracks branching off the main road offering good camping. You'll come to a signed fork in the road. 0525854 E, 4351696 N Z12 NAD83.

The left fork goes northeast for 1 mile to the Cleveland-Lloyd Dinosaur Quarry (0526923 E, 4352652 N Z12 NAD83).

8.9   Take the right fork to continue to Humbug Canyon. Follow this medium-clearance dirt road generally east. There are numerous tracks branching off at various angles. Stay with the main road. You will be passing through a section of private property, no camping. Though only fenced on the north side of the road, this property extends to the south side as well. After the road goes through a low ridge you will come to a fork on the edge of Lucky Flats. 0531560 E, 4351156 N Z12 NAD83.

10.9   Go right (S) and follow the road south across Lucky Flats to the edge of Humbug Canyon and the top of the Jump Trail. There are many places to camp. This is the trailhead for Humbug Canyon Hike #1. 0531443 E, 4348090 N Z12 NAD83.

6.7   Continue going south on EM215/Cedar Overlook Scenic Backway. Soon the road heads southwest and parallels the top of a ridge above Dry Wash. The road turns south again and you will come to a signed, four-way intersection. To the left is the Cedar Overlook Scenic Backway. If you continue heading south you will intersect the Green River Cutoff Road. If you turn right (NW) this road leads to the town of Cleveland. 0515934 E, 4348954 N Z12 NAD83.

Cedar Overlook Scenic Backway

0.0   Mileage begins at the four-way intersection. 0515934 E, 4348954 N Z12 NAD83.

1.5   Turn left (SE) onto EM206/Cedar Overlook Scenic Backway. Follow this graded dirt road generally southeast. Before the road begins ascending Cedar Mountain you will pass a dirt road on the right. This double track goes into the lower end of Bull Hollow and continues as a rough high-clearance 4WD track to the trailhead for Hike #2. 0518275 E, 4348239 N Z12 NAD83.

4.8   Continue on the main road as it leads you up the mountain. You'll intersect an unmarked dirt road on the right that leads to the Staker Spring trailhead for Hike #2. 0522340 E, 4346442 N Z12 NAD83.

Side road to Staker Spring trailhead, Hike #2

0.0   Mileage begins at the junction with EM206/Cedar Overlook Scenic Backway. 0522340 E, 4346442 N Z12 NAD83.

0.2   Head south on this medium-clearance double track to a parking area. This is the Staker
Spring trailhead for Bull Hollow Hike #2.
0522244 E, 4346105 N Z12 NAD83.

8.1   Keep following the road southeast. On the right (SW) is
a fenced sagebrush test plot. It was fenced in 1936. This is
worth a look to see the difference between natural vegetation and that grazed by cattle. 0526235 E, 4342939 N Z12
NAD83.

9.7   The road continues generally southeast. Just after it turns
to the south is a dirt road on the right that leads to the Bob
Hill Spring trailhead for Hike #2. 0527773 E, 4340875 N.

Side road to Bob Hill Spring trailhead, Hike #2

0.0   Mileage begins at the junction with EM206/
Cedar Overlook Scenic Backway. 0527773 E,
4340875 N Z12 NAD83.

0.2   Head southwest on this good dirt road. Cross
one wash then park near the second, just
before the road climbs a hill. If you are doing a
mountain bike shuttle for Hike #2, cache your
bike here. The Bob Hill Spring Trail begins
here and descends into the head of Bull Hollow
to the northwest. 0527515 E, 4340740 N Z12
NAD83.

10.6   Follow the road generally south. A dirt road on the right
(W) leads to Bob Hill Flat and Knoll. 0527608 E, 4339331 N
Z12 NAD83.

14.7   The road continues south then turns and heads southeast,
paralleling the rim of Cedar Mountain. You will come to
a Cedar Mountain Recreation Area sign and an overlook
on the right (S). This is a worthy stop. The view is fantastic.
There are interpretive signs and maps that will help orient
you to the area. 0531185 E, 4336289 N Z12 NAD83.

15.3   Keep following the road along the rim. On the right (S)
is a picnic area with an outhouse, garbage cans, picnic

tables, and fire grates (bring your own wood). There is no water. A short nature trail goes to a piece of petrified wood embedded in a conglomerate cliff. Youngsters may enjoy the narrow slots, caves, and rock formations. Bouldering is available throughout the area. 0532232 E, 4336081 N Z12 NAD83.

15.6 The road deteriorates quickly after passing an area of radio and telephone towers. 0532820 E, 4335856 N Z12 NAD83.

8.8 Continue following EM215 south. You will come to another intersection. Coming in from the town of Lawrence on the right (NW), and carrying through the intersection on the left (SE), is EM332/Lawrence-to-Tan Seeps Road. The faint double track to the southwest is B6768. 0515318 E, 4345714 N Z12 NAD83.

12.3 Head southeast then south on EM332/Lawrence-to-Tan Seeps Road. On the left will be the junction with EM335/Lower Cedar Mountain Road. This high-clearance double track runs generally southeast along the base of Cedar Mountain and connects with EM401/Green River Cutoff Road. It is very sandy in places and is for 4WDs only. Some interesting rock art sites along the way (45-degree Rock, Daisy Chain Rock, Silent Sentinel) make this a worthy side trip. 0516611 E, 4340761 N Z12 NAD83.

15.4 Continue generally south on the main road and you will reach EM401/Green River Cutoff Road at the Buckhorn Well Intersection. 0518022 E, 4336293 N Z12 NAD83.

Hike #1: Humbug Canyon

SEASON:	Any. There is much boulder hopping so no snow.
TIME AND DISTANCE:	Part 1: Two hours (2.4 miles). Part 2: Four to five hours (7 miles).
WATER:	There is always some water in Humbug Canyon. Bring your own drinking water.
MAPS:	Cow Flats, Flattop Mountain, Bob Hill Knoll. (Huntington.)
LOOP HIKE:	No.
SKILL LEVEL:	Part 1: (1A) Easy route finding. [Class 1] walking. Part 2: (1A) Easy/moderate route finding. [Class 3+] scrambling.

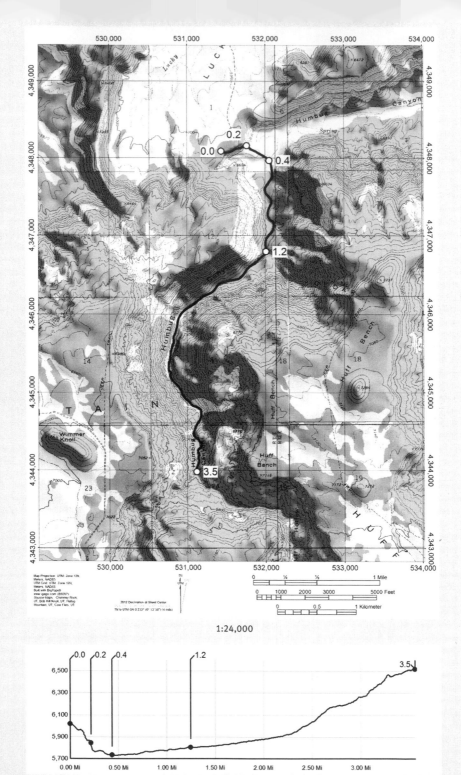

Elev Gain 502 Ft; Climb 957 Ft; Drop −454 Ft; Max Elev 6520 Ft; Min Elev 5729 Ft; Map Dist 3.563 Mi; Ground Dist 3.585 Mi

Humbug Canyon is a pleasant surprise. Its walls are composed of a variety of sandstone layers that are not normally seen in the San Rafael Swell: the Summerville, Morrison, Cedar Mountain, and Dakota formations. The canyon contains a medley of sparkling, spring-fed pools and is often choked with huge conglomerate boulders, some containing petrified logs.

The route comes in two parts. Part 1 starts at the Jump Trail, a constructed cattle trail going down a 200-foot cliff into Humbug Canyon. It then goes up Humbug Canyon until the going gets rough. Part 2 continues up the canyon past several challenging obstacles and returns the same way.

Part 1

0.0   Mileage begins at the parking area at the top of the Jump Trail. 0531443 E, 4348090 N Z12 NAD83.

0.2   Hike down the Jump Trail into Humbug Canyon. It goes generally west and is easy to follow. It cuts through a half-dozen different sandstone layers as it diagonals down the cliff face. Near the bottom you will go through a wire gate. Whether opened or closed, please leave the gate as you found it. You will end up on a bench above the floor of the canyon. 0531763 E, 4348162 N Z12 NAD83.

0.4   Head southeast across the bench and drop down into the wash on the canyon floor. 0532053 E, 4347970 N Z12 NAD83.

1.2   Now head south up Humbug Canyon. The sandy wash is easy walking at first. After a small drainage enters from the left (E) the going gets rougher. The wash becomes boulder choked up ahead. 0532011 E, 4346797 N Z12 NAD83.

2.4   Go as far up the canyon as you feel comfortable, then return to the trailhead the way you came. 0531443 E, 4348090 N Z12 NAD83.

Part 2

Mileage resumes from mile 1.2

3.5   The canyon turns and trends to the southwest for a while. Pick your way through or around large conglomerate boulders [Class 3+]. Watch for petrified logs embedded in them. A seasonal stream runs in and around the boulders, forming pools and small waterfalls. Climbers can have a blast here. The canyon turns south again then enters a park-like area and divides. The southwest fork is called Johnson Hollow and the southeast fork is called Huff Hollow. 0531118 E, 4343978 N Z12 NAD83.

7.0   Return to the trailhead the way you came. 0531443 E, 4348090 N Z12 NAD83.

Hike #2: Bull Hollow

SEASON:	Any. There is much boulder hopping so no snow.
TIME AND DISTANCE:	Four to five hours if you use a bike shuttle or five to six hours if you walk the whole way (11.1 miles).
WATER:	Perennial springs throughout Bull Hollow. Bring your own drinking water.
MAPS:	Bob Hill Knoll, Cow Flats. (Huntington.)
LOOP HIKE:	Yes.
SKILLLEVEL:	(1A) Easy/moderate route finding. [Class 3] scrambling.

Often routes are appreciated for the grandeur of their surroundings. The far view is what catches the eye. In Bull Hollow the far view is fair to middling. The view up close, especially while going by a series of springs and pools surrounded by huge boulders, is captivating.

The route goes down an old cattle trail, by Staker Spring, and into Bull Hollow. It is a shallow canyon that has eroded through the conglomerate crust that overlays all of Cedar Mountain. The route then goes up Bull Hollow and exits at Bob Hill Spring. The return journey is either by hiking along the northeast rim of Bull Hollow or by mountain biking back to the Staker Spring trailhead on the main road.

> *Historical note:* Alma Staker (1837–1922) moved to Castle Valley in 1880, eventually settling near Lawrence. He had a sawmill business and helped build canals for the new Castle Valley communities. Robert Hill moved to Huntington in 1879. He ran cattle here.

Before starting, if you are going to ride a mountain bike on the final leg, cache it at the Bob Hill Spring trailhead. You can lock your bike to a tree or to the fence a short way down the trail.

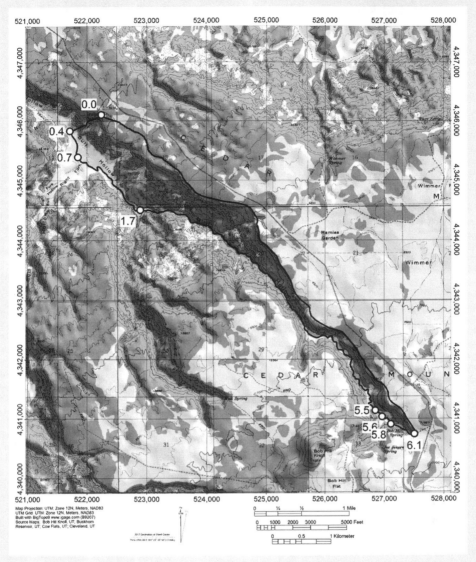

1:24,000

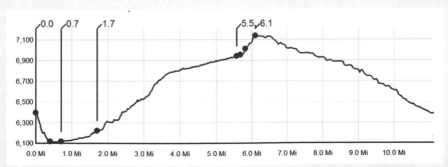

Elev Loss −7 Ft; Climb 1407 Ft; Drop −1413 Ft; Max Elev 7139 Ft; Min Elev 6111 Ft; Map Dist 11.090 Mi; Ground Dist 11.119 Mi

0.0   Mileage begins at the parking area and trailhead at the top of the signed Staker Spring Trail. 0522244 E, 4346105 N Z12 NAD83.

0.4   Hike southwest down the easy to follow Staker Spring Trail (now an ORV scar), past the spring, and down to the floor of Bull Hollow. 0521718 E, 4345830 N Z12 NAD83.

0.7   Head south-southeast up Bull Hollow, either along the ORV scar or in the sandy wash. The canyon divides, with the Right Fork heading to the southwest. 0521851 E, 4345389 N Z12 NAD83.

1.7   Follow the main canyon southeast. The ORV scar peters out and becomes a network of cattle trails. The [Class 3] canyon becomes intermittently choked with boulders from here on up. Often these are thirty to forty feet high and can be a challenge to ascend, though there is always an easy way around them. Climbers will have fun confronting these obstacles more directly. There are small springs that sometimes run like a stream and form small pools. At a wide spot the canyon divides. It may be hard to determine, but the main canyon goes east. 0522895 E, 4344506 N Z12 NAD83.

5.5   Head east then southeast up the main canyon. The canyon divides several times. Always head southeast to stay with Bull Hollow. The canyon gradually narrows and becomes shallower. The walking becomes easier on cattle trails or in the wash itself. As the canyon begins to end it divides one more time. 0526851 E, 4341136 N Z12 NAD83.

5.6   Go up the left (SE) fork. Soon you will come to a dirt road that comes in from the left (E) and crosses the wash. (It heads south onto the low peninsula that divides the canyon. On the peninsula are a stock pond and some stock tanks.) 0526967 E, 4341032 N Z12 NAD83.

5.8   Continue hiking southeast up the wash. Before it gets too rough, leave the wash and head south to intersect a track that parallels it. This is the Bob Hill Spring Trail. 0527117 E, 4340905 N Z12 NAD83.

6.1   Head east-southeast up the track, past Bob Hill Spring, to the dirt road on the canyon rim. 0527515 E, 4340740 N Z12 NAD83.

11.1   If you stashed a bike here, ride it northeast a short way to 206/Cedar Overlook Scenic Backway, then northwest on the Backway to the Staker Spring trailhead. If you are walking back, head northwest along the rim of Bull Hollow and follow it back to the start. 0522244 E, 4346105 N Z12 NAD83.

2 | THE NORTHERN REEF AND MEXICAN MOUNTAIN

The Northern Reef and the Mexican Mountain areas are in the northeastern part of the San Rafael Swell. They are bounded by the Cottonwood Wash Road on the west, Interstate 70 on the south, the Tidwell Draw Road on the east, and Cedar Mountain on the north.

The Northern Reef, located on the eastern edge of the Swell, is readily visible from Interstate 70 and Highway 6/191. It is a compact area that has seen little use by canyoneers. Deep, rarely explored canyons, seldom-visited arches, towers, pinnacles, and slickrock domes provide an opportunity for exceptional and often solitary hiking.

The Mexican Mountain area is to the west of the Northern Reef. It is dominated by the San Rafael River as it sweeps through the Mexican Bend, around Mexican Mountain, and exits the Reef to the north of Black Dragon Wash. The area is most well-known for the Upper and Lower Black Boxes. These are sections of the San Rafael River where the river has cut deeply into the Coconino Sandstone, leaving narrow, high-walled canyons behind. The Boxes are beautiful and challenging to negotiate, a canyoneer's dream.

The Northern Reef and the Mexican Mountain areas are well suited for day hiking, though there are several backpacking trips described. With the use of the guide other multiday trips will be easy to design. Both areas are in the Mexican Mountain Wilderness Study Area.

The Buckhorn Draw, Mexican Mountain, and Black Dragon Wash Roads are used heavily by ORVs in the summer and on most holiday weekends. The track from the end of the Mexican Mountain Road to Mexican Bend is closed to vehicles.

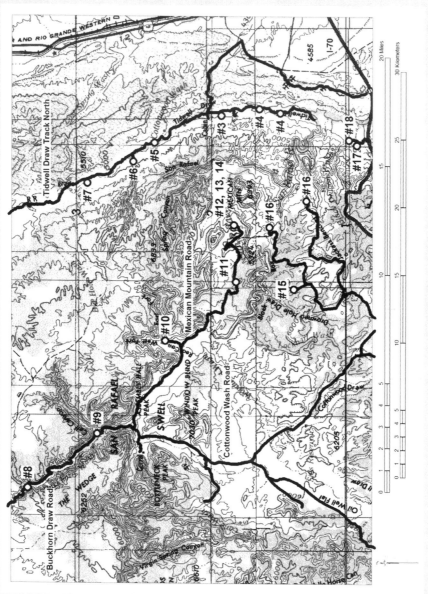

1:250,000

Peering down into the Lower Black Box from the heights of Mexican Mountain.

Historically the Northern Reef and Mexican Mountain areas are steeped in local lore. They were roamed by Butch Cassidy and his Hole-in-the-Wall Gang in the 1880s. Spring Canyon, north of Mexican Bend, was the site of a shootout between one gang member, Joe Walker, and the local sheriff. The Horse Thief Trail, to the east of the Bend, was used to bring stolen livestock from Tidwell Draw and the San Rafael Desert over the Reef and into the Bend.

The Old Spanish Trail followed the east side of the Northern Reef. It was a single-track trail until 1849 when Mormon pioneers started using four-wheeled wagons. The main trail went along the east face of the Northern Reef, passing Trail Spring near Tidwell Draw. This was called Akanaquint Spring by the Utes. It then went north to the Big Holes in Pack Saddle Gulch and west, under Cedar Mountain, by the Little Holes, and finally to Red Seep. From there the trail dropped off the Swell into Castle Valley. Other versions went through Buckhorn Wash and Spotted Wolf Canyon, where Interstate 70 now cuts through the Reef.

Signs of Native American habitation are visible at the many pictograph and petroglyph panels that are scattered throughout the Northern Reef and Mexican Mountain area. The most famous pictograph panel, at mile 5.6 on the Buckhorn Draw Road, had been vandalized but was extensively restored in 1996. The Cattle Guard panel, at mile 2.3 on the Buckhorn Draw Road, the pictograph panels in Black Dragon Wash, the large panel in Cottonwood Wash, and the petroglyph panels at the mouth of Spring Canyon at Mexican Bend are some other noteworthy rock art sites in the area.

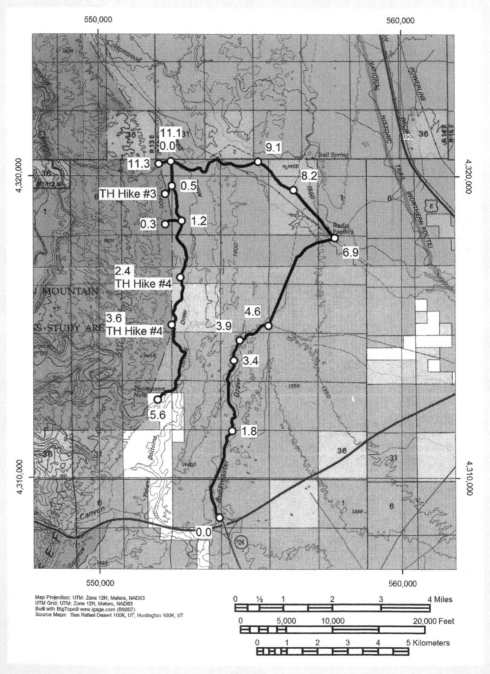

Map Projection: UTM Zone 12N, Meters, NAD83
UTM Grid: UTM Zone 12N, Meters, NAD83
Built with BigTopo9 www.igage.com (B9207)
Source Maps: San Rafael Desert 100K, UT; Huntington 100K, UT

1:100,000

EM1029/Buckmaster Draw Road Section

Access to Hikes #3 through #7.

Access is from Interstate 70.

Provides access to Tidwell Draw Track—South and B6809/Tidwell Draw Track—North.

1:100,000 maps: San Rafael Desert, Huntington.

This road goes north from exit 149 on Interstate 70 and intersects the Tidwell Draw Track—South and B6809/Tidwell Draw Track—North near the Smith cabin. Exit 149 is 11 miles west of Green River and is the same for Highway 24, which goes south to the hikes in the Temple Mountain, Southern Reef, and Eastern Reef areas (detailed in volume 2) and then eventually to Hanksville and Capitol Reef National Park. Though Highway 24 does not continue north from here, the graded Buckmaster Draw Road does and it is suitable for medium-clearance vehicles. The road, though not particularly scenic, is suitable for mountain bikes and there is camping along the way.

> *Historical note:* The Buckmaster name has two possible derivations. First, a man named Buckmaster mined here during the uranium years of the 1950s–60s. Second, unattributed: "John W. Buckmaster (1847–1917) was a Civil War veteran, serving with the Cavalry. Apparently Buckmaster Draw north of Elgin [Green River] was named after him."

From exit 149 on I-70 turn north onto EM1029/Buckmaster Draw Road.

0.0   Mileage begins at the end of the pavement on EM1029. 0553955 E, 4308680 N Z12 NAD83.

1.8   Go generally north up Buckmaster Draw. You will pass a corral on the left (W). 0554400 E, 4311527 N Z12 NAD83.

Corral behind the Smith cabin.

3.4   There is a large sign on the left (W) warning of the dangers of open mines, radon gas and unused explosives. 0554453 E, 4313866 N Z12 NAD83.

For a short hike and spectacular views of the Northern and Eastern Reefs, hike up the hill to the west of the sign. The Archtower is visible halfway up the face of the reef directly to the west. It is possible to get to Archtower Canyon from here by making your way down several cliff bands and crossing the strike valley to the west.

3.9   Cross Buckmaster Draw wash. 0554695 E, 4314558 N Z12 NAD83.

4.6   The road climbs out of Buckmaster Draw and turns to the east before reaching an intersection. Turn left (N) onto EM1032. 0555604 E, 4315032 N Z12 NAD83.

The road to the right (S) goes to Buckmaster Reservoir. The road going straight ahead (E) is EM1029/Four Corners Mine Road and intersects Highway 6/191 a mile north of I-70 at 0565418 E, 4315761 N Z12 NAD83.

6.9   Follow EM1032 north-northeast then east to the junction with EM1030. There is a sign here that says "Trail Spring, Tidwell, and Buckmaster Reservoir." Turn left (NW) onto EM1030. 0557700 E, 4317933 N Z12 NAD83.

It is 2.5mi to Hwy 6/191 if you go straight (NE) on EM1030. You'll end up 4.8 miles north of I-70 exit 158 (0560596 E, 4319812 N Z12 NAD83).

8.2 Head northwest on EM1030. You will reach the junction with EM1031 on the right (N). 0556411 E, 4319519 N Z12 NAD83.

9.1 Go left (NW) and continue following EM1030. You will reach the intersection with a dirt road and the old 1881 railroad grade. 0555221 E, 4320466 N Z12 NAD83.

11.1 EM1030 turns and heads west. Follow it to another intersection. B6809/Tidwell Draw Track—North is on the right (N). The Tidwell Draw Track—South is on the left (S). 0552373 E, 4320453 N Z12 NAD83.

11.3 Go straight (W) for 0.2 mile to get to the Smith cabin. On the Mexican Mountain 7.5 minute map the cabin is shown a quarter mile west of elevation 4548 at a marked spring but is unlabeled. 0551988 E, 4320398 N Z12 NAD83.

> *Historical note:* The first to run cattle in this general area was Alt Thompson. Next was the Thomas Tidwell family. For a short time the Joe Biddlecome family settled here. Millie Biddlecome: "We lived the winter out at the springs.... We had tents, Nate, his wife and three kids. . . . We had the nicest spring. The boys had made a little spout high enough to stick a bucket under and there was quite a stream of the nicest clearest water you ever saw—good water too, there."
>
> Thomas William Smith arrived next, in 1922. Attracted by the spring, he built a small house and a corral here by 1930. In 1933 his son, Wayne, and Wayne's wife, Betty, took over the ranch. Betty Smith: "We planted peach trees, apricot trees, and these two cherry trees. We raised enough cherries that a dozen families from Green River came out and picked cherries. Enough for everyone. And we had a little garden. Hard work."
>
> Betty described the end of the ranch in the 1940s: "A seismograph crew came through and drilled north and south of the cabin and it dried up our spring at the corral. So, there's no water, no more cattails, and I loved the cattails. . . . No more fruit trees, no more gardens. No more hay."

Tidwell Draw—South Road Section

Access to Hikes #3 and #4.

Access is from EM1029/Buckmaster Draw Road.

1:100,000 maps: San Rafael Desert, Huntington.

Also known simply as the Tidwell Draw Track, this rough dirt road starts just east of the Smith cabin and goes south along the foot of the Northern Reef to the San Rafael River. The area from the Smith cabin south to the San Rafael River is considered Tidwell Draw. The area south of there is called Tidwell Bottoms. Medium-clearance vehicles may be able to get to mile 1.2, high-clearance vehicles can get to about mile 2.4. Beyond that the track is for high-clearance 4WDs and mountain bikes if the rider is willing to negotiate several sandy sections. This road is impassable if wet or snowy. There is camping in the area.

> *Historical note:* Green River pioneer John Thomas Farrer, Sr.: "In the summer of 1880–1881 Thomas Tidwell moved his family and sons, Philamon and Frank. Both had families. And also Tidwell's son-in-law, Burdick, and his father, Alden Burdick. They squatted on the San Rafael River.... Where we lived [Green River] they had a hard name and seemed to be proud of it. They did not want anybody over there.... These Tidwells had cattle and horses but could not leave other people's alone." The Tidwells were forced off the bottoms in 1884–85 and moved to Colorado. Several old maps dating to 1885 show a settlement on Tidwell Bottoms called Tidwell. H. L. A. Culmer in 1909: "We are soon at the old Mormon Tidwell ranch, made by one who is now a bishop of American Fork. [This was Thomas Tidwell.] The cabin was built some thirty years ago and there Tidwell kept several wives and lived an adventurous life." There is nothing left of Tidwell.

0.0   Mileage begins 0.2 mile east of the Smith cabin at the intersection. 0552373 E, 4320453 N Z12 NAD83.

0.5   Go south down Tidwell Draw. You will reach the junction with a track leading to a drill hole and the start of Hike #3 on the right (E). 0552401 E, 4319675 N Z12 NAD83.

Side road to Hike #3

     0.0   Mileage begins at the junction. 0552401 E, 4319675 N Z12 NAD83.

     0.2   Go southwest on this medium-clearance track to the drill hole and trailhead parking. Start of Acer's Arch and Horse Thief Trail Canyon Hike #3. 0552190 E, 4319410 N Z12 NAD83.

1.2   Continue going south down Tidwell Draw. The junction with the dirt road to Horse Thief Trail Canyon will be on the right (E). 0552674 E, 4318503 N Z12 NAD83.

Side road to Horse Thief Trail Canyon

     0.0   Mileage begins at the junction. 0552674 E, 4318503 N Z12 NAD83.

     0.3   Go west then southwest on this medium-clearance track to a parking area at the mouth of the canyon. This is a great place from which to explore the lower box of the canyon. 0552186 E, 4318402 N Z12 NAD83.

2.4   Just before the road goes down into a wash, the mouths of three canyons can be seen exiting the reef to the west. The one farthest left (S) is Archtower Canyon. Most high-clearance vehicles will make it this far. The road gets very rough beyond this point. For practical purposes, this will be described as the trailhead for Sheep Cave and Archtower Canyons Hike #4. Park near here before the track enters the wash. 0552692 E, 4316630 N Z12 NAD83.

3.6   Those in serious, high-clearance 4WDs may wish to continue on down the track to the mouth of Sheep Cave Canyon and park there. 0552397 E, 4315058 N Z12 NAD83.

5.6   The rough 4WD track continues south past Sheep Cave Canyon and reaches the San Rafael River just east of Thompson Hole (Hike #18).

Many rarely explored canyons can be accessed from this part of Tidwell Draw. 0551935 E, 4312564 N Z12 NAD83.

Hike #3: Acer's Arch and Horse Thief Trail Canyon

SEASON:	Any. Summer can be hot.
TIME AND DISTANCE:	Four to six hours (Alternate 1—5.4 miles, Alternate 2—6.7 miles).
WATER:	Seasonal potholes. Bring your own water.
MAPS:	Mexican Mountain. (San Rafael Desert, Huntington.)
LOOP HIKE:	Yes.
SKILL LEVEL:	1A). Moderate route finding. [Class 3+] scrambling.

The hike to Acer's Arch is different, perhaps sublime. It winds its way up small canyons, around Navajo domes, in and out of sandy washes, and climaxes at the top of the Northern Reef with thrilling panoramas, intriguing outlaw history, and a seldom-visited arch. The possibilities for route variations here are countless and one can easily link this to several other hikes.

0.0   Mileage begins at the trailhead at the drill pipe. 0552190 E, 4319410 N Z12 NAD83.

0.7   From the trailhead you will see two small buttresses to the west and southwest. Go west up the shallow drainage that goes between them. You will be entering the Mexican Mountain Wilderness Study Area. Contour above the drainage on the right (N) side to avoid a small fall. You will end up on a flat knoll just west of elevation 4982 on the Mexican Mountain map. The scene to the west is a maze of Navajo Sandstone domes. You will ultimately be aiming for the left (S) side of the farthest dome to the left (S) that is shaped like a dorsal fin. 0551205 E, 4319418 N Z12 NAD83.

0.9   Head southwest down a small draw into the wash below you that follows a north to south running fault. Cairns may show the way. This fault is an important landmark and will be used again. 0550988 E, 4319199 N Z12 NAD83.

> *Digression:* Heading north up the wash and over a divide for 0.5 mile along the fault brings you to the drainage in Alternate

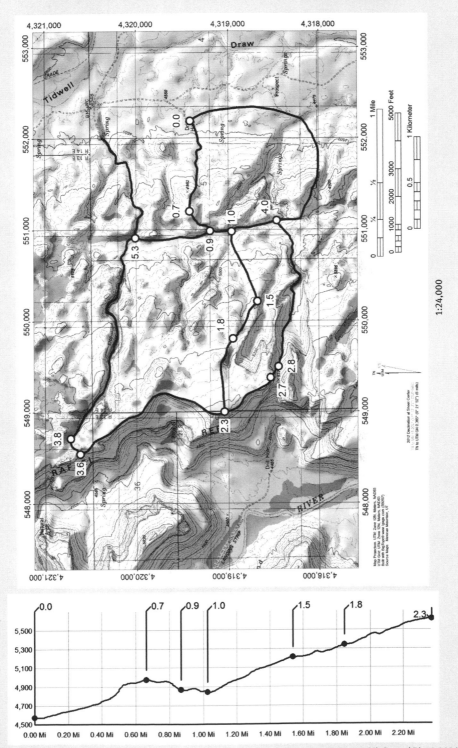

Elev Gain 1047 Ft; Climb 1270 Ft; Drop −223 Ft; Max Elev 5618 Ft; Min Elev 4569 Ft; Map Dist 2.370 Mi; Ground Dist 2.395 Mi

2. 0550915 E, 4320011 N Z12 NAD83. You can go west up the drainage for 1.5 miles to the rim of Spring Canyon. 0548758 E, 4320294 N Z12 NAD83. Or you can head east down the drainage for 1 mile and you will arrive at the Smith cabin. A stock trail leads the way (see Alternate 2 for details). 0551988 E, 4320398 N Z12 NAD83.

1.0   Go left (S) down the wash. The left (E) side of the wash is formed by a towering cliff. Just before the end of the cliff a wash comes in from the right (NE). 0550983 E, 4318962 N Z12 NAD83.

Digression: If you continue south down the wash for another 0.3 mile you will intersect Horse Thief Trail Canyon just above the keeper pothole (see Alternate 1 for details). 0551107 E, 4318462 N Z12 NAD83.

1.5   From this junction head west-southwest and contour past the dorsal fin–shaped dome to the rim of the right-hand fork of Horse Thief Trail Canyon. 0550218 E, 4318683 N Z12 NAD83.

1.8   Go northwest to skirt the canyon. You will be heading toward a dome with a small knob on its top. Intersect a small draw on the left (W) and go northwest up it to a cairn at its head. 0549808 E, 4318949 N Z12 NAD83.

2.3   When you come out of the draw the dome with the knob will be right before you to the northwest. To the left (S) of the dome is a short drainage. Continue going northwest and skirt the drainage on the right (N) side to bypass a fall. You will be passing between the dome and the drainage. When you are on the far side of the dome begin heading west until you reach the rim of the escarpment. The view is staggering. Once there you will be looking 900 feet down at the San Rafael River as it makes the Mexican Bend around Mexican Mountain. You can see a uranium-era airstrip paralleling the river. Coming into the bend from the right (N) is Spring Canyon (Hikes #6 and #14). 0549005 E, 4319044 N Z12 NAD83.

To return, there are two alternatives. Alternate 1 is technically harder, but is shorter and goes past Acer's Arch and down the eastern section of the Horse Thief Trail. Alternate 2 is a couple of miles longer, but is a must for the photographer as it follows the rim of

Spring Canyon for a mile, always showing a new face to the camera enthusiast.

Alternate 1

Resumes from mile 2.3.

2.7 Go southeast, staying close to the rim of the escarpment, until you reach the rim of Horse Thief Trail Canyon. You'll be right above and just north of the saddle at the head of the canyon marked elevation 5370 on the Mexican Mountain map. The saddle is the top of the route down to Mexican Bend via the western section of the Horse Thief Trail (Hike #13). Follow the rim as it turns to the east. An unlikely looking cleft appears with a cairn at its head. 0549379 E, 4318536 N Z12 NAD83.

2.8 Scramble southeast down the steep cleft [Class 3+, 20'] until the small, double Acer's Arch is reached. Large packs will need to be lowered. From the arch you can clearly see the route down Horse Thief Trail Canyon. The slope below the arch looks worse than it is. Follow a sometimes trail down the rubble to the floor of the canyon. 0549502 E, 4318446 N Z12 NAD83.

> *Historical note:* Green River rancher Ted Ekker: "When they were working on the railroad [in the early 1880s], a few of the old boys had a bright idea that they could slip down and steal some of the horses and take them over to Mexican Bend and hide them in that country. And that was called the Horsethief [*sic*] Trail."

4.0 Follow a use-trail generally east down the floor of the canyon. You will intersect a north to south running wash. (This is the same wash as at mile 0.9.) 0551107 E, 4318462 N Z12 NAD83.

> *Digression:* If you keep going down Horse Thief Trail Canyon it goes south then turns abruptly to the east. 0551120 E, 4318384 N Z12 NAD83. You will soon come to a large keeper pothole followed shortly by an 80-foot pour-off. Do not jump into this pothole unless you have a way back out. You can, however, skirt

all of this to the south. Back-track to the point where the canyon turns east. Go south up the fault and then contour your way around to the east, passing to the north of elevation 4900 on the Mexican Mountain map. 0551408 E, 4318077 N Z12 NAD83. Continue working your way east down the gradually sloping face of the reef until you can intersect the wash coming from Horse Thief Trail Canyon. 0552134 E, 4318264 N Z12 NAD83. The box section of the canyon is worth exploring and the springs inside the mouth of the canyon are often flowing. Return by following the face of the reef north back to the trailhead. 0552190 E, 4319410 N Z12 NAD83. From the fault to the trailhead this way is 1.5 miles.

4.5   Turn left (N) and follow the wash north back to the bottom of the draw (from mile 0.9 of the route). 0550988 E, 4319199 N Z12 NAD83.

5.4   Retrace your steps back to the trailhead at the drill pipe. 0552190 E, 4319410 N Z12 NAD83.

Alternate 2

Resumes from mile 2.3.

3.6   Go right (N), perhaps after a short excursion to Acer's Arch, and follow a bumpy course generally north along the rim. There are varied views of Spring Canyon as the Mexican Bend is left behind. For the next fifty minutes try to stay as close to the rim as possible, veering away now and again to negotiate obstacles. You will come to a slick-rock ridge that impedes progress. It is characterized by six domelike humps, with a seal-shaped pinnacle in the middle of them. (These are shown 0.25 mile south-southeast of elevation 5642.) 0548524 E, 4320641 N Z12 NAD83.

Deep in Spring Canyon you will see a freestanding, pinnacled fin. This fin is near the division of Spring and Nates Canyons (Hikes #6 and #14). To the south of the fin on the far wall, visible only if the light is right, is Delicate Arch.

3.8   Go northeast to the head of a southeast running canyon. 0548800 E, 4320473 N Z12 NAD83.

5.3   Descend this canyon. You will have to work your way past several [Class 2] boulder fields. As the canyon widens several plunge pools appear. After 1.5 miles you will encounter a north to south running fault. This is the same as in the digression at mile 0.9. 0550915 E, 4320011 N Z12 NAD83.

> *Digression:* You can continue heading generally east down the drainage for another mile, bypassing a fall on either side, and end up at the Smith cabin. 0551988 E, 4320398 N Z12 NAD83.

5.8   Head south along the fault, over a divide, and down the wash on the other side until you intersect the draw from mile 0.9. 0550988 E, 4319199 N Z12 NAD83.

6.7   Retrace your steps from here back to the trailhead at the drill pipe. 0552190 E, 4319410 N Z12 NAD83.

Hike #4: Sheep Cave and Archtower Canyons

SEASON:	Any. Spring and fall are best.
TIME AND DISTANCE:	Six to eight hours. Add one to one and one-half hours if you start hiking at mile 2.4 (7.4 miles).
WATER:	Seasonal. There are springs extending halfway up Sheep Cave Canyon. There are small springs in lower Archtower Canyon. Bring your own water.
MAPS:	Spotted Wolf Canyon, Mexican Mountain. (San Rafael Desert, Huntington.)
LOOP HIKE:	Yes.
SKILL LEVEL:	(2A). Moderate route finding. [Class 3] scrambling. This can be a long day.

Often the far view of an area does not reveal its hidden treasures. From a distance this part of the Northern Reef does not look like it has much to offer. The canyons that run into and through it are hidden in a tangle of Navajo slickrock faces and domes. Both Sheep Cave and Archtower Canyons do not stand out. But once you have found your way into them, they are true gems.

The hike goes up Sheep Cave Canyon, under one of the few natural bridges in the San Rafael Swell, to the rim of an escarpment that overlooks

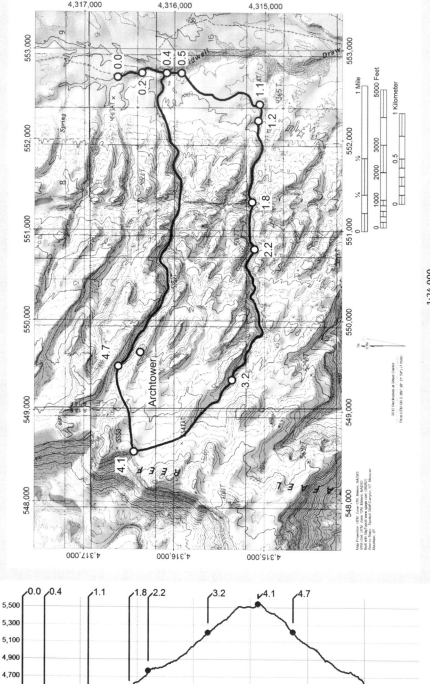

1:24,000

Elev Loss −44 Ft; Climb 1513 Ft; Drop −1557 Ft; Max Elev 5549 Ft; Min Elev 4353 Ft; Map Dist 6.987 Mi; Ground Dist 7.032 Mi

the San Rafael River, with spectacular views of Mexican Mountain and Mexican Bend. To return, the route drops into Archtower Canyon and passes the Archtower before exiting back onto the Tidwell Draw Track.

0.0	Mileage begins at mile 2.4 on the Tidwell Draw Track—South. 0552692 E, 4316630 N Z12 NAD83.
0.2	Head south down the track. The track has entered a wash. This is Tidwell Draw. 0552740 E, 4316360 N Z12 NAD83.
0.4	Continue south down the track. A wash entering from the right (W) is coming from Archtower Canyon. This hike can be done in either direction from here. If you can drive to this point you will save yourself 0.8 miles of walking. 0552738 E, 4316084 N Z12 NAD83.
0.5	Just beyond the wash the track divides. To the left (E) is the section of road shown on the Spotted Wolf Canyon map. (It climbs out of Tidwell Draw wash and parallels it on the east side.) Continue south down the wash a little farther. The track leaves the wash and climbs the bench to the southwest. The remainder of the track is not shown on the Spotted Wolf Canyon map. 0552739 E, 4315921 N Z12 NAD83.
1.1	Follow the track south-southwest across this bench. Just before intersecting Sheep Cave Canyon wash you will reach a junction near benchmark 4343. If you've driven this far, park near here. 0552397 E, 4315058 N Z12 NAD83.
1.2	Turn right (W) and head up the wash into the Mexican Mountain Wilderness Study Area. Soon the shallow canyon divides. 0552218 E, 4315073 N Z12 NAD83.
1.8	Stay left. A minute later, at the top of a grassy section, the canyon seems to end. Go left (SW) up a triangular slickrock ramp. It ends in fifty yards. Continue up the shallow wash. After passing an area of springs the canyon narrows. A series of large potholes is encountered. Above the potholes the canyon enters a park and divides at a north to south running fault. 0551318 E, 4315139 N Z12 NAD83.
2.2	Continue going straight (W). Pass a fall on either side. The Sheep Cave is high on the hillside to the right (N). As is evidenced by the amount of bighorn scat in the cave, it is apparent that this is a favorite bighorn getaway. It is probably best to not disturb this site. The next falls are just beyond the cave, are terraced, and can be passed on the right (N) with a tough [Class 3] move made easier with a

friend. Soloists may find this especially challenging. At the top of the fall the canyon divides. Find your way into the canyon to the left (S). 0550797 E, 4315112 N Z12 NAD83.

3.2   Head generally west up this canyon. After a half hour of glorious walking, much of it on slickrock, pass under the undocumented Ednah Natural Bridge. This is a great lunch spot. It should take two to two and a half hours to reach the bridge. 0549348 E, 4315359 N Z12 NAD83.

4.1   On up. Within ten minutes the now shallow canyon nearly ends in a park-like area. Continue northwest staying with the main channel. As the canyon tapers to nothing, a ridge to the west comes into view. It is characterized by a pinnacle on its left side and two triangular-shaped domes on its right side. Pass the ridge heading north until the rim of the escarpment is reached just south of elevation 5553 on the Spotted Wolf Canyon map. The view is expansive. Below you is the San Rafael River as it makes the Mexican Bend around Mexican Mountain. A route heads west down several ledges and then down a talus ramp to the river. Looking southwest one can see the start of the Lower Black Box and Swaseys Leap (Hike #16). To the north is the wide, barren mouth of Spring Canyon (Hikes #6 and #14). 0548552 E, 4316445 N Z12 NAD83.

> *Historical note:* Two similar name derivations are given for Mexican Bend. First, H. L. A. Culmer in 1909: "Mexican Bend is so named because a Mexican dared to follow some thieves who had stolen his cattle down in Old Mexico, and although they disposed of a number of them at the settlements on their way up, they still had a goodly bunch when they reached San Rafael.... That was the last of the Mexican. He was murdered at the [Mexican] bend in the river...." Second, Owen McClenahan: "At one time, a Mexican who raised horses lived here. He was murdered for money that he was supposed to have. Then his body was thrown into the river by the murderers...."

4.7   To the northeast is a brown cliff band running northwest to southeast. Beneath the cliff is the top of Archtower Canyon, the descent route. Hike east-northeast toward the brown cliff, crossing washes and gullies. Drop into the canyon just north of the Archtower. The

Archtower is a Northern Reef surprise. It is a 200-foot-tall pinnacle, spectacular in itself, but it also contains a large arch. 0549496 E, 4316618 N Z12 NAD83.

> *Rock climber's note:* The Archtower, made of Navajo Sandstone, has several excellent route possibilities, especially for off-width specialists. 0549652 E, 4316377 N Z12 NAD83.

7.0   Head southeast down the canyon. Below a beautiful set of slickrock potholes the canyon merges with several other canyons and trends to the east. The drop here can be passed on the right. The next fall [Class 4] can be descended to the right of center or up and around to the left (N). Watch for a small prehistoric animal trackway on the near-vertical surface of a boulder in the wash. From here the hiking is easy. Springs appear as you approach Tidwell Draw and the junction at mile 0.4. 0552738 E, 4316084 N Z12 NAD83.

7.4   Head north on the track back up to the trailhead. 0552692 E, 4316630 N Z12 NAD83.

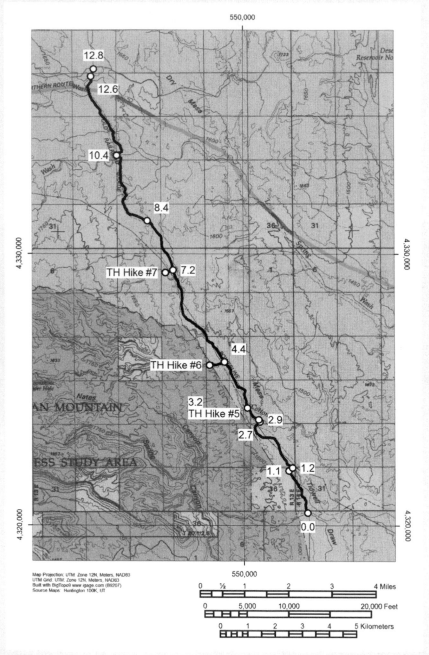

1:100,000

B6809/Tidwell Draw—North Road Section

Access to Hikes #5 through #7.

Access is from EM1029/Buckmaster Draw Road and EM401/Green River Cutoff Road.

1:100,000 maps: San Rafael Desert, Huntington.

This rough dirt road starts east of the Smith cabin and goes generally northwest along the foot of the Northern Reef to EM401/Green River Cutoff Road. The Old Spanish Trail paralleled the track, though signs of it have been obliterated by time. The track is for high-clearance vehicles and is impassable when wet or snowy. There is plenty of good camping in the area. Except for some sandy spots, this section of road would be great for mountain bikes.

0.0	Mileage begins 0.2 mile east of the Smith cabin at the intersection. 0552373 E, 4320453 N Z12 NAD83.
1.1	Go through a gate and generally northwest up Tidwell Draw to a junction with a dirt road to the northwest. 0551665 E, 4322001 N Z12 NAD83.
1.2	Go right (NE) and then through another gate. The road turns again to the northwest. 0551815 E, 04322115 N Z12 NAD83.
2.7	The Old Spanish Trail sign. 0550606 E, 4323812 N Z12 NAD83.
2.9	Cross Cottonwood Wash. The wash rarely has more than a couple of inches of water in it so should not be difficult to ford. The Old Spanish Trail went along Cottonwood Wash, though it did not enter the canyon itself. There are small pools along Cottonwood Wash in the mile above the crossing. 0550574 E, 4323894 N Z12 NAD83.
3.2	Start of Pinnacle Canyon Hike #5. Park just before the road climbs out of the wash in the vicinity of power pole #1061. (For the next several miles the track follows a line of power poles. Each pole has a number on a small silver plaque). 0550152 E, 4324327 N Z12 NAD83.

Nates Canyon.

4.4   Continue northwest to the junction with a track on the left (W). At the end of this medium-clearance spur is the start of Cottonwood Wash Hike #6. 0549319 E, 4326021 N Z12 NAD83.

Side road to Hike #6

0.0   Mileage begins at the junction. 0549319 E, 4326021 N Z12 NAD83.

0.4   Go west on this sandy double track to the trailhead and a parking area just inside the mouth of the canyon part of Cottonwood Wash. There is good camping here. Start of Hike #6. 0548776 E, 4325908 N Z12 NAD83.

7.2   As you continue generally northwest, the track winds under the power lines. You will come to the junction with a track on the left (W). Down this medium-clearance track is the trailhead for Grotto Canyon Hike #7. 0547416 E, 4329398 N Z12 NAD83.

Side road to Hike #7

0.0   Mileage begins at the junction. 0547416 E, 4329398 N Z12 NAD83.

0.2   Take this double track west under the power lines (just south of pole #1034) to a small parking area on the far side. Start of Grotto Canyon Hike #7. 0547176 E, 4329312 N Z12 NAD83.

8.4   You have been paralleling an old railroad grade. 0546506 E, 4331196 N Z12 NAD83.

> *Historical note:* The railroad from Grand Junction to Price was a part of the Denver and Rio Grande system and was called the Rio Grande Western. The initial route of the railroad was going to be from Grand Junction, through Green River, up the east side of the northern San Rafael Reef along Cottonwood Wash, then under the south end of Cedar Mountain (parallel to today's Green River Cutoff Road) to the Buckhorn Flat area. There it was to divide; one route going north to Ogden, the other going south to Utah's Dixie and beyond. To that end, construction was started and a railbed was built from Grand Junction to Buckhorn Flat. During construction, though, it was decided that a different route should be used. The new route was the same to Green River, but it then went straight up to Woodside, along the Price River to Wellington, and on to Price. Long sections of the old railbed can still be found. On some of the USGS 7.5 series maps, it is shown as the "Old Railroad Grade."

10.4   You will cross Big Hole Wash at what is shown as "cement crossing" on the Dry Mesa map. 0545395 E, 4333586 N Z12 NAD83.

You can do a short, easy hike up the canyon section of Big Hole Wash by following the wash west. From here it is 3.6 miles up the wash to the junction with Pack Saddle Gulch and another mile to Big Hole. Look for a small rock art panel as you make your way up the wash.

12.6   El Rancho Not So Grande to the right (E). 0544463 E, 4336523 N Z12 NAD83. This is PRIVATE PROPERTY.

> *Historical note:* Wayne and Betty Smith bought the land at El Rancho Not So Grande from a Mr. Nottingham in the early 1940s and built a small cabin there. Betty is credited with naming the ranch: "Dick and Edith Gardner—we called her 'Pete,'—came from California during the uranium boom and they went out there and staked a claim at El Rancho and they lived in a tent. We had a cabin out there and so they decided that they

wanted to build this rock house. All of us got together, Wayne and I and Pete and Dick, and gathered rocks, and gathered rocks for months and finally had enough that we thought we'd start construction…and we finally got it together…. I wrote a note [that we posted in the house] that said: 'this is a fun place to come and stop and get out of the weather and stay overnight if you need to, but please leave it as you find it.' Nobody ever did. They just make a big mess."

The final insult to the ranch happened recently. Betty Smith: "We went there one time, Wayne and I, and there was two big semi-trucks and two men with chain saws and you know there's a little cabin to the side of the rock house? They were gonna saw it in two and take it!"

12.8   Junction with EM401/Green River Cutoff Road. 0544546 E, 4336787 N Z12 NAD83.

Hike #5: Pinnacle Canyon

Season:	Any. No snow.
Time and distance:	Two to three hours, add one to two hours for digressions (3.8 miles).
Water:	Seasonal potholes. Bring your own water.
Maps:	Mexican Mountain. (Huntington.)
Loop hike:	Yes.
Skill level:	(2A). Advanced route finding. [Class 3] scrambling, [Class 5.4] climbing. Rock climbers only. Those less experienced will need a rope.

This short "after dinner" hike is designed for the adventurous rock climber. Physical challenges combine with a beautiful backdrop to set the tone for the hike.

The route ascends the face of the Northern Reef while following a shallow canyon. After an out and back digression to a jaw-dropping view into Nates Canyon, the route ascends a steep slab and enters a park-like area containing a 125-foot-tall pinnacle. A second digression leads to another breath-taking view and an alternate return to the start.

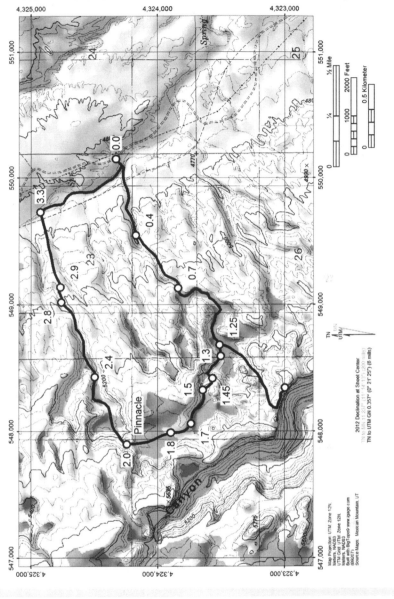

1:24,000

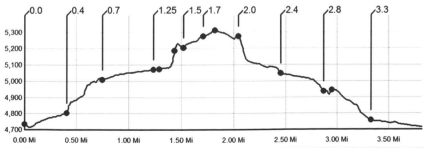

Elev Loss −21 Ft; Climb 755 Ft; Drop −776 Ft; Max Elev 5309 Ft; Min Elev 4714 Ft; Map Dist 3.818 Mi; Ground Dist 3.846 Mi

0.0   Mileage begins at mile 3.2 on the Tidwell Draw Track—North near power pole #1061 (each pole is numbered with a small, metal plaque). 0550152 E, 4324327 N Z12 NAD83.

0.4   Go southwest across Cottonwood Wash and then generally west-southwest up the wash on the other side of it. You will cross into the Mexican Mountain Wilderness Study Area. The wash quickly deepens into a shallow canyon and after 0.4 mile you'll come to the first of three pour-offs. Just before you reach the first pour-off is the start of the "triple bypass" route on the left (SW). 0549550 E, 4324171 N Z12 NAD83.

0.7   Follow a faint trail up onto and then along the bench above the canyon floor. The route slopes back down to the floor of the canyon above the third pour-off. 0549134 E, 4323845 N Z12 NAD83.

1.25   Continue generally southwest then west up the wash as it goes through a couple of park-like areas to a wash junction on the western side of a large Navajo dome. 0548686 E, 4323517 N Z12 NAD83.

> *Digression:* You can go left (S) at this junction and follow this short and steep [Class 3] drainage generally southwest for 0.5 mile (with a gain of 350 feet) to its head and a stunning peek down into Nates Canyon (Hike #6). 0548268 E, 4323024 N Z12 NAD83. After taking in the views from the top of the flat plateau to the east (traverse the northern side to find steep routes up through the caprock), return to the wash junction the way you came. 1.0 mile round trip. This could also be used as the end of a 3.8-mile round trip out-and-back hike for those not wanting or able to do the slab climb.

1.3   Go right (W) and follow the wash west a short way to another wash junction. 0548598 E, 4323507 N Z12 NAD83.

1.45   Now turn right (NW) and go northwest up the wash to where the quickly deepening canyon ends. The only outlet is a steep slickrock gully to the west. Scramble northwest up this [Class 3] gully to its end. To the left (SW) is the slab climb [5.4, 30']. The easiest way is to angle left after you step up onto the thin black ledge. Some more vertically challenged people may find that next crucial handhold a little out of reach, thereby rendering the climb's rating a bit higher for them. 0548421 E, 4323573 N Z12 NAD83.

1.5 From the top of the climb follow the ledge northwest back into the wash right above the big pour-off you just bypassed. 0548329 E, 4323648 N Z12 NAD83.

1.7 Continue up the wash generally west-northwest, going straight (W) through the first wash junction to the second wash junction. 0548063 E, 4323743 N Z12 NAD83.

1.8 Turn right (NW) and follow an indistinct gully northwest until you reach a saddle in a park-like area. You will see the pinnacle to the north-northwest. 0547992 E, 4323900 N Z12 NAD83.

> *Rock climber's note:* 0.1 mile southwest of the pinnacle is a small gully going through the western wall. It can provide some climbing fun. Chimney up the start of the gully which invariably has water in it. Surmount a yellow-striped friction slab to the north [5.6, 35']. Continue southwest to the rim of Nates Canyon (Hike #6). After enjoying the views return to the saddle the way you came. Round trip is 0.8 mile. If you don't want to down-climb the route, you can go northeast around the double-headed Pinnacle Canyon and follow the shallower canyon that's to the north of it west back down to Cottonwood Wash and then south to the start. From the pinnacle back to the start this way is 3 miles.

2.0 Go north-northwest to the head of the canyon that starts on the north side of the pinnacle. This is Pinnacle Canyon. 0547901 E, 4324241 N Z12 NAD83.

2.4 Now go east-northeast down Pinnacle Canyon, passing twin balanced rocks on the left, to a pour-off. 0548431 E, 4324492 N Z12 NAD83.

2.8 Pass this pour-off to the right or left and continue east-northeast down the wash to another pour-off. 0549021 E, 4324758 N Z12 NAD83.

2.9 Go right around this one and traverse east across a sloping bench above the canyon, angling gradually up until you find a notch leading the rest of the way through the caprock to the canyon rim. 0549141 E, 4324767 N Z12 NAD83.

3.3 Now head east-northeast down this flat, gentle slope until you intersect the bottom of Cottonwood Wash. 0549731 E, 4324926 N Z12 NAD83.

3.8   Turn right and follow Cottonwood Wash generally south-southeast back to the parking area at the start. 0550152 E, 4324327 N Z12 NAD83.

Hike #6: Cottonwood Wash

SEASON:	Any but summer. It is best in early spring, spring, or fall. Water can be a problem on the first two days, so try to do this hike after a rain.
TIME AND DISTANCE:	Three to seven days. This will depend on which digressions you choose to do (23.5 miles without digressions). The first couple of miles would make for an easy and pleasant short day hike.
WATER:	Seasonal. There is always water in the first mile of Cottonwood Wash and seasonal water in its upper reaches. The area adjacent to the Thin Man Pinnacle in Sulphur Canyon has seasonal pothole water but don't count on it. It may be necessary to carry enough water for the first two days of this hike, from Cottonwood Wash to the reliable springs in Spring Canyon, a distance of 18 miles. There is always water flowing in the San Rafael River, but it is questionable at best. Use it only if you must.
MAPS:	Mexican Mountain, Devils Hole. (Huntington, San Rafael Desert.)
LOOP HIKE:	Yes
SKILL LEVEL:	(2A). Moderate/advanced route finding. Difficult [Class 4] climbing. Possibility of little water along the route. Familiarity with low-impact camping techniques is essential. A short rope will be necessary for lowering packs.

This is a classic canyoneering trip. Variety, views, deep canyons, wide-open bench lands, arches, and pinnacles give character to these little-known and seldom-visited masterpieces. For the canyoneer there are falls to surmount, route-finding difficulties, a seasonal lack of water, and at several places a touch of the climbing challenge. There are some big elevation changes. Though a bit stiff, the rewards are exceptional. Some of the best rock art in

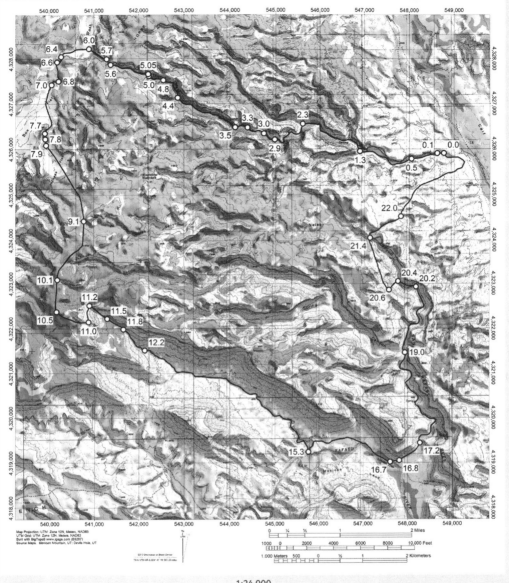

1:24,000

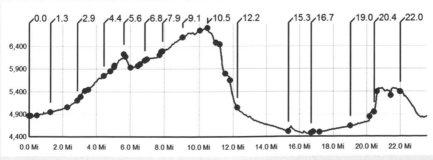

Elev Loss −15 Ft; Climb 4779 Ft; Drop −4794 Ft; Max Elev 6807 Ft; Min Elev 4467 Ft; Map Dist 23.550 Mi; Ground Dist 23.757 Mi

the Swell can be found along the way. This trip could undoubtedly be hiked in three days, but four days allow for a more relaxed pace. With side adventures abounding, this could easily be extended to a week. Side-trip possibilities will be mentioned.

The route goes to the top of Cottonwood Wash (a canyon) and drops onto Box Flat. This is crossed to the top of Sulphur Canyon, which is descended to the San Rafael River. The river is followed to Mexican Bend. From there the route goes up Spring Canyon and into Nates Canyon, which you ascend to the top of the reef back to the start.

0.0   Mileage begins at the trailhead at the end of the spur road. 0548776 E, 4325908 N Z12 NAD83.

0.1   From the trailhead go west and drop down into the wash. You will be entering the Mexican Mountain Wilderness Study Area. Continue west up the wash a short way then follow a use-trail onto the low bench on the north side of the wash. 0548633 E, 4325907 N Z12 NAD83.

> *Historical note:* Another use-trail branches off on the right (N). Follow this trail west-northwest as it angles up to the base of the brown Navajo cliffs. There are some interesting, faded petroglyphs on the wall. Though well worn by time, they have not been vandalized. Please don't be the first. After visiting the rock art return to the use-trail on the bench.

0.5   Keep following the trail generally west up the deepening canyon. On the right (N) wall of the canyon is a large alcove at the top of a talus slope. 0548052 E, 4325783 N Z12 NAD83.

> *Historical note:* This alcove contains numerous petroglyphs and pictographs and shows signs of heavy prehistoric use. There are also some historic inscriptions from the 1800s. A use-trail leads you north from the wash up through the talus to the base of the alcove. There are rock art panels all along the base of the cliff.

1.3   Continue heading generally west up the canyon until it divides. This first section would be an ideal, short day hike on easy terrain for those less active or with young children. 0546905 E, 4325956 N Z12 NAD83.

2.3   Go right (NW) and follow the canyon northwest, passing a small hanging canyon that comes in on the right (N). You may find some seasonal water. The canyon divides again. 0545613 E, 4326555 N Z12 NAD83.

2.9   Go left (S) and follow the narrowing and now bouldery canyon generally southwest. A large hanging canyon enters from the southwest. 0544981 E, 4326210 N Z12 NAD83.

3.0   Keep heading up the canyon as it turns to the northwest. After a short way the canyon floor is blocked by a large fall and pool. Just a little bit farther above it is another one. Before you reach the pool is a bypass route on the left (W) marked by cairns. Head up it onto the bench above. 0544745 E, 4326342 N Z12 NAD83.

3.3   Traverse generally northwest following cairns along benches until you rejoin the canyon floor above the second pour-off. 0544385 E, 4326473 N Z12 NAD83.

3.5   Continue heading up the canyon, now generally west, until it divides. 0544096 E, 4326475 N Z12 NAD83.

4.4   Go right (NW) and head northwest up the canyon until it divides again. 0542846 E, 4327132 N Z12 NAD83.

4.8   Turn right (N) and go up this canyon heading generally northwest. A short way up is a lovely seasonal pool and hanging garden. Just beyond that the canyon splits again at a small pour-off. 0542549 E, 4327520 N Z12 NAD83.

5.0   Bypass the fall on the right (N) and make your way into the right-hand (NW) drainage, staying with Cottonwood Wash. Head west then northwest up the canyon, bypassing a fall on the right, to another junction. 0542229 E, 4327610 N Z12 NAD83.

5.05   Go up the right (N) fork. You will quickly encounter a pour-off. A small seasonal spring just before it might offer some bonus water. If there is water here and you are planning on at least four days, a nearby overhang offers pleasant, shady camping. 0542213 E, 4327658 N Z12 NAD83.

5.6   Bypass the pour-off by going left (S) behind a large flake [Class 3]. Continue up the canyon heading west-northwest. Bypass another fall on the left. You will temporarily be leaving the Mexican Mountain WSA. The canyon enters a park at its head. The walls are weather-worn and twisted. Hike west up steep slickrock to a pinyon and juniper covered saddle. 0541375 E, 4327863 N Z12 NAD83.

5.7   Head north-northwest across the saddle to the head of a steep draw that runs northwest. You will see Big Hole Wash down below and Cedar Mountain behind it. If you have enough water to see you to Spring Canyon (or the San Rafael River at the very least) and you aren't pressed for time, then this area between the saddle and the draw would make a fine place to camp with great views. 0541284 E, 4327990 N Z12 NAD83.

6.0   Go northwest down the steep draw, passing a series of drops on the right, until you intersect Big Hole Wash. Note the arch on the left (S). 0540894 E, 4328221 N Z12 NAD83.

6.4   Follow Big Hole Wash west then south. As the walls of the wash begin to close in, notice the small arch on the right (NW). The wash becomes blocked by a fall. Backtrack a little way and bypass this on the left (E) following a use-trail. 0540270 E, 4328047 N Z12 NAD83.

6.6   Once you are on the rim, follow it southwest a short way until you rejoin the wash. Three washes merge just above the fall. The one on the left (ESE) is unnamed. The middle one (S) is Box Flat Wash. The one on the right (SW) is the continuation of Big Hole Wash. 0540181 E, 4327928 N Z12 NAD83.

6.8   Go south up Box Flat Wash. Bypass a pour-off on the right (W). When you get to the top of this pour-off the wash turns to the right (W). 0540214 E, 4327501 N Z12 NAD83.

7.0   Be careful not to continue south here. Follow the wash as it swings to the northwest then southwest. You'll pass a seasonal pothole and stock pond just as you reach the northern end of Box Flat. 0540060 E, 4327420 N Z12 NAD83.

Coming into Box Flat from the northwest is the high-clearance 4WD Box Flat Road. A mile to the south-southwest, on the far end of the flat, are the gaps between the Navajo buttresses from Hike #10. Beyond them is the head of the East Fork of Red Canyon.

7.7   Go south-southwest on cattle trails onto Box Flat a short way then head south-southeast into the draw that is east of the point marked 6315 on the Devils Hole map. After entering the draw follow a use-trail southwest along the base of the cliff on the right (W) to bypass

a pour-off with a seasonal stock pond below it. 0539913 E, 4326381
N Z12 NAD83.

7.8 Just past the pour-off the bouldery drainage turns southeast and
ends in a low cliff. Go into the head of the draw.

> *Historical note:* At the base of the cliff to the east, hiding behind
> the giant boulders, is the mouth of a deep cave. Just inside the
> entrance is a small pictograph panel on the ceiling. The cave is
> well protected from the elements, and vandals, and would be a
> nice, cool place to take a siesta on a boiling hot afternoon.

From the cave continue southeast up the rubble to exit the draw.
0539922 E, 4326223 N Z12 NAD83.

7.9 You will be at the continuation of the wash that runs through the
draw. Follow the wash south onto Jackass Flat. 0539940 E, 4326085
N Z12 NAD83.

9.1 To the southeast is a long, seemingly continuous, ridge with the
land form labeled Nates 6833 on the Devils Hole map at its southern end. Go south-southeast across Jackass Flat, crossing back
into the Mexican Mountain WSA, then over slickrock and sandy
benches heading to the southwest side of Nates. (To save confusion, 6485 is the dome with the nob on top, Nates is the one that
looks like a castle.) You will be on a saddle between Nates Canyon
and the East Fork of Red Canyon (Hike #10). 0540780 E, 4324423
N Z12 NAD83.

> *Digression:* You can head 5 miles east down Nates Canyon and
> intersect the route at mile 21.4 (0547128 E, 4324052 N). You
> could then head south down to Spring Canyon or northeast
> back to the trailhead. There are falls to negotiate, but all are easy.

10.1 Head generally south-southwest along the divide between Nates
and Spring Canyons and the East Fork of Red Canyon on a cattle
trail/ORV scar. Intersect the head of the North Fork of Spring Canyon (Hike #14) 0.25 mile west of elevation 6735 on the Devils Hole
map. 0540164 E, 4323089 N Z12 NAD83.

The route into Sulphur Canyon.

10.5   Now head south until you come to the edge of a ridge with a grand view. You will be between elevations 6832 and 6814 on the Devils Hole map. 0540149 E, 4322373 N Z12 NAD83.

11.0   Below you is the San Rafael River. Far down the canyon to the east is the Mexican Bend sweeping around Mexican Mountain. That is your destination. Go southeast down small ledges then across slickrock to the rim of Sulphur Canyon. 0540872 E, 4322144 N Z12 NAD83.

11.2   Follow the rim north until you come to the head of Sulphur Canyon. You will intersect Hike #14 here. 0540888 E, 4322510 N Z12 NAD83.

> *Digression:* To go down the South Fork of Spring Canyon, go north-northeast onto a saddle between Sulphur Canyon and the North Fork of Spring Canyon 0540943 E, 4322669 N Z12 NAD83. (You could also go down the North Fork, but some of the down-climbing would be laborious in that direction.) There are two big Navajo domes to the east. The one to the south is elevation 6842 on the Devils Hole map. Between the domes is

the head of the South Fork (see Hike #14 for details). 0541961 E, 4322483 N Z12 NAD83.

11.5   Descend into Sulphur Canyon by going southeast down the head of the canyon toward a large detached flake. Climb down a short chute behind the flake [difficult Class 4, 20']. A rope or webbing is a must here for lowering packs. Beginners may want a belay. Now scramble down a steep rubble slope [Class 3, 750'], following occasional cairns, to a wonderful flat area. The 175-foot-tall Thin Man Pinnacle is to the right (S). If there is pothole water here, this is a delightful camping area. 0541289 E, 4322218 N Z12 NAD83

11.8   Head southeast across the pinyon and juniper covered plaza, following the wash to the top of the next descent. 0541653 E, 4321981 N Z12 NAD83.

12.2   Go southeast down a cool little stone stairway [Class 4, 15'], followed by 950 feet of arduous [Class 4] boulder-hopping to reach the canyon floor. 0542133 E, 4321514 N Z12 NAD83.

15.3   The going is easy as you hike southeast down Sulphur Canyon the rest of the way. Just before you exit the mouth of the canyon you will intersect the old, closed portion of the Mexican Mountain Road. (You will also be intersecting Hike #13 here.) 0545765 E, 4319242 N Z12 NAD83.

If you are really desperate for water, continue down the wash to the river. If you can hang on a little farther, the sweet pools in Spring Canyon are only 2 miles away.

Digression: The mouth of the Upper Black Box (Hike #11) and the Mexican Mountain Ascent (Hike #12) are a half-mile upriver. The trailhead parking (Hikes #11, #12, #13, and #14) at the end of the usable portion of the Mexican Mountain Road is 1.3 miles southwest on the old dirt track. 0544307 E, 4318542 N Z12 NAD83.

16.7   Follow the old road. It heads northeast out of the canyon onto the bench above, then east and southeast, paralleling the river, to the wind vane next to the airstrip at Mexican Bend. The airstrip is actively used so don't mess with it and whatever you do, don't camp on it. 0547608 E, 4319016 N Z12 NAD83.

Hike #13 veers away here and continues southeast up the Horse Thief Trail. Swazys Leap and the Lower Black Box (Hike #16) are 3 miles down the river.

16.8   Follow a use-trail east-northeast from the wind vane up onto a low, boulder-studded bench. 0547817 E, 4319048 N Z12 NAD83.

> *Historical note:* Several of the large, patinated boulders atop the bench are adorned with excellent Fremont style petroglyphs, one of the best sites in the area. Be sure to look on all surfaces of the boulders. Some of the more intriguing images are also some of the less readily visible.

17.2   Take the use-trail northeast into the mouth of Spring Canyon. You should find good water here. If the cattle aren't around and the bugs aren't too bad, there is good camping in the area. 0548286 E, 4319438 N Z12 NAD83.

19.0   Go generally north up Spring Canyon along the trail. You will pass some springs and see Delicate Arch (also known as Bumpy Road or Leaning Arch) on the left (W). Just past the arch is a short drainage coming in from the left (W) followed by a distinct, castle-like fin. On the far side of the fin is the junction with Nates Canyon. 0547940 E, 4321462 N Z12 NAD83.

Hike #14 diverges here and continues up Spring Canyon. If you haven't found good water by now, you should find some just inside the mouth of Nates Canyon or a short way up Spring Canyon.

> *Historical note:* Nate Biddlecome ran cattle in the canyon in the early 1900s. Millie Biddlecome described Nate: "[He was] a big fat cuss—just as lazy as a guy could get and had all of the angles figured out to ease up on the work."

20.2   Turn right (N) at the junction and head up Nates Canyon. The canyon winds back and forth several times but goes generally north. After 1.2 miles the canyon turns to the west for the first time. Look for an exit route on the right (N) going up steep rubble to the bench above [Class 3]. A cairn sits at the top. 0548192 E, 4322927 N Z12 NAD83.

Don't worry if you miss the exit at first. Within a quarter-mile you will be stopped by an impressive dry-fall with a long, thin, seasonal pool at its base. Backtrack until you find the route.

20.4   Traverse east-northeast on ledges to the top of the fall. As there is another fall three-quarters of a mile up ahead, you will exit the canyon here. 0547784 E, 4323052 N Z12 NAD83.

Digression: It is worth a quick side trip up the canyon to see the many gemlike, seasonal pools. If they are full, there is excellent camping in the area.

20.6   Head southwest and scramble 500 feet up a steep, bouldery slope then climb through a break in the caprock to the rim of the canyon [Class 3]. 0547583 E, 4322860 N Z12 NAD83.

21.4   Follow the rim northwest and intersect the wash on the floor of Nates Canyon again above the dry-fall. 0547128 E, 4324052 N Z12 NAD83.

From the top of the fall, Nates Canyon, now shallower, continues upward to the northwest. This is where the digression from mile 9.1 intersects the canyon.

22.0   There is a gully coming into the wash from the north. Go up it a short way until you see an open area to the right (E). Head east-northeast through a gap between sandstone domes until you are standing on the rim of Pinnacle Canyon (Hike #5). 0547816 E, 4324523 N Z12 NAD83.

23.5   Start angling generally northeast down the gradually sloping face of the reef. If you try to stay on top and not go down any drainages until the very end, you will rejoin Cottonwood Wash just below the trailhead. 0548776 E, 4325908 N Z12 NAD83.

Hike #7: Grotto Canyon

SEASON:	Early spring, spring, or fall. No snow.
TIME AND DISTANCE:	Part 1: Two hours (2.2 miles). Part 2: Five to seven hours (4.3 miles).
WATER:	Seasonal, though there is usually some water in the grotto. Bring your own water.
MAPS:	Mexican Mountain. (Huntington, San Rafael Desert.)

LOOP HIKE: Part 1: No. Part 2: Yes.

SKILL LEVEL: (2B). Moderate route-finding. [Class 3] scrambling. If you are
not a rock climber, bring wading shoes.

Sometimes a hike can surprise you. This one starts with nothing to recommend it. In fact the start, a flat plain and nondescript hills, is discouraging. With a little faith and perseverance, this changes quickly as you enter one of the finest short canyons in the Northern Reef.

The hike comes in two parts. Part 1 goes to the grotto, a large pothole nestled below a dry-fall. The route is short, varied, and should be especially fun for youngsters. Part 2 goes out the top of Grotto Canyon, across a corner of Horse Heaven, visits an old cabin and a natural bridge, then descends a charming canyon.

Part 1

0.0   Mileage begins at the small parking area on the west side of the power poles (near the pole with plaque #1034). 0547176 E, 4329312 N Z12 NAD83.

0.6   Follow an ORV scar west-southwest down into the wash. You'll be at the junction of two washes. Go straight up the westerly wash. It narrows for a bit then divides into three at a section of purple slickrock. 0546371 E, 4329159 N Z12 NAD83.

0.8   Turn left (S) and follow the canyon south then southwest. Bypass a pour-off on the left (S) following cairns. Rejoin the canyon where a side canyon enters from the left (S). 0546103 E, 4328925 N Z12 NAD83.

0.9   Go straight (W) up the main canyon. You'll pass the exit route for Part 2 on the left (S). 0545940 E, 4328905 N Z12 NAD83.

1.1   The canyon becomes corridor-like and is easy walking for several hundred yards. As you near the grotto at its end, there are several sections that must be waded. For climbers this section can easily be chimneyed [Class 5.0]. The grotto itself is exquisite—a special place. 0545673 E, 4328890 N Z12 NAD83.

2.2   If you are just doing Part 1, return to the trailhead the way you came. 0547176 E, 4329312 N Z12 NAD83.

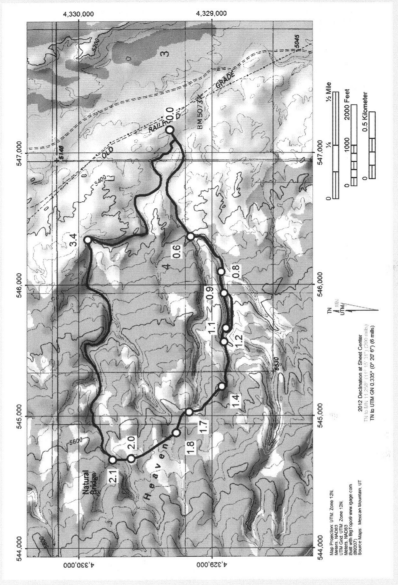

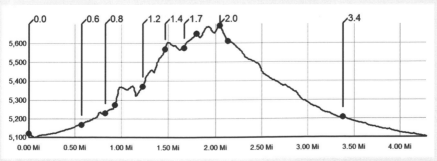

Elev Loss −20 Ft; Climb 852 Ft; Drop −871 Ft; Max Elev 5693 Ft; Min Elev 5100 Ft; Map Dist 4.283 Mi; Ground Dist 4.310 Mi

Grotto Canyon narrows.

Part 2

Mileage resumes from mile 0.9 at the bottom of the exit route.

1.2   Go south up to the rim and then follow it west until you can rejoin the canyon just above the grotto. Now head west up the canyon. Soon the canyon divides just past side-by-side falls. 0545568 E, 4328905 N Z12 NAD83.

1.4   Scramble up steep slickrock into the right-hand drainage (W). After five minutes ascend a slickrock slab [Class 3]. Shortly thereafter the canyon essentially dies at a half circle of low overhangs. Exit the canyon to the right (N). 0545940 E, 4328905 N Z12 NAD83.

1.7   Follow your compass northwest toward the rim of a red-and-white, Navajo-walled canyon. Two washes coming from the west converge here to form the head of the canyon. Go to the northernmost wash. 0545033 E, 4329169 N Z12 NAD83.

1.8   A short way to the north, on the divide between this wash and the next one to the north, is an ORV scar. (This is the same track that you started on from the trailhead. You could easily follow it east back to the start.) Follow it west-northwest to the ruins of an old cabin. A lot of artifacts still remain. Please don't take anything so others can enjoy these interesting relics. 0544875 E, 4329265 N Z12 NAD83.

2.0   From the cabin head northwest. You'll be crossing a section of Horse Heaven. Soon you'll cross a shallow wash and go up a hillside to another divide. Note the cowboy cairn on top of a small knoll. 0544679 E, 4329604 N Z12 NAD83.

2.1   From the divide drop down into the canyon to the north. You'll be at or near a side canyon coming in from the northwest. 6544669 E, 4329743 N Z12 NAD83.

   Digression: Just 0.2 mile northwest up this side canyon is a small natural bridge. 0544410 E, 4329852 N Z12 NAD83.

3.4   Now head generally east down the main canyon. There are occasional obstacles, all easy to negotiate. There is a huge pool at the base of a big drop. Pass this to the right (S). The next half-mile contains a succession of tantalizing pools. 0546346 E, 4329930 N Z12 NAD83.

4.3   The canyon gets shallower once you exit the reef and begins trending to the southeast. You will come to the junction with the wash and ORV scar next to the trailhead. Turn east-northeast out of the wash and back to the start. 0547176 E, 4329312 N Z12 NAD83.

EM401/Green River Cutoff Road Section

Alternate access to Hike #8.

Access is from Highway 10 and Highway 6/191.

Provides access to B6767/Fuller Bottom Road, EM405/Wedge Overlook Road, EM332/Buckhorn Draw Road (Hikes #6 and #7), EM320/Mexican Mountain Road (Hikes #8 through #12) and the Tidwell Draw Tracks (Hikes #1 through #5).

1:100,000 map: Huntington.

County Road EM401, also known as the Green River Cutoff Road, is a major artery for exploration in the northern part of the San Rafael Swell. One mile north of Castle Dale on Highway 10, on the east side of the road between mileposts 39 and 40, is the junction with this well-groomed dirt road. It runs west to east from Highway 10, past Cedar Mountain, to Highway 6/191, and is suitable for most vehicles unless wet or snowy. The unmarked eastern end of this road is 0.5 mile north of milepost 284 on Highway 6/191, which is 17 miles north of the junction with I-70 and 4.8 miles south of Woodside.

Although this is a scenic road, mountain bikers may find the dusty traffic intolerable. Numerous side roads can be used for camping.

> *Historical note:* The route of the Green River Cutoff Road was a part of the Old Spanish Trail. Bert J. Silliman noted that the Elk Mountain Mission of 1855 was told of this route by the Ute Indians. It was called the Old Trail as it probably predated the Old Spanish Trail.
>
> The Green River Cutoff Road was fifty percent shorter than taking the main road up to Price and down Castle Valley. The road, a rough track dating from the early days, was improved by the CCC in 1938.

0.0   Mileage begins on EM401/Green River Cutoff Road at the cattle guard just off of Highway 10. 0500251 E, 4341272 N Z12 NAD83.

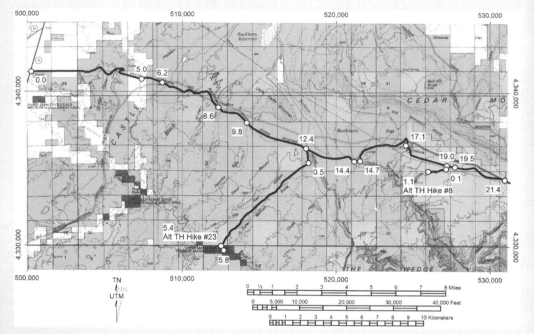

From Mile 0.0 to 21.4. 1:100,000

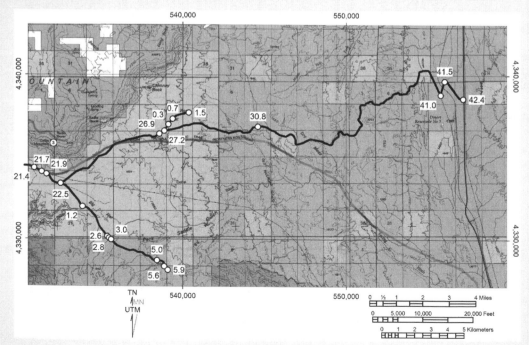

From Mile 21.4 to 42.4. 1:100,000

5.0   Head generally east. The road gradually climbs to the top of Oil Well Dome then, not so gradually, descends the eastern side and crosses a bridge over Huntington Creek. 0507325 E, 4340794 N Z12 NAD83.

6.2   Continue following the road generally east. You will come to the junction with B6768 on the left (N). This track goes northeast through Cedar Hollow to EM332/Lawrence-to-Tan Seeps Road. Continue east-southeast. 0508736 E, 4340563 N Z12 NAD83.

8.6   The road begins trending to the southeast and you will reach an intersection. EM402/Red Seep Road on the left (N) goes up Red Seep Wash to EM332/Lawrence-to-Tan Seeps Road. The track on the right (S) goes down Red Seep Wash. 0512420 E, 4338864 N Z12 NAD83.

9.8   Keep following the main road southeast. The junction with EM404/Hambrick Bottom Road will be on the right (S) at White Rocks. This track goes south then southwest from White Rocks, past Favorite Hills to the San Rafael River at Hambrick Bottom. 0514152 E, 4337982 N Z12 NAD83.

12.4   Continue heading southeast on the main road to the Buckhorn Well Intersection. There is a large parking area, pit toilet, some small buildings, and signs here.

> *Historical note:* The well was drilled by the BLM in 1945 as a water source for the MK Tunnels. The water is now used for livestock. Owen McClenahan: "This water lies in the Gypsum Formation and is so hard that if soap flakes were mixed with it, it would curdle. A man can drink it for about two days only; after that time, he has to avoid any sudden moves."

EM332/Lawrence-to-Tan Seeps Road on the left (N) comes in from Huntington (see the Cedar Mountain and Cleveland-Lloyd Dinosaur Quarry Road Section). EM405/Wedge Road is on the Right (S) and leads to the Wedge Overlook. 0518022 E, 4336293 N Z12 NAD83.

The road to the Wedge Overlook is 6.4 miles long, is easy to navigate, and is suitable for most vehicles. The view from the overlook is astounding. There are several side tracks along the way leading to good camping.

A short way down the Wedge Overlook Road is the junction with the Fuller Bottom Road. This medium-clearance dirt road is often used by river-runners to reach the San Rafael River. There is good camping on several spur roads. The area near the river has unimproved campsites, but it is often buggy. This can also be used as a way to access the trailhead for Hike #23 by those with high-clearance 4WDs (provided the river is low enough to ford) or for accessing the alternate trailhead for Hike #23 at Fuller Bottom (see the Sids Mountain chapter for details on Hike #23).

B6767/Fuller Bottom Road

0.0   Mileage begins at the Buckhorn Well intersection. Go south on EM405/Wedge Road. (The first mile of the Wedge Road has been realigned since the Buckhorn Reservoir and Huntington maps were made so this part is not shown accurately on them.) 0518022 E, 4336293 N Z12 NAD83.

0.5   Junction with B6767/Fuller Bottom Road on right (S). Take the right (S) fork. The road becomes red in color and soon turns to the southwest. 0518220 E, 4335465 N Z12 NAD83.

5.4   The road heads south for a short way then southwest. Just before you reach the river will be the alternate trailhead parking for Hike #23 and an info kiosk on left (SE). 0512524 E, 4329984 N Z12 NAD83.

5.8   Follow the road generally south to the San Rafael River Ford. The river should only be crossed during low water! The bottom is made of shifting gravel. Only high-clearance 4WD vehicles should attempt to cross it. If in doubt, wade across the river first. This could save much aggravation. On the other side of the river the road becomes B6770 (see the Dutch Flat to Fuller Bottom Road Section in the Sids Mountain chapter for details). 0512601 E, 4329625 N Z12 NAD83.

Historical note: Muriel Smith noted that Bob Fuller settled on the bottom in the early days. Ben R. Hite, the brother of Cass Hite, in 1893: "Where the San Rafael River cuts through the reef there is a little bar formed on the east side . . . and Bob Fuller, a ranchman of good reputation in that country told me just a week ago that they had found good placer gold on that bar...." Fuller was killed in a shoot-out over a bull.

14.4   Go straight (ESE) through the intersection on the Green River Cutoff Road. The road then starts heading east. You will reach the junction with EM4406/Wedge Cutoff Road on the right (SE). 0521122 E, 4335470 N Z12 NAD83.

14.7   Keep heading generally east to the junction with EM332/Buckhorn Draw Road on the right (SE). EM401/Green River Cutoff Road continues to the northeast. 0521483 E, 4335772 N Z12 NAD83.

The Buckhorn Draw Road is really a section of EM332/Lawrence-to-Tan Seeps Road. It provides access to Hikes #8 and #9, is suitable for most vehicles, and has some great camping at designated sites. The road becomes EM332/Cottonwood Wash Road at the bridge over the San Rafael River (see the Buckhorn Draw Road Section for details).

17.1   Follow the Green River Cutoff Road generally northeast. The road then swings south and crosses Furniture Draw. There is an interesting, washed-out bridge here. 0524493 E, 4336526 N Z12 NAD83.

19.0   Now the road heads east-southeast. You will come to the junction with the Wedge Spur Road on the right (S). This track leads to the alternate trailhead for Little Holes Canyon Hike #8. 0527135 E, 4335203 N Z12 NAD83.

Wedge Spur Road

0.0   Mileage begins at the junction with the Green River Cutoff Road. 0527135 E, 4335203 N Z12 NAD83.

0.1   Go south on the medium-clearance Wedge Spur Road to the junction with a dirt road on the right (W) at Little Holes stock pond. 0527166 E, 4335017 N Z12 NAD83.

Medium-clearance vehicles park here. There is a faint trail that follows the bench between the white rim of the inner canyon and the short, brown cliff band above and goes west for 1.0 mile to the pinnacles.

1.1   Turn right (W) onto this high-clearance double track and go generally west along the rim for 1.0 mile. Park just east of the Twin Conquistadors Pinnacles at the top of the exit route marked by a small cairn. This is the alternate trailhead for Little Holes Canyon Hike #8. This track parallels the faint trail that's on the bench below, but along the top of the cliffs. 0525992 E, 4334809 N Z12 NAD83.

19.5   The road continues running east-southeast. The junction with EM335/Lower Cedar Mountain Road is on the left (N). This high-clearance double track runs generally northwest along the base of Cedar Mountain and connects with EM332/Lawrence-to-Tan Seeps Road. It is very sandy in places and is for 4WDs only. Some interesting rock art sites along the way (45-degree Rock, Daisy Chain Rock, Silent Sentinel) make this a worthy side trip. 0527581 E, 4335113 N Z12 NAD83.

21.4   Keep heading down the main road. You will come to the junction with EM409 on the right (S). 0530936 E, 4334277 N Z12 NAD83.

This high-clearance track goes southwest for 3.2 miles to an overlook on the rim of Calf Canyon and has lots of camping. It continues on as a rough, rocky, high-clearance 4WD track for another 1.2 miles to a grand overlook above the junction of Calf Canyon and Buckhorn Wash (0527815 E, 4329587 N Z12 NAD83). Even with some sandy spots, this would be a great mountain bike ride.

21.7   Continue heading east-southeast on the main road. You will pass Summit Pond on the left (N). On the right (S) is the head of Calf Canyon, which is just a wash at this point. 0531427 E, 4334041 N Z12 NAD83.

21.9   Just after the wash is the junction with a dirt road on the right (S). 0531729 E, 4333890 N Z12 NAD83. This track goes south for 1.6 miles to a great overlook above the junction of Calf and Cow Canyons (0531933 E, 4331545 N Z12 NAD83).

22.5   Keep following the main road to the junction with EM410/Big Flat Road on the right (SE). 0532530 E, 4333335 N Z12 NAD83.

EM410/Big Flat Road

0.0   Mileage starts at the junction. 0532530 E, 4333335 N Z12 NAD83.

1.2   Go southeast on EM410/Big Flat Road. You will reach the junction with TR628 on the right (S). (This track goes south to Cow Canyon wash just above the exit route on the Calf, Cow, and Pine Canyons Hike #9.) 0533920 E, 4331922 N Z12 NAD83.

2.6   Continue heading southeast. You will come to an intersection and cattle guard. The dirt track on the left (E) goes to the Big Holes in Pack Saddle Gulch. The high-clearance

4WD track on the right (W) heads out to Prickly Pear Flat and the edge of an escarpment high above the San Rafael River. 0535326 E, 4330061 N Z12 NAD83.

2.8   Just past the intersection is the junction with a track on the right (SW). This track heads southwest to a stock pond. 0535420 E, 4329928 N Z12 NAD83.

3.0   Just a little farther is another junction with a faint track on the right (S). 0535643 E, 4329847 N Z12 NAD83.

This high-clearance double track goes south for 2.3 miles to a great view on the rim of the West Fork of Red Canyon near the top of the exit route on Hike #10. (0535314 E, 4326528 N Z12 NAD83).

5.0   Continue heading generally southeast on the Big Flat Road. The road is now going down Big Hole Wash. You will pass a corral on the left (N). 0538437 E, 4328696 N Z12 NAD83.

5.6   After the corral is the junction with a track on the right (SW). This goes southwest into a wonderful Zane Grey-style box canyon, well worth the one-half hour hike. 0538849 E, 4328310 N Z12 NAD83.

5.9   Continue heading southeast to the end of the graded dirt road at a turnaround. There are good views of Nates Ridge in the distance. 0539006 E, 4328158 N Z12 NAD83.

If you continued on foot down Big Hole Wash for another mile, you would intersect Hike #6 at the three-way wash junction above the dry-fall.

The road carries on south-southeast from the turnaround as a rough, high-clearance 4WD track for another 1.7 miles. It ends at the Mexican Mountain WSA boundary in Box Flat near the route into the East Fork of Red Canyon on Hike #10.

26.9   The Green River Cutoff Road swings to the northeast. You will come to the junction with a track on the right (S) going to Lews Hole and the Big Holes in Pack Saddle Gulch. 0538541 E, 4336375 N Z12 NAD83.

This high-clearance track goes south for 4.8 miles to a parking area above the Big Holes, which usually have water (0541327 E, 4330947 N Z12 NAD83).

Historical note: The Big Holes in Pack Saddle Gulch were an important stop on the Old Spanish Trail. Clarence Dutton's Powell Survey map of 1879 shows this as "Water Pocket."

Orville C. Pratt followed the Old Spanish Trail in 1848: "Found water in a canion to the left [Big Hole].... Left a pack saddle today, worn out."

27.2   Next you'll come to the junction with a track on the left (NE). This high-clearance track goes to Chimney Rock and the old 1881 railroad grade and the ruins of a Chinese work camp. 0538800 E, 4336536 N Z12 NAD83.

Side road

0.0   Mileage starts at junction. 0538800 E, 4336536 N Z12 NAD83.

0.3   Head northeast to a "Y" junction. Stay right (NE) to the railroad grade and the remains of the work camp. (Go left for a mile on this high-clearance 4WD track to Chimney Rock.) 0539097 E, 4336933 N Z12 NAD83.

0.5   A stock pond is on the left. 0539329 E, 4337235 N Z12 NAD83.

0.7   A track comes in on the right. Stay to the left. 0539518 E, 4337355 N Z12 NAD83.

1.4   Go through a road cut. This is part of the old railroad bed. The road then turns to the north and passes two side roads that come in on the left. After the road turns east is a junction with a dirt road on the right (S). 0540343 E, 4337797 N Z12 NAD83.

1.5   Turn south down this road to the railroad grade. The railbed was built in the early 1880s but was never used. Chinese laborers were imported to do the manual labor. Piles of rubble and the remains of the work camp can be seen in this area. 0540376 E, 4337691 N Z12 NAD83.

30.8   Follow the main road as it heads generally east to the unmarked intersection with B6707 on the left (N) and B6809/Tidwell Draw Track—North on the right (S). B6809 leads to the Smith cabin and

Hikes #3 through #7 (see Tidwell Draw Track—North Road Section for details). 0544542 E, 4336788 N Z12 NAD83.

41.0   The road continues east then heads northeast as it exits the Swell. The road divides on a plain. 0555689 E, 4338819 N Z12 NAD83.

41.5   Follow the road left (N) under the railroad tracks to another junction. 0555689 E, 4338819 N Z12 NAD83.

42.4   Now go right (SE) to the junction with Hwy 6/191. 0557118 E, 4338540 N Z12 NAD83.

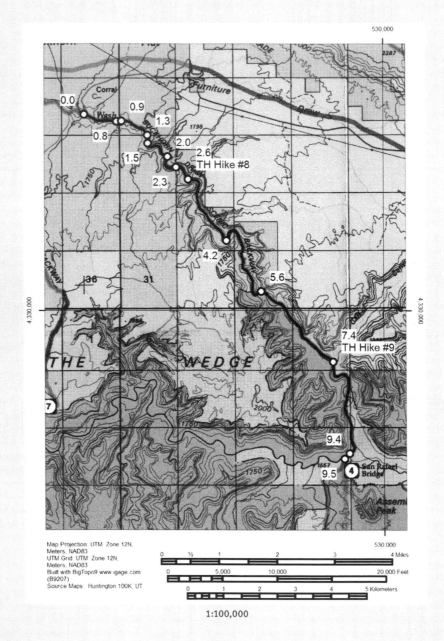

1:100,000

EM332/Buckhorn Draw Road Section

Access to Hikes #8 and #9.

Provides access to EM320/Mexican Mountain Road (Hikes #10 through #14) and EM332/Cottonwood Wash Road (Hikes #19 and #20)

Access is from the Green River Cutoff and Cottonwood Wash Roads.

1:100,000 map: Huntington.

This good dirt road goes generally southeast down Buckhorn Wash from EM401/Green River Cutoff Road to the San Rafael River bridge and campground. This section of County Road 332 (Lawrence-to-Tan-Seeps Road) is called the Cottonwood Wash Road south of the bridge. The road is well maintained and is suitable for most vehicles unless wet or snowy. This is an excellent mountain bike road in the off-season, but during the ORV season it can be noisy and busy. There is excellent free camping in Buckhorn Wash at designated, primitive campsites only. The campground at the river is a self-pay fee area with picnic tables, fire rings, and pit-toilets.

0.0   Mileage begins at the Buckhorn Draw Road junction at mile 14.7 on EM401/Green River Cutoff Road. 0521483 E, 4335772 N Z12 NAD83.

0.8   Go southeast down Buckhorn Wash. You will come to the junction with a track on the right (S) with an interpretive sign. Beyond the sign is a fenced-off tunnel entrance. This is the site of the MK Tunnel Project. Created in 1948 by the Morrison Knudsen Corporation for the Department of Defense, the tunnels were a top secret project utilizing surface planted explosives. 0522560 E, 4335226 N Z12 NAD83.

0.9   Junction with track on left (N). There is a fenced-off mine shaft at the end of the spur road. The fence runs east across a flat area to the sandstone wall of the canyon. From the east end of the fence walk right (SE) along the wall to a small petroglyph panel. 0522669 E, 4335225 N Z12 NAD83.

1.3   A track to the left (NE) goes to the mouth of Furniture Draw. An easy hike, suitable for everyone, goes up this short canyon. There is a section of narrows and several small obstacles to surmount (Class 2+). Round trip will take two hours. Some water is possible in the narrows. 0523324 E, 4334884 N Z12 NAD83.

1.5   There is a dinosaur footprint here that can be sort of hard to find. Just past the mouth of Furniture Draw the road swings to the south and comes up against the east side of Buckhorn Wash. There is a gray track angling off of the main road to the right (W) and a small place to park. The track leads to a large designated camping area. From the parking area walk east across the road and follow a trail up through a 12-foot-high cliff band to a ledge. The ledge is wider in one area and is bare sandstone. The print is at the backside of the ledge (away from the road) and sometimes well-meaning people will cover it with a small slab of sandstone. 0523394 E, 4334620 N Z12 NAD83.

2.0   Continuing down the Buckhorn Draw Road you will come to a designated campsite on the left (NE) at the mouth of Triangle Canyon. There is a nice "after dinner hike" up the canyon that will take about thirty minutes round trip. There is a small petroglyph panel located at the mouth of the canyon that is easily visible from the campsite. 0523923 E, 4334234 N Z12 NAD83.

2.3   Just around the bend from Triangle Canyon are the Cattle Guard Petroglyphs. Immediately past the cattle guard is a small place to park on the left (N). Take a use-trail north up to the base of the cliff to a good panel of pictographs and petroglyphs. 0524137 E, 4333981 N Z12 NAD83.

2.6   The mouth of Little Holes Canyon is on the left (NE) and a large designated camping area is on the right (SW). This is the start of Little Holes Canyon Hike #8. 0524455 E, 4333648 N Z12 NAD83.

4.2   Continue down Buckhorn Draw. The Mat Warner inscription is on the left (W). After rounding a jutting peninsula of rock the road swings around to the north. Just past the point of the peninsula are two small places to park on either side of the road. To the left (W) and fifty feet up on a cliff band is the inscription. It is easy to spot from the road. 0525642 E, 4332053 N Z12 NAD83.

Historical note: Mat was one of the Hole-in-the-Wall Gang who used to roam the San Rafael Swell and the Robbers Roost country in the 1880s. Warner's claim to fame was in helping Butch Cassidy rob the Telluride Bank. He also led a gang called the "Invincible Three" in Oregon, Washington, Wyoming, and Utah. Later, after quitting his outlaw ways, he became the Marshal of Price.

5.6   After rounding a bend the Buckhorn Draw Pictographs will be on the left (N). This is one of the finest Barrier Canyon style pictograph panels in the Swell and was recently and extensively restored. Please slow down as you approach the site to keep dust from the road from damaging the art. 0526459 E, 4330519 N Z12 NAD83.

7.4   Next is the junction with a track on the left (NE) at the mouth of Calf Canyon and a designated campsite. This is the start of Calf, Cow, and Pine Canyons Hike #9. 0528488 E, 4328555 N Z12 NAD83.

You can either park here near the campsite or, if you have a high-clearance vehicle and the wash is dry, follow the double track 0.4 miles northeast up Calf Canyon to the junction with Pine Canyon.

9.4   The junction with EM320/Mexican Mountain Road is on the left (SE). There is a large self-pay camping area here. 0529047 E, 4326029 N Z12 NAD83.

9.5   Just past the junction with EM320 and the camping area is the San Rafael River bridge. The road continues south beyond the bridge as EM332 but is known as the Cottonwood Wash Road. 0528860 E, 4325828 N Z12 NAD83.

Historical note: In 1921 an oil company built a road from Buckhorn Flat, through Buckhorn Wash, to the San Rafael River. A bridge—no longer standing—was constructed. The road continued south to Sinbad Country. A geology report from 1928 noted that the road was rarely used and was the best route to Sinbad Country. In 1935 the CCC improved the road and in 1937 built the still-standing, but no-longer-used, suspension bridge. This bridge was listed on the National Register of Historic Places in 1996. A new bridge was built in the late 1990s.

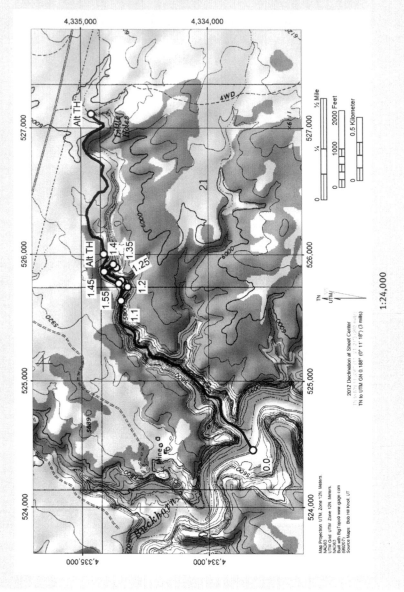

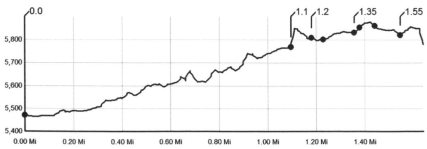

Elev Gain 300 Ft; Climb 859 Ft; Drop −559 Ft; Max Elev 5877 Ft; Min Elev 5464 Ft; Map Dist 1.641 Mi; Ground Dist 1.688 Mi

Hike #8: Little Holes Canyon

SEASON:	Any.
TIME AND DISTANCE:	One and a half to three hours (2.75 miles).
WATER:	Seasonal, though the canyon is rarely completely dry. Bring your own water.
MAPS:	Bob Hill Knoll. (Huntington). Little Holes Canyon is not named on the map but the Little Holes are. They are at the head of the canyon and include the stock pond at the alternate parking area.
LOOP HIKE:	No. This is either done as an "out and back" or as a through hike with a vehicle or mountain bike shuttle.
SKILL LEVEL:	(1A) Easy route finding. [Class 3] scrambling.

This is a short but rewarding hike through a beautiful canyon. With its easy access, fun route, high Wingate walls, two pinnacles and a seasonal stream, it is surprising that this canyon is so rarely visited.

The route ascends Little Holes Canyon from Buckhorn Wash, visits the Twin Conquistadors Pinnacles, and then returns the way it came. You could also do this as a through-hike by setting up a shuttle at the top of the canyon, but the lower canyon is the best part and is worth seeing twice. (See the Green River Cutoff Road Section for directions to the alternate trailhead parking areas.)

0.0   Mileage begins at the trailhead parking area and designated campsite at mile 2.6 on EM332/Buckhorn Draw Road. 0524455 E, 4333648 N Z12 NAD83.

1.1   Go northeast up Little Holes Canyon. At first there is a good trail but it quickly fades and the canyon becomes bouldery. The canyon turns to the east and is blocked by a major constriction. 0525638 E, 4334688 N Z12 NAD83.

1.2   Bypass the constriction by climbing up the [Class 3] cleft on the left (N) onto a sandstone bench. Now follow the bench east-southeast a short way until you can return to the canyon floor. You will see the pinnacles straight ahead to the northeast. 0525747 E, 4334635 N Z12 NAD83.

1.25   Go northeast up the wash. You will quickly come to a cairned exit route on the left (NW). This route hooks up with the exit to the double track and the path that follows the rim of the canyon to Little

Holes. If you are through-hiking to either of these points, exit the inner canyon here. 0525798 E, 4334686 N Z12 NAD83.

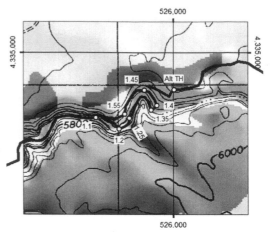

Hike #8. Detail from Mile 1.1 to 1.55. 1:24,000.

1.35   Continue going northeast up the wash. The canyon narrows as it swings around to the south. Once you are on the eastern side of the pinnacles, there is another cairned exit route on the left (NE). 0525899 E, 4334724 N Z12 NAD83.

If you pass this exit you will soon come to a very brushy section of the canyon blocked by dual chimney routes [5.5, 12'] that bypass either side of a large chockstone that's plugging the canyon floor. This would be a very difficult down-climb from above. If you are going to hike down the canyon floor from Little Holes, be prepared to do a short rappel here and wear long sleeves and pants. The rest of the canyon is equally brush-choked and brambly almost all the way to the Little Holes and you'll likely have to get your feet wet.

1.4   Go east-northeast up this exit route to the sandstone bench above. 0525928 E, 4334734 N Z12 NAD83.

1.45   Now follow the bench northwest a short way until you are standing due north of the pinnacles. Here is where the routes converge. 0525867 E, 4334820 N Z12 NAD83.

> *Digression:* If you go right (E) and follow a gradually rising trail east for a short way, you will come to the cairned exit route that leads through the final caprock to the alternate parking on the double track above (0525992 E, 4334808 N Z12 NAD83). Or you can continue generally east along the trail that follows the bench on the rim of the inner canyon for 1 mile to the alternate parking at the Little Holes stock pond (0527118 E, 4334916 N Z12 NAD83).

Historical note: The Little Holes at the head of the canyon were a stopping spot on the Old Spanish Trail as there was usually water there. It is fitting that the pinnacles have a name with a Spanish flair.

1.55 Continue on the bench as it swings southwest to the west side of the pinnacles. Now contour south down to the bench below. You will be at the top of the first exit route. 0525774 E, 4334704 N Z12 NAD83.

1.65 Instead of going down, stay on the bench and follow this layer southwest then around to the northwest as you slope down to the top of the constriction bypass. 0525638 E, 4334688 N Z12 NAD83.

2.75 Down-climb the bypass and follow the canyon southwest for 1.1 miles back to the start. 0524455 E, 4333648 N Z12 NAD83.

Hike #9: Calf, Cow, and Pine Canyons

SEASON:	Best in fall, winter if there is no snow, or spring.
TIME AND DISTANCE:	Eight to ten hours (12.2 miles). With much exploring to do, this could be done as an overnight hike, though water would have to be carried.
WATER:	Seasonal springs in all three canyons. Bring your own water.
MAPS:	Bob Hill Knoll, Bottleneck Peak, Chimney Rock, Devils Hole. (Huntington).
LOOP HIKE:	Yes.
SKILL LEVEL:	(2A) Difficult route finding. [Class 5.2] climbing. This is a long day hike. Competent canyoneers only. The less experienced will find a rope useful.

This is one of the most demanding day hikes described. It is a classic canyoneering route that goes through two marvelous canyons and high along the rimrock on the edge of an escarpment. Technical and mental challenges await the dauntless hiker.

The route goes up Calf Canyon, into Cow Canyon, and out its top. It then crosses a long sage, juniper, and pinyon plain to a large, rarely visited Barrier Canyon style pictograph panel. You will walk along a ridge to the head of Pine Canyon and descend it back to the start. The canyons are superb, the views from the top are unbeatable, and the route captivating.

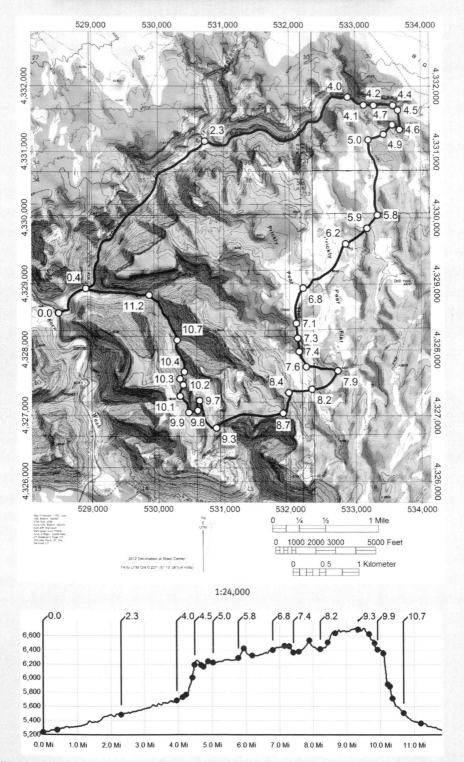

1:24,000

Elev Gain 36 Ft; Climb 2525 Ft; Drop −2489 Ft; Max Elev 6706 Ft; Min Elev 5231 Ft; Map Dist 11.806 Mi; Ground Dist 11.920 Mi

0.0   Mileage begins at the trailhead parking area and designated camp-site at mile 7.4 on EM332/Buckhorn Draw Road. 0528488 E, 4328555 N Z12 NAD83.

0.4   Follow the double track northeast up Calf Canyon to the confluence with Pine Canyon. The track divides. 0528912 E, 4328929 N Z12 NAD83.

2.3   Continue northeast up Calf Canyon on the track. After thirty minutes the canyon opens into a park. Toward the end of the park, past double caves, the canyon divides. Calf Canyon continues to the northeast and ends shortly, while Cow Canyon and the track head to the east. The very accessible double caves are a worthy goal for those looking for a short day hike. 0530722 E, 4331160 N Z12 NAD83.

4.0   Head east up Cow Canyon. The track soon ends. Continue generally northeast up the canyon on a use-trail. The canyon divides. 0532895 E, 4331833 N Z12 NAD83.

4.1   Stay right (E) with the main canyon. Soon a short, steep side canyon enters from the right (S). 0533137 E, 4331712 N Z12 NAD83.

4.2   Continue east. After a short way the canyon divides again. 0533291 E, 4331707 N Z12 NAD83.

4.4   Once again, continue heading east up the main canyon. The canyon ends in a quarter-mile, so as you head up look for an emerging use-trail on the right (S). Follow the trail as it angles up the talus to the right (W) side of a cliff band that is halfway to the rim. 0533584 E, 4331707 N Z12 NAD83.

4.5   Climb up a break in the cliff to its top [Class 3]. Now angle up and left (SE) through more talus to a cleft at the base of the final cliff layer. Climb up this cleft [Class 4, 50'] through the caprock to a large cairn sitting on the rim. 0533656 E, 4331634 N Z12 NAD83.

It is a half mile from here to EM410/Big Flat Road at mile 1.2 (see the Green River Cutoff Road Section for details). You can follow the rim of the canyon northeast to its head, go southeast up the shallow wash to a parking area on TR628, and follow this double track north to the junction (0533920 E, 4331922 N Z12 NAD83).

4.6   Head south over a small rise and drop immediately into the shallow drainage to the south. 0533684 E, 4331339 N Z12 NAD83.

4.7   Go west-northwest down the drainage. It will quickly make a hard left (SSW). 0533571 E, 4331411 N Z12 NAD83.

On the rim of Cow Canyon at the top of the exit route.

4.9   From the bend continue south-southwest down the wash. Continue on this course as the wash swings to the right (WNW) and leave the drainage. Soon you will come to the top of a sandy rise. 0533440 E, 4331265 N Z12 NAD83.

5.0   Now head west-southwest and intersect a wide, shallow valley running north to south. 0533206 E, 4331183 N Z12 NAD83.

5.8   Go south, following the wash up this valley until you reach its head. The valley ends here but the wash continues. 0533343 E, 4330043 N Z12 NAD83.

5.9   Head southwest out of the valley and work your way up to the top of a rise. Just to the northwest you will see an old fence line made of brush. To the southwest is a wide plain with a dirt road running through it. This is Prickly Pear Flat. 0533183 E, 4329844 N Z12 NAD83.

6.2   Continue heading southwest down onto the flat and to the dirt road, aiming for a junction. 0532860 E, 4329607 N Z12 NAD83.

6.8   From the junction follow the track southwest across the flat to another junction. 0532209 E, 4328939 N Z12 NAD83.

7.1   Turn left (SE) and head southeast then south on the track. You will be entering the Mexican Mountain Wilderness Study Area. You will come to a point where Prickly Pear Flat gets pinched between low cliffs to the east and the head of the North Fork of Pine Canyon to the west. 0532103 E, 4328403 N Z12 NAD83.

7.3   Keep following the track south. You will soon come to the edge of a valley. 0532123 E, 4328177 N Z12 NAD83.

7.4   Continue following the track down slickrock into the wash below. 0532146 E, 4327973 N Z12 NAD83.

Digression: An alternate way back to the start is via the North Fork of Pine Canyon. It is the shortest way back and skips the [Class 5.2] down-climbs, but misses some of the best scenery. Go northwest down the wash to the apex of the canyon. Head left (NW) along the rim for several hundred yards to the top of a gully with several trees in it. Scramble down the gully. The rest of the canyon has several falls and seasonal pools that can all be passed on the right. After a mile of laborious boulder-hopping intersect Pine Canyon. Head down the canyon back to the start. It is 2.5 miles from the rim of the canyon to the trailhead this way.

7.6   Head south-southeast down the wash a short way to intersect a track. 0532250 E, 4327745 N Z12 NAD83.

7.9   Turn left onto the track and follow it generally east to the corralled-off area you can see at the base of the cliffs on the eastern edge of the valley. 0532736 E, 4327682 N Z12 NAD83.

Historical note: Behind the fence is a large alcove containing a wonderful Barrier Canyon style pictograph panel. Though smaller in magnitude, it bears a resemblance to the panels in Buckhorn Wash. Please be kind to these fragile art works and refrain from touching them or building fires inside the alcove.

8.2   The track turns away from the cliff here and runs southwest across the valley. Follow it and intersect the wash again, this time at the southern end of the valley. 0532337 E, 4327403 N Z12 NAD83.

8.4   To the southwest is a slickrock-lined gully that enters the valley above a short drop. This will be your route out of the valley. Head west up the talus to the base of the cliffs and into the bottom of the gully. 0531984 E, 4327348 N Z12 NAD83.

8.7   Go south up the gully until you can turn west onto the divide between the valley to the east and the left-hand (E) fork of the South Fork of Pine Canyon to the northwest. 0531896 E, 4327037 N Z12 NAD83.

9.3   Now cruise west staying on top of the pinyon and juniper-studded rim of the escarpment. You will gradually be forced southwest onto a narrow land bridge to traverse around the head of the canyon to the west (part of the South Fork of Pine Canyon) characterized by a white slickrock dome in its middle. (The dome is shown as elevation 6630 on the Bottleneck Peak map.) You will have stunning views of Window Blind Peak and the San Rafael River to the south. 0530879 E, 4326811 N Z12 NAD83.

9.7   Continue circling around the head of the canyon, first northwest then north. You will wind up on a peninsula. Find the break down through the caprock on the northwestern end of the peninsula. The large pinnacle to the southwest is Bottleneck Peak. 0530627 E, 4327224 N Z12 NAD83.

The big canyon system to the northwest is the South Fork of Pine Canyon, which you will descend. To the west is a three-humped Navajo slickrock ridge heading away from you (also 6630 on the Bottleneck Peak map, but the western one). You want to work your way down to the valley between the peninsula and the ridge.

9.8   Go northwest through the break in the caprock then left (SW) down a steep slab [Class 5.1, 20'] to a bench below. Now head south on this bench until it starts to peter out, then carefully pick your way down another slab [Class 5.2, 50'] to the valley below. 0530596 E, 4327074 N Z12 NAD83.

9.9   Head west and you will quickly be on the rim of the apex of the South Fork of Pine Canyon. 0530465 E, 4327044 N Z12 NAD83.

10.1   Now go northwest along the rim of the canyon a short way until you find a steep slot going down into the canyon. 0530335 E, 4327294 N Z12 NAD83.

10.2   Carefully climb down the slot/chimney [Class 5.2, 60']. From the bottom go straight down the steep rubble [Class 3+]. This looks improbable, but avoids cliffs on either side. You will soon end up at the top of a large fall. 0530382 E, 4327464 N Z12 NAD83.

10.3   Traverse left (NW) to the top of a large rubble slide. 0530333 E, 4327555 N Z12 NAD83.

10.4   Scramble northeast down the slide to the bottom of the drainage. 0530400 E, 4327664 N Z12 NAD83.

10.7   Head generally northwest down the bouldery canyon to the confluence with the left-hand (E) fork. 0530291 E, 4328145 N Z12 NAD83.

11.2   Continue northwest down the canyon to the confluence with the North Fork of Pine Canyon. 0529865 E, 4328831 N Z12 NAD83.

11.8   Intersect the double track and follow it west down Pine Canyon to the junction with Calf Canyon. 0528912 E, 4328929 N Z12 NAD83.

12.2   Now follow the track southwest down Calf Canyon to the trailhead. 0528488 E, 4328555 N.

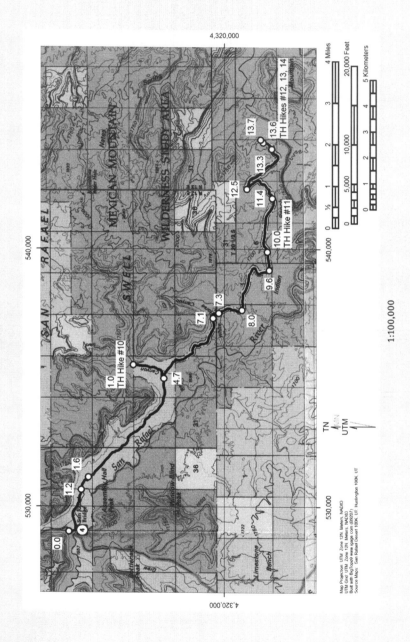

EM320/Mexican Mountain Road Section

Access to Hikes #10 through #14.

Access is from EM332/Buckhorn Draw and EM332/Cottonwood Wash Roads.

1:100,000 map: Huntington, San Rafael Desert.

This dirt road starts just northeast of the San Rafael River bridge on EM332/ Buckhorn Draw Road and is suitable for medium-clearance vehicles unless wet or snowy. This is a popular mountain bike ride, but ride it in the fall or midweek when there is little vehicle traffic. The road goes southeast, paralleling the river on its northern side, to a gate and parking area near the Lower Black Box. Beyond the gate the road is closed to vehicles and mountain bikes. There are many short side roads in the first five miles that are good for camping.

0.0   Mileage begins at the junction at mile 9.4 on the Buckhorn Draw Road. 0529047 E, 4326029 N Z12 NAD83.

1.2   After initially going south then northeast for a short distance, the road runs generally southeast beneath the massive cliffs that stand to the northeast. You will see Assembly Hall Peak to the right (S) with Bottleneck Peak in the background. You will come to a box canyon and corral on the left (N). 0530664 E, 4325517N Z12 NAD83.

> *Historical note:* Assembly Hall Peak was named for its resemblance to the LDS assembly hall in Salt Lake City. Old maps show it as Sawtooth Butte. The corral is called both the Sinbad Cowboy Stock Corral and the Judd Corral. It was built by Paul Judd in the early 1900s and is still in use.

1.6   After the corral you will come to an intersection on a hilltop. Window Blind Peak is to the south-southeast. It is the dominant landmark in the northern part of the Swell and is among the world's largest freestanding monoliths. 0531118 E, 4325240 N Z12 NAD83.

> *Historical note:* Early visitors called this Window Blind Castle for its resemblance to a castle with big windows and drawn blinds. Later, it was informally given the name Lon Chaney Peak, a "mountain with a thousand faces." Pearl Baker: "There was a place on the peak that looked like a window. He [an unnamed surveyor] called it a Blind Window, so it's Blind Window Peak. Then the Bureau of Land Management has it Window Blind Peak which makes me see red!"

4.7   You will pass several side roads coming in from the right (S) then reach the junction with a dirt road on the left (N). 0534995 E, 4322381 N Z12 NAD83.

The start of the Red Canyon—West Fork to East Fork Hike #10 is up this medium-clearance track. Drive north for 1.0 mile up into the mouth of Red Canyon, mostly in the wash, until the road ends where the canyon divides. Park someplace where a flash flood won't take your car away. (0535490 E, 4323540 N Z12 NAD83).

7.1   Continue heading southeast on the main road. You will go through a gate just before reaching White Horse Canyon. 0537343 E, 4320408 N Z12 NAD83.

7.3   The road then crosses White Horse Canyon wash. 0537494 E, 4320207 N Z12 NAD83.

For a short hike to the San Rafael River, walk west-southwest down White Horse Canyon to a fall. Follow a ledge on the left of the fall (S) until it narrows; then go straight down [Class 3, some exposure]. One hour round trip.

8.0   The road goes south then turns east at the head of Lockhart Box. There is a BLM sign here. This is one way of starting the Upper Black Box Hike #11, but adds two to three hours to an already long day. 0537623 E, 4319284 N Z12 NAD83.

A hike into Lockhart Box is worthwhile, though. Park by the roadside and walk southwest down the wash. At a pour-off, backtrack fifty yards and ascend a steep white gully to the west (0537251 E, 4318684 N Z12 NAD83). At the top is a saddle. Traverse 100 yards south on rocky terrain before descending a long, loose slope to the edge of a wide plain. A wash runs south along the edge of the plain. Follow it down to the river (0536988 E, 4318331 N Z12 NAD83). There are several nice swimming holes here. Return the way you came. Two miles round trip.

> *Historical note:* A man named Lockhart tried ranching in Lockhart Box. Many old maps show the Lockhart cabins.

9.6   The road heads generally east. You'll reach the junction with a closed dirt road on the right (S). This is another alternate start of the Upper Black Box Hike #11. (Unless you have a vehicle shuttle, this adds unnecessary time and distance.) 0539174 E, 4318195 N Z12 NAD83.

10.0   Continue a little farther east down the road to the Upper Black Box Hike #11 trailhead. There is a parking area and information kiosk on the right (S). 0539919 E, 4318292 N Z12 NAD83.

11.4   You will pass through another wire gate with an unobstructed view of Lone Rock straight ahead. The Thin Man Pinnacle, near the head of Sulphur Canyon, can be faintly seen to the north-northwest. 0541975 E, 4318112 N Z12 NAD83.

12.5   The road then takes a jog to the north and crosses a wash that runs southeast. 0542724 E, 4318805 N Z12 NAD83.

13.3   The road heads southeast and you will pass the junction with a closed dirt road on the right (S). 0543882 E, 4318099 N Z12 NAD83.

13.6   After the road turns to the northeast you will reach a large parking area and a closed track on the right (SE). This is the shuttle parking for Hike #11 and the trailhead parking for Hikes #12, #13 and #14. The road is closed to all vehicles just ahead. 0544129 E, 4318477 N Z12 NAD83.

13.7   The open portion of the Mexican Mountain Road ends here at a gate. Beyond the gate is the Mexican Mountain Wilderness Study Area. 0544235 E, 4318581 N Z12 NAD83.

The closed road, though deteriorating, continues on for another two and a half miles to Mexican Bend (for details see Hike #13 or #14).

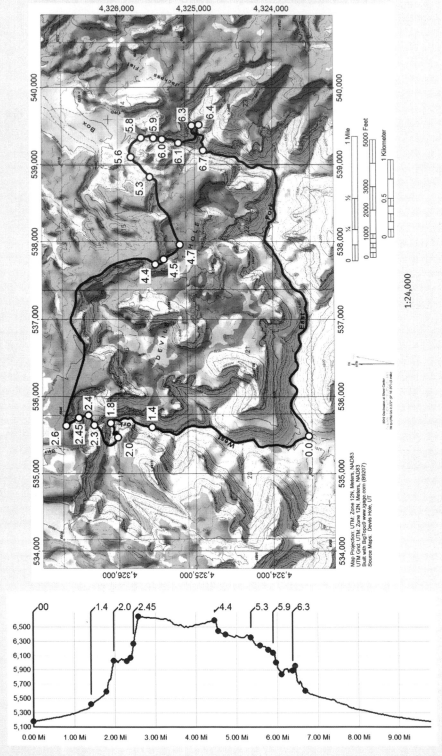

Elev Gain 0 Ft; Climb 2243 Ft; Drop −2243 Ft; Max Elev 6646 Ft; Min Elev 5176 Ft; Map Dist 9.775 Mi; Ground Dist 9.901 Mi

Hike #10: Red Canyon—West Fork to East Fork

SEASON:	Any. Spring and fall are best. No snow. It might be worrisome to leave your car parked in Red Canyon Wash during the summer monsoon.
TIME AND DISTANCE:	Seven to nine hours (9.8 miles).
WATER:	Seasonal potholes. The East Fork has a seasonal spring in its upper reaches. Bring your own water.
MAPS:	Devils Hole. (Huntington).
LOOP HIKE:	Yes.
SKILL LEVEL:	(2A) Moderate route finding. [Class 4] climbing. This is a long day hike with some rough terrain.

This is a demanding hike that forces you to work for your just rewards . . . and the rewards are plentiful. The hike includes two incredible canyons, a handful of pinnacles, terrific views and great hiking along the rimrock.

The route goes to the end of the West Fork of Red Canyon, exits the canyon by way of a steep, two-pitched route, follows the rimrock above Devils Hole, goes out to Box Flat and then heads down the spectacular East Fork of Red Canyon back to the start.

0.0   Mileage begins at the end of the track coming up Red Canyon Wash at the junction of the forks. This is the Mexican Mountain Wilderness Study Area boundary. 0535490 E, 4323540 N Z12 NAD83.

1.4   Go north up the sandy wash of the West Fork of Red Canyon until you are stopped by a 25-foot pour-off. 0535605 E, 4325569 N Z12 NAD83.

1.8   Pass the pour-off on the right (E). The canyon floor becomes bouldery. Continue heading north up the canyon until it divides and ends. 0535657 E, 4326105 N Z12 NAD83.

> *Rock climber's note:* The draw to the right (E) is the "climbers' route" to the Kayenta bench at the top of the Wingate cliffs. It goes north up steep slabs, several 20-foot steps [Class 5.0], then exits through a V-slot [5.5, 12'] to the bench. 0535619 E, 4326216 N Z12 NAD83.

2.0   From the end of the canyon where the two draws divide, go left up the steep rubble to the southwest. Climb up through loose rubble and

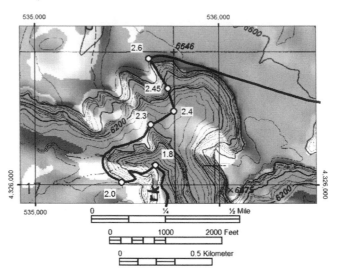

Hike #10. Detail from Mile 1.8 to 2.6. 1:24,000

small ledges until one-third of the way up you get stopped by a long, steep sandstone wall. Traverse right (W) on a ledge at the base of the wall until it starts to peter out and the ledge disappears under very steep dirt. Now look for a ledge/fault angling up through the sandstone wall from the east. Follow this ledge/fault east as it slopes up to the top of the wall. You'll be three-quarters of the way to the top of the Wingate cliffs. Now go west and angle up some more ledges to the base of the final caprock. Traverse west until you find the final [Class 4] moves behind a large boulder that is detached from the rim (see map above). 0535472 E, 4326012 N Z12 NAD83.

2.3   Now follow the bench, staying close to the rim of the inner canyon, first northwest then around to the northeast to the head of the draw containing the "climbers' route." This is the bottom of the second pitch of the ascent. You will temporarily be leaving the Mexican Mountain WSA. 0535632 E, 4326323 N Z12 NAD83.

> *Digression:* Instead of climbing the rest of the way to the rim, you can stay on this layer and follow Devils Hole to rejoin the route. Though you'll save yourself from a long scramble to the rim, you'll miss some of the best views. The mileage is the same. Contour southeast on the broken Kayenta bench for 0.6 mile and then swing east around the point marked 6675 and into

Devils Hole. Now go up Devils Hole on an old ORV scar for 2.0 miles, first to the northeast, then south-southeast (around the buttress marked 6664) and then finally east until you intersect the route again at mile 4.7.

2.4 Start angling upward and northeast until you are at the bottom of a steep, rocky chute with a pine tree near its top. 0535758 E, 4326398 N Z12 NAD83.

2.45 Go north-northwest up through the rubble and ascend the [Class 4] chute, passing behind the tree. 0535726 E, 4326522 N Z12 NAD83.

2.6 Continue climbing north-northwest as the chute turns into a steep, rocky [Class 4] gully. Stay close to the wall on the left (SW) as you work your way up the steep rubble to a hands-on finish at the rim. 0535623 E, 4326686 N Z12 NAD83.

4.4 Now take in the sweeping views as you rim-walk through the pinyons and junipers above Devils Hole for 2 miles, first to the east then south, as you work your way out to the southern end of a long, gently rising point. 0537711 E, 4325514 N Z12 NAD83.

4.5 Go south off the end of the point and follow a trail down through the caprock into the eastern end of Devils Hole. You will be re-entering the Mexican Mountain WSA. 0537777 E, 4325406 N Z12 NAD83.

4.7 Now go southeast, past a "horned" fin, and intersect an ORV scar running east and west. (The return of the digression is here by way of the scar coming from the east and Devils Hole.) 0537964 E, 4325199 N Z12 NAD83.

5.3 Follow the sometimes-track/sometimes-trail east-northeast, staying close to the base of the cliffs to the north, to a well-cairned pass leading into Box Flat. 0538838 E, 4325583 N Z12 NAD83.

5.6 Go between the big cairns and head northeast down the wash toward the southern end of Box Flat. (This is the same flat mentioned in Cottonwood Wash Hike #6.) 0539096 E, 4325828 N Z12 NAD83.

5.8 Start circling east then southeast on a stock trail around the Navajo domes that are to the right (S) and intersect the East Fork of Red Canyon Wash. 0539344 E, 4325695 N Z12 NAD83.

5.9 Head south down the wash between the big domes to the apex of a huge dry fall and a fence. 0539341 E, 4325531 N Z12 NAD83.

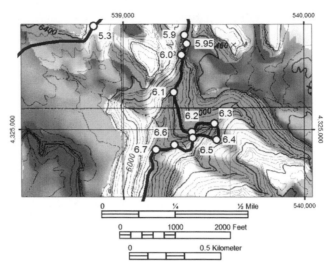

Hike #10. Detail from Mile 5.9 to 6.7. 1:24,000

5.95   Go south on a stock trail a little way past the fence to the top of the bypass route. It is marked by a small cairn and is the first steep gully to the southeast of the pour-off (see map above). 0539353 E, 4325482 N Z12 NAD83.

6.0   Descend the steep gully [Class 4, 240'] on loose rocks to the south-southwest until you reach the bottom of the canyon. 0539325 E, 4325420 N Z12 NAD83.

6.1   Follow the steep canyon floor south past several small pour-offs to the top of a big pour-off. 0539279 E, 4325209 N Z12 NAD83.

6.2   To bypass the pour-off go south then east on benches that contour into the side canyon that's coming in from the northeast. 0539379 E, 4324986 N Z12 NAD83.

6.3   Now follow the bench east-northeast up the side canyon a short way until you intersect its wash. Stay close to the rim of the inner canyon and as you go into the side canyon study the steep, rocky gully across from you to the southeast. This is the next descent route. 0539505 E, 4325034 N Z12 NAD83.

6.4   Cross the wash and go south-southeast to the top of the descent route. You'll have to go uphill a little bit before you find the huge cairn marking the entry into the steep gully. 0539516 E, 4324943 N Z12 NAD83.

6.5   Go west down this loose, rocky gully [Class 4, 220'] to the top of a big pour-off on the floor of the side canyon. 0539386 E, 4324954 N Z12 NAD83.

6.6   Bypass the pour-off on the left (S) and contour around to the southwest then northwest a short way before dropping down into the floor of the side canyon again. 0539283 E, 4324914 N Z12 NAD83.

6.7   Continue going west down this canyon. Soon you will come to the junction with the East Fork of Red Canyon. 0539181 E, 4324887 N Z12 NAD83.

9.8   Now follow the East Fork of Red Canyon, first south-southwest then generally east, enjoying the easy walking back to the start. 0535490 E, 4323540 N Z12 NAD83.

Hike #11: Upper Black Box

SEASON:	Best done in late April to mid-May and August through October. Can be too cold in late fall, winter, and early spring. Warmest water temperatures will be found in late summer and early fall. Skip the summer monsoon season altogether. Extreme flash flood danger. River level must be very low.
TIME AND DISTANCE:	Nine to twelve hours (8.8 miles with a car or mountain bike shuttle, 12.5 miles if you walk the whole way).
WATER:	San Rafael River. You will be in the river most of the time, but only drink from it if you must (it is known to have a laxative effect on some people). Bring your own drinking water.
MAPS:	Mexican Mountain, Spotted Wolf Canyon, Devils Hole, Drowned Hole Draw. (Huntington, San Rafael Desert.)
LOOP HIKE:	Yes.
SKILL LEVEL:	(3 B/C) Easy route finding. [Class 4] scrambling. [Class 5, 15'] down-climb/rappel. This can be a very long day hike. Good wading shoes are essential. Carefully read the additional material below.

At the trailhead is a bright red sign posted by the BLM that states: "WARNING! EXTREME FLASH FLOODING AND HYPOTHERMIA DANGER DURING THE SPRING, SUMMER, FALL AND WINTER MONTHS. ENTER AT YOUR OWN RISK!! TWO DEATHS OCCURRED IN THE

Deep in the Upper Black Box. Photo courtesy Ryan Choi.

BLACK BOXES IN 1999. DON'T LET THE NEXT ONE BE YOU!" The quote accurately sets the tone for this hike. Numerous parties have underestimated the difficulty of this trip and have been rescued from the canyon, sometimes not until twenty-four long, wet, and cold hours later. Danger, of course, can be invigorating if you are properly prepared, both physically and mentally. With a little forethought and preparation this trip is a blast.

Before reading the route description you should have a better understanding of what you are getting into.

1.   Water flow in the river should be below 30 cubic feet per second (cfs). The flow rate can be checked on the Daily Recreational River Report at 801-539-1311 or online at waterdata.usgs.gov.

2.   There is nothing easy about any of the hike. You will be constantly boulder-hopping, wading and probing, bushwhacking, or swimming. Everyone must be a good swimmer.

3.   Be prepared for a vertical drop off a fifteen-foot-high boulder into a pool of water. Do not jump down this. You won't be able to see what lurks beneath the murky water and an injury at this spot would be devastating. (There have been MANY injuries at this spot.) You will need a strong rope or length of webbing to create a handline. Tie

knots in it for better handholds. Wait until you are at the drop to see where they are needed. For those less-experienced or without sufficient arm strength for the handline, you will need to set up a rappel or sitting belay. If you don't know how, learn this skill somewhere else. A log has been used for years to tie-in to. If it disappears a large boulder, though a bit more awkward, will do. You may find old ropes or slings left behind by others. Please cut them down and pack them out as trash. Never use an old rope or webbing; you don't know their history. Removing them will prevent others from being tempted.

4. You will need a walking stick for probing pools. Sticks can be found everywhere along the river in the first few miles. It is nice to know when you are going to have to swim.

5. Everybody needs something that floats well to aid in swimming. Some people use inner tubes, but they can be cumbersome when not being used. The best method is to line your day-pack with doubled plastic bags (trash compactor bags are extra heavy duty and work well), fill the bags with your gear, and tie them off. Not only will this keep the things inside your pack dry, but now it will float like a cork. Wear a life jacket under the pack for the watery sections and you will be both mobile and buoyant.

6. If your dog hasn't been hiking and climbing regularly, leave him behind. He will slow you down. He should be accustomed to being lowered on a rope. He will not be able to jump down the "big drop."

7. Leave out the weak members. If they are still picking their way down the cattle trail an hour after everybody else, they will get your party into trouble when the going gets really tough up ahead. Send them back. There is no egress from the canyon for seven miles once started.

8. On a cold day hypothermia, which is life threatening, is a real possibility. Even on an 80-degree day you will be chilled inside the box. Sunlight doesn't reach the bottom of the canyon very often. Some people wear wetsuits when the water temperature is not optimal (you can check at the bridge on the Buckhorn Draw Road).

9. No children. Very strong and experienced teens may do okay at very low water levels.

10. Sturdy shoes you can hike, wade, and swim in are a must. No sandals or flip-flops. It would be wise to pack dry shoes and socks for the walk out.

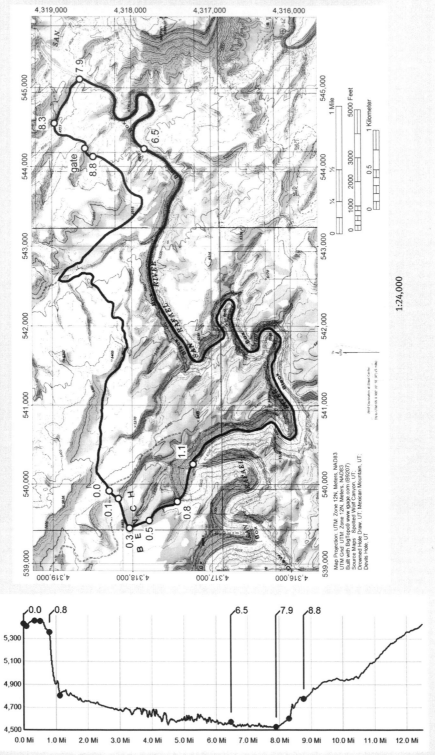

Elev Gain 0 Ft; Climb 3342 Ft; Drop −3342 Ft; Max Elev 5453 Ft; Min Elev 4524 Ft; Map Dist 12.488 Mi; Ground Dist 12.644 Mi

11. It would be advisable to have a car or mountain bike shuttle parked at the end of the Mexican Mountain Road (mile 13.6). Otherwise, the walk back to the trailhead at mile 10.0 on the Mexican Mountain Road will take about one-and-a-half hours. If you are walking the entire route, park at the trailhead and save the road for the end of the day. You'll be able to walk the road in the dark a lot easier than the canyon if you become delayed.

12. In the past this hike has been done by various youth groups with bad results. The larger the group, the slower it will move. A better alternative is Lower Black Box Hike #16

The hike starts on the flat plain called Indian Bench, goes down an old cattle trail to the San Rafael River, and follows its course through a deep and spectacular Coconino-walled canyon. The Mexican Mountain Road is then followed back to the start.

0.0 Mileage begins at the trailhead parking area at mile 10.0 on EM320/ Mexican Mountain Road. You will be entering the Mexican Mountain Wilderness Study Area. 0539919 E, 4318292 N Z12 NAD83.

0.1 Go southwest on a faint trail. You will soon come to a stock pond at the head of a shallow wash running to the southeast. 0539820 E, 4318176 N Z12 NAD83.

0.3 From the stock pond follow the trail west-southwest to intercept the head of a second, larger wash also flowing southeast. There are some cairns here. 0539451 E, 4318040 N Z12 NAD83.

0.5 Now turn left and head south-southeast to the top of another shallow wash and more cairns. This is the head of the access drainage. (If you've parked at the alternate start at mile 9.6 on the Mexican Mountain Road you can join the route here.) 0539545 E, 4317788 N Z12 NAD83.

0.8 Take the emerging trail southeast down the wash. The wash deepens and you will quickly come to the edge of the San Rafael River canyon at the top of a huge slide. 0539785 E, 4317437 N Z12 NAD83.

1.1 Follow a well-cairned trail that zigzags 600 feet down the rubble to the river's edge. 0540256 E, 4317236 N Z12 NAD83.

6.5 Head downstream, at first along a use-trail and then by hiking mostly in the river itself. The canyon winds back-and-forth a great deal, but generally follows a northeasterly course. There are countless small obstacles to negotiate as you head deeper into the canyon. You will begin to enter the narrow part of the Black Box after 4 miles. After 5.4 miles you will come to the infamous "big drop" [Class 5, 15']. 0544228 E, 4317831 N Z12 NAD83.

> *Note:* At the top of the rubble above the "big drop," on the left (N), is a very steep chute leading up to the canyon rim. It has been suggested by some that this route is a quick solution for tired and cold hikers. *This chute should not be construed as an escape from the canyon.* It is 250 feet high, has a lot of loose rock, and several vertical sections. It is [Class 5.3 to 5.4] and is three pitches in length. There are few spots for placing protection. A rope and a skilled leader are essential for those attempting the route. If you fall when halfway up, you will not stop until you hit bottom. The people who need to escape the canyon—the tired, cold, and inexperienced—are the least likely candidates for attempting the climb.

> *Digression:* Climbers and advanced canyoneers only. This same chute mentioned above is also a handy way to access the lower part of the Black Box. If you can safely execute a 200-foot rappel, you can turn a 12.5-mile round trip into a 3-mile one and still see some of the best parts of the canyon. Park at mile 13.3 on the Mexican Mountain Road at the closed track (0543882 E, 4318099 N Z12 NAD83). The track heads southeast out onto a limestone ridge. To the south of the junction is the head of a canyon paralleling the closed track. Follow the rim of the forming canyon southeast until you can work your way down to its floor. Go down the canyon 0.25 mile to the top of the chute. There is a trail that leads down into the rocky chute. Carefully down-climb to a flat ledge. There are bolts and chains on the right (SW). Rappel the remaining 200 feet to the top of the rubble above the "big drop". Some people will leave their rope fixed here and then retrieve it after their hike. If you find such a rope hanging here, please leave it alone.

7.9   Carefully descend the big drop (see additional material above, item #3) into the pool of water beneath it. You'll have to start swimming here and again at several more places ahead. After swimming a final, long pool, the canyon ends rather abruptly with a willowy wash entering from the left (NW). 0545112 E, 4318644 N Z12 NAD83.

8.3   Head northwest up this wash until you intersect the closed portion of the Mexican Mountain Road. 0544550 E, 4318962 N Z12 NAD83.

8.8   Turn left (W) and follow the road generally southwest, past the gate to the parking area (mile 13.6 on the Mexican Mountain Road). 0544129 E, 4318477 N Z12 NAD83.

12.5   If you are parked at the trailhead (mile 10.0 on the Mexican Mountain Road), it is another 3.6 miles, generally west up the road, back to the start. 0539919 E, 4318292 N Z12 NAD83.

Historical note: Proposals to dam the Upper Black Box at its mouth at Mexican Bend were made in 1909 and 1925.

Hike #12: Mexican Mountain Ascent

SEASON:	Any. No snow.
TIME AND DISTANCE:	Five to six hours (5.8 miles).
WATER:	You will have to wade across the San Rafael River. None on the mountain. Bring your own water.
MAPS:	Mexican Mountain. (Huntington, San Rafael Desert.)
LOOP HIKE:	No.
SKILL LEVEL:	Moderate route finding. Much [Class 3] scrambling. Some exposure. Climbing to [Class 5.0, 30']. Most will want to rappel this pitch on the way back. Beginners will need to be belayed.

Views, Views, Views. Mexican Mountain is the king of the area. Its summit, rarely trodden, provides unparalleled vistas of the San Rafael Swell. The route itself is a stiff, long scramble that cuts through the Moenkopi, Chinle, Wingate, Kayenta, and Navajo Formations. Though there are several sections of easy rock climbing, the inexperienced should have no problems if there is competent leadership.

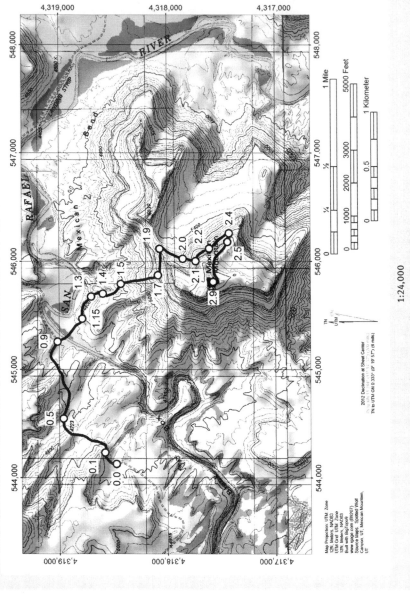

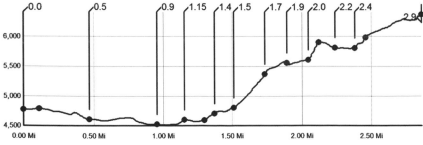

Elev Gain 1602 Ft; Climb 2224 Ft; Drop −622 Ft; Max Elev 6376 Ft; Min Elev 4516 Ft; Map Dist 2.864 Mi; Ground Dist 2.965 Mi

0.0   Mileage begins at the trailhead parking area at mile 13.6 on EM320/ Mexican Mountain Road. 0544129 E, 4318477 N Z12 NAD83.

0.1   Head northeast on the Mexican Mountain Road. Soon you will come to a gate blocking the road. 0544235 E, 4318581 N Z12 NAD83.

The road is closed to vehicles beyond this point, but continues on, in one form or another, to the drill pipe at Mexican Bend. You will be entering the Mexican Mountain Wilderness Study Area.

0.5   Follow the road north-northeast. When it turns to the east it crosses (and parallels for a short time) a wash running to the southeast. This wash is the same one used to return to the trailhead at the end of the Upper Black Box Hike #11. 0544550 E, 4318962 N Z12 NAD83.

0.9   Continue hiking along the old road, now generally east, to the first place it comes close to the cottonwood-lined San Rafael River.

Look south toward Mexican Mountain as you hike along. Notice that low cliffs rise up from near river level forming a bench. From the bench is steep talus (Moenkopi) heading up to a persistent, red cliff band. There is a long, triangular-shaped rubble ramp in the talus slope that appears to break through the cliff. The route goes straight up it. Above the red cliff band is another talus apron (Chinle) leading up to the base of the giant Wingate cliffs.

Leave the road when it begins to parallel the river and turn to the left (NE). 0545262 E, 4319015 N Z12 NAD83.

1.15   Head southeast to the river and wade across (0545289 E, 4318947 N Z12 NAD83). From the crossing you can see the route up through the first low cliffs. It begins in the small wash to the southeast. Head up this wash and follow an emerging trail southeast onto a bench. 0545473 E, 4318788 N Z12 NAD83.

1.3   Now traverse east-southeast across this bench until you can work your way into the bottom of a steep draw that leads southeast up to a break in the next low cliffs. 0545677 E, 4318705 N Z12 NAD83.

1.4   Hike southeast up this draw and then climb through an easy break in the cliffs to the wide bench above. A large cairn waits at the top. You'll have a great view of the talus ramp from here. 0545706 E, 4318599 N Z12 NAD83.

1.5   Follow a faint use-trail south-southeast across the bench to the bottom of a cairned route at the base of the ramp. 0545795 E, 4318432 N Z12 NAD83.

Mexican Mountain is a worthy challenge.

1.7   Scramble south up this arduous slide [Class 3], following cairns and a use-trail when you can, until you reach it's very top at the base of the red cliff band (see map on page 149). 0545875 E, 4318086 N Z12 NAD83.

1.9   Climb up through a broken part of the cliff [5.0, 30']. The route is fairly obvious. Beginners will want a belay or the use of a handline. At the top of the cliff is a faint use-trail that angles up and left (E) across sloping talus. Follow it up to the base of the huge Wingate wall near its eastern end. Traverse left (E) along the wall to a saddle. 0546120 E, 4318071 N Z12 NAD83.

2.0   Follow the faint trail around the corner of the Wingate wall to the southwest. Below you, to the south, is a bouldery gully. Contour south-southwest along the trail to a cairn in the bottom of the gully. 0546027 E, 4317855 N Z12 NAD83.

2.1   Scramble up the steep gully [Class 3], following occasional cairns generally south, to the base of a cliff band (Kayenta). 0546005 E, 4317734 N Z12 NAD83.

2.2   Traverse left (SE) until forced onto a large expanse of candy-striped slickrock (Wingate Sandstone). Go out onto a red ledge that traverses the slickrock slab. There are several prevalent red ledges here. Find the highest one that appears reasonable. 0546122 E, 4317607 N Z12 NAD83.

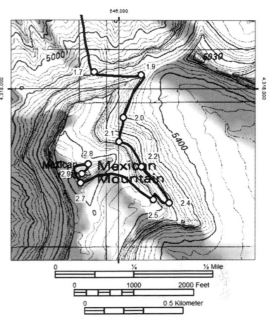

Hike #12. Detail from Mile 1.7 to 2.9. 1:24,000

2.4   Follow the narrow ledge southeast. As you do, look for a cairn. You'll climb to the top of the Kayenta cliffs from here. 0546262 E, 4317424 N Z12 NAD83.

If you miss the cairn, the red ledge quickly widens and ends in a spectacular balcony with several large, white boulders sitting on it. (0546274 E, 4317373 N Z12 NAD83). The red ledge ends in a drop here. This is a perfect spot for a break. Backtrack on the red ledge for seventy-five yards or to the cairn.

2.5   Go west and ascend steep slickrock until a white cliff band is reached (Kayenta). Climb up a nice crack to a ledge. Take the ledge north a short way then zigzag up a series of ledges, following cairns, to the top of the cliff [Class 4]. Note where you come out on top so you will be able to find it on your way back. 0546182 E, 4317439 N Z12 NAD83.

2.7   Hike northwest toward the summit ridge (Navajo) and then west along the bench below it until you are just south of the summit. 0545807 E, 4317525 N Z12 NAD83.

2.8   Go north, then east, and circle around to the north side of the summit ridge. A steep gully with a cairn leads south up through the wall. 0545845 E, 4317620 N Z12 NAD83.

2.9   Ascend the gully [Class 4, 40'] then zip to the summit (6393'). 0545815 E, 4317571 N Z12 NAD83.

5.8   After enjoying the splendid views, return to the start the way you came. 0544129 E, 4318477 N Z12 NAD83.

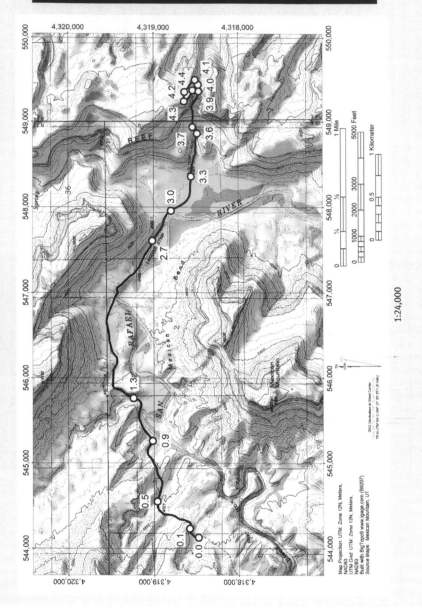

1:24,000

Map Projection: UTM, Zone 12N, Meters.
NAD83
UTM Grid UTM Zone 12N. Meters.
NAD83
Built with BigTopo9 www.igage.com (B9207)
Source Maps: Mexican Mountain, UT

2012 Declination at Sheet Center
11s to USK Grid 0.349° (0° 20' 25") (4 miles)

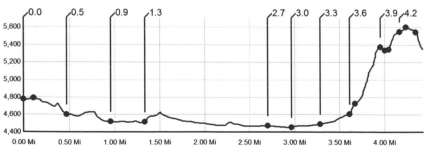

Elev Gain 573 Ft; Climb 1517 Ft; Drop −944 Ft; Max Elev 5604 Ft; Min Elev 4451 Ft; Map Dist 4.426 Mi; Ground Dist 4.502 Mi

Hike #13: Mexican Bend and the Horse Thief Trail

SEASON:	Any.
TIME AND DISTANCE:	Six to eight hours (8.6 miles). Could easily be combined with other hikes to make a longer, multiday trip.
WATER:	San Rafael River if you must. Good springs nearby in Spring Canyon. Bring your own water.
MAPS:	Mexican Mountain. (Huntington, San Rafael Desert.)
LOOP HIKE:	No.
SKILL LEVEL:	(1A). Easy route finding. [Class 3+] scrambling.

Visions of dusty trails, the hoot of cowboys, and the bawling of cattle come alive when hiking the Horse Thief Trail. One can just imagine a herd of cattle winding their way down the steep trail. The hike follows the trail through the towering west wall of the Northern Reef and returns the same way. It connects with Hikes #3, #6, #12 and #14, making for many possible digressions.

> *Historical note:* The Horse Thief Trail was used to move cattle and horses, often stolen, from the Tidwell Draw area to Mexican Bend. Butch Cassidy and his Hole-in-the-Wall Gang are known to have used the trail, as well as local ranchers. It has not been used for many years. There are bits and pieces of the old trail still visible, though most of it has disappeared. It is most distinct just before topping out.

0.0   Mileage begins at the trailhead parking area at mile 13.6 on EM320/ Mexican Mountain Road. 0544129 E, 4318477 N Z12 NAD83.

0.1   Head northeast on the Mexican Mountain Road. Soon you will come to a gate blocking the road. 0544235 E, 4318581 N Z12 NAD83.

The road is closed to vehicles beyond this point, but continues on, in one form or another, to the drill pipe at Mexican Bend. You will be entering the Mexican Mountain Wilderness Study Area.

0.5   Follow the road north-northeast. When it turns to the east it crosses (and parallels for a short time) a wash running to the southeast. This wash is the same one used to return to the trailhead at the end of the Upper Black Box Hike #11. 0544550 E, 4318962 N Z12 NAD83.

0.9   Continue hiking along the old road, now generally east, to the first place it comes close to the cottonwood-lined San Rafael River.

Hike #12 diverges here and heads south across the river. 0545262 E, 4319015 N Z12 NAD83.

1.3   Keep following the road. It turns and goes northeast along the river and then into the mouth of Sulphur Canyon. Hike #6 joins here, coming down the canyon. 0545765 E, 4319242 N Z12 NAD83.

2.7   The old road heads northeast out of the canyon and onto the bench above. It then goes east and southeast, paralleling the river, to the wind vane next to the airstrip at Mexican Bend. The airstrip is actively used so don't mess with it and whatever you do, don't camp on it. 0547608 E, 4319016 N Z12 NAD83.

> *Historical note:* Follow a use-trail east-northeast from the wind vane up onto a low, boulder-studded bench. Several of the large, patinated boulders atop the bench are adorned with excellent Fremont style petroglyphs, one of the best sites in the area. Be sure to look on all surfaces of the boulders. Some of the more intriguing images are also some of the less readily visible.

3.0   Hikes #6 and #14 diverge here and go up Spring Canyon to the north. From the wind vane continue following the deteriorating old track southeast. You will cross the wash coming from Spring Canyon just before it joins the San Rafael River. If there are no cattle around and the bugs aren't too bad, there is some excellent camping in the area. This zone would make a good base camp location for extended journeys. Good spring water can normally be found in the first mile of Spring Canyon. 0547959 E, 4318799 N Z12 NAD83.

3.3   Keep going southeast along the track (it's really nothing more than a road-grade at this point). It soon ends at a drill pipe. You'll be able to see the route of the Horse Thief Trail going up a rubble gully on the face of the Northern Reef to the east. 0548359 E, 4318558 N Z12 NAD83.

3.6   There is a shallow wash running west from the bottom of the gully that goes right past the drill pipe on its way to the river. Head east up the wash until you reach the bottom of the first low cliff band at the base of the Reef. A trail begins to emerge as you do. There is a cairn where the trail leaves the wash to head up through the cliffs (see map on page 153). 0548866 E, 4318481 N Z12 NAD83.

3.7 Take the trail east through a break in the cliffs, then north to the bottom of the rubble gully. Cairns show the way. 0548942 E, 4318538 N Z12 NAD83.

3.9 Now follow the well-cairned trail generally east up the steep rubble (850 feet) to the saddle above. Signs of the constructed portions of the Horse

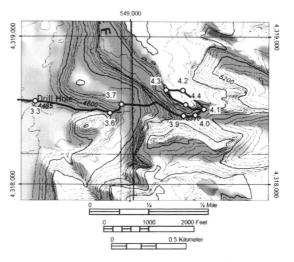

Hike #13. Detail of Mile 3.3 to 4.4. 1:24,000

Thief Trail can be seen along the way. At the saddle you will be able to see Acer's Arch to the north. The top of Horse Thief Trail Canyon is to the east. The route intersects Hike #3 (Alternate 1) here. 0549366 E, 4318461 N Z12 NAD83.

4.0 To continue to the top of the Reef, follow the use-trail east from the saddle down into the head of Horse Thief Trail Canyon. A dry-fall is quickly reached. 0549445 E, 4318467 N Z12 NAD83.

4.1 The trail swings to the left (NE) and traverses to the base of a rubble slope coming down from a break in the cliffs above. 0549504 E, 4318506 N Z12 NAD83.

4.2 Go northwest along the trail, up the [Class 3] rubble and through the break in the cliffs. Once on top the break turns into a shallow gully. Follow the gully, still northwest, until it is easy to exit the gully to the left (W). 0549359 E, 4318633 N Z12 NAD83.

4.3 Head west across slickrock a short way to the high point at the rim of the Reef. The view is staggering. You will be looking 900 feet down at the San Rafael River as it makes the Mexican Bend around Mexican Mountain. You can see the airstrip paralleling the river. Coming into the bend from the right (N) is Spring Canyon. 0549248 E, 4318637 N Z12 NAD83.

4.4 Go southeast, staying close to the rim of the escarpment, until you reach the rim of Horse Thief Trail Canyon. You'll be right above and just north of the saddle. Follow the rim as it turns to the east.

An unlikely looking cleft appears with a cairn at its head. 0549379 E, 4318536 N Z12 NAD83.

4.5 Scramble southeast down the steep cleft [Class 3+, 20'] until the small, double Acer's Arch is reached. Large packs will need to be lowered. From the arch you can clearly see the route down into Horse Thief Trail Canyon. The slope below the arch looks worse than it is. Keep scrambling down until you reach some ledges. Traverse left (E) until you can intersect the use-trail again at the base of the rubble. 0549504 E, 4318506 N Z12 NAD83.

8.6 Follow the trail southwest to the saddle then retrace your steps back to the trailhead. 0544129 E, 4318477 N Z12 NAD83.

Hike #14: Spring Canyon to Sulphur Canyon

Season:	Any. Spring and fall are best.
Time and distance:	Two to three days (15.9 miles).
Water:	San Rafael River if you must. Reliable springs in Spring Canyon. Seasonal water in both forks of Spring Canyon and Nates Canyon.
Maps:	Mexican Mountain, Devils Hole. (Huntington, San Rafael Desert.)
Loop hike:	Yes.
Skill level:	(1A). Advanced route finding. [Class 4] scrambling. A rope or webbing for lowering packs will be a must. Familiarity with low-impact camping techniques is essential.

Rabid dogs can be out of control. Downhill skiers can be out of control. Can the Spring Canyon to Sulphur Canyon loop hike be out of control? To find out, treat yourself to this fabulous route as it wends its way through deep, Wingate-walled canyons, around Navajo domes, and past two large arches.

The route goes up the North Fork of Spring Canyon, crosses a broken plateau with outstanding views, and descends Sulphur Canyon before returning to the start. It ties into Hikes #6 and #13 making many possible variations.

0.0 Mileage begins at the trailhead parking area at mile 13.6 on EM320/ Mexican Mountain Road. 0544129 E, 4318477 N Z12 NAD83.

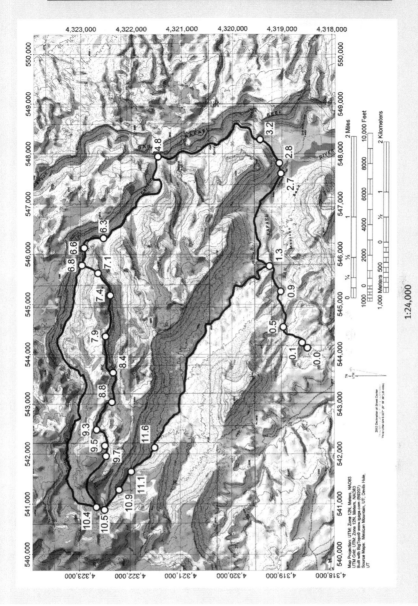

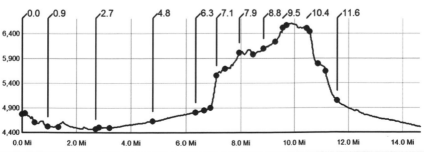

Elev Loss −260 Ft; Climb 3184 Ft; Drop −3444 Ft; Max Elev 6603 Ft; Min Elev 4467 Ft; Map Dist 14.639 Mi; Ground Dist 14.799 Mi

0.1   Head northeast on the Mexican Mountain Road. Soon you will come to a gate blocking the road. 0544235 E, 4318581 N Z12 NAD83.

'The road is closed to vehicles beyond this point, but continues on, in one form or another, to the drill pipe at Mexican Bend. You will be entering the Mexican Mountain Wilderness Study Area.

0.5   Follow the road north-northeast. When it turns to the east it crosses (and parallels for a short time) a wash running to the southeast. This wash is the same one used to return to the trailhead at the end of the Upper Black Box Hike #11. 0544550 E, 4318962 N Z12 NAD83.

0.9   Continue hiking along the old road, now generally east, to the first place it comes close to the cottonwood-lined San Rafael River. Hike #12 diverges here and heads south across the river. 0545262 E, 4319015 N Z12 NAD83.

1.3   Keep following the road. It turns and goes northeast along the river and then into the mouth of Sulphur Canyon. Hike #6 joins here, coming down the canyon. 0545765 E, 4319242 N Z12 NAD83.

2.7   The old road heads northeast out of the canyon and onto the bench above. It then goes east and southeast, paralleling the river, to the wind vane next to the airstrip at Mexican Bend. The airstrip is actively used so don't mess with it and whatever you do, don't camp on it. Hike #13 diverges here and heads southeast up the Horse Thief Trail. 0547608 E, 4319016 N Z12 NAD83.

2.8   Take a use-trail east-northeast from the wind vane up onto a low, boulder-studded bench. 0547817 E, 4319048 N Z12 NAD83.

> *Historical note:* Several of the large, patinated boulders atop the bench are adorned with excellent Fremont style petroglyphs, one of the best sites in the area. Be sure to look on all surfaces of the boulders. Some of the more intriguing images are also some of the less readily visible.

3.2   Follow the use-trail northeast into the mouth of Spring Canyon. You may find good water here. If the cattle aren't around and the bugs aren't too bad, there is good camping in the area. This zone would make a good base camp location for extended journeys. 0548286 E, 4319438 N Z12 NAD83.

4.8   Go generally north up Spring Canyon along the trail. You will pass some springs and see Delicate Arch (also known as Bumpy Road or

Leaning Arch) on the left (W). Just past the arch is a short drainage coming in from the left (W) followed by a distinct, castle-like fin. On the far side of the fin is the junction with Nates Canyon. 0547940 E, 4321462 N Z12 NAD83.

Hike #6 diverges here and goes north up Nates Canyon. If you haven't found good water by now, you should find some just inside the mouth of Nates Canyon or farther up Spring Canyon. If cattle have fouled the springs, there may be seasonal pothole water above a bovine-stopping dry-fall a short way up Nates Canyon.

6.3 Turn left (W) and continue hiking northwest up Spring Canyon. The inner canyon within the bigger canyon opens up. After 1.5 miles the canyon divides. The North Fork is on the right (N) and the South Fork on the left (W). 0546320 E, 4322541 N Z12 NAD83.

6.6 Turn right and follow the North Fork. It only goes north a short way before turning to the west. There is a spring and nice camping near a very large boulder with "BLASTING. KEEP OUT" whitewashed on it. If doing the hike in two days, this makes a fine place to spend the night. 0546125 E, 4322922 N Z12 NAD83.

6.8 Keep following the canyon west. As you do, look for a long talus ramp on the left (S) that leads up to the rim of the inner canyon. A cairned trail begins at the bottom of the talus. 0545781 E, 4322964 N Z12 NAD83.

> *Digression:* You can continue up the North Fork and eventually exit the canyon. Those who are base camped in Spring Canyon, and can safely negotiate a short [Class 5] friction climb, can turn the North and South Forks into a worthwhile, day-long loop. Go generally west up the North Fork. Pick your way past giant boulders as you work your way up the brushy canyon [Class 3]. This can be tedious. The canyon ahead is blocked by a large dry-fall. Once you pass an alcove with a pinnacle in it that's on the right (N), there is a cairned trail leading up steep rubble on the left (S). 0543766 E, 4323214 N Z12 NAD83. Follow the faint trail as you angle up the rubble to the base of a cliff band. 0543680 E, 4323038 N Z12 NAD83. Traverse right (W) along the cliff as far as you can. Above you in the cliff will be three unlikely looking

concavities, one atop the other. This is the way up. 0543573 E, 4322984 N Z12 NAD83. Friction-climb this first part [Class 5, 15'] then zigzag south up several small cliffs to cairns waiting at the top. 0543591 E, 4322940 N Z12 NAD83. Now traverse west across a white slickrock bench and rejoin the floor of the North Fork above another medium-sized pour-off. 0542628 E, 4323103 N Z12 NAD83. Hike generally west up the much shallower canyon. Go left (S) around two small falls before the wash divides. 0541506 E, 4323278 N Z12 NAD83. Head up the southwest fork. Pass a double-tiered fall on the left. The wash opens up into a big slickrock area 0541023 E, 4323031 N Z12 NAD83. To the left (S) are two domes. Scramble south up to a saddle in between the domes and rejoin the standard route. 0540943 E, 4322669 N Z12 NAD83. From the North Fork to this point is 3.6 miles. To the south is the head of Sulphur Canyon (Hike #6). To the east are the large domes standing at the head of the South Fork of Spring Canyon. Follow the standard route description in reverse to return to the North Fork at the start of the digression. 0545781 E, 4322964 N Z12 NAD83. The North Fork to South Fork section is 6.2 miles round trip.

7.1   Scramble south-southwest up the cairned trail to the top of the talus ramp and through a break in the caprock to the rim of the inner canyon [Class 3]. A large cairn sits at the top. 0545624 E, 4322647 N Z12 NAD83.

7.4   You will be on the large, flat peninsula that separates the North and South Forks. Sitting on the peninsula to the west is a large dome (elevation 5885 on the Mexican Mountain map). Head southwest and follow the rim of the South Fork. As you pass south of the dome, the canyon turns west. 0545185 E, 4322404 N Z12 NAD83.

7.9   Follow the rim west. Eventually you will be forced to angle up to the top of white ledges. Look for the very large Spring Canyon Arch across the canyon. It can only be seen through a gap in the fin that divides the canyon to the southwest. It is the largest in the Swell but is easily missed. As you continue along the rim you will see the massive dry-fall below that blocks the canyon. 0544363 E, 4322498 N Z12 NAD83.

8.4   Continue heading west, contouring across a series of ledges, until you can drop southwest into the South Fork just above the big dry-fall. 0543637 E, 4322344 N Z12 NAD83.

8.8   Head west up the canyon past several easy obstacles. Soon the canyon divides. 0543045 E, 4322364 N Z12 NAD83.

9.3   Go right (N) and follow the canyon northwest for another 0.5 mile, past more easy obstacles, until it divides again. 0542490 E, 4322670 N Z12 NAD83.

9.5   Now go left (S). Head southwest up this fork. It ends in a dry-fall just after turning to the west. Scramble up steep rubble that leads to the bottom of a cleft to the right (N). Climb up this chimney [Class 4] to the top of the fall. 0542172 E, 4322504 N Z12 NAD83.

9.7   Head west between two big Navajo Domes (the one to the south is elevation 6842 on the Devils Hole map) and quickly exit the head of the canyon. You will be on the divide between Sulphur Canyon to the south and the North Fork of Spring Canyon to the north. 0541961 E, 4322483 N Z12 NAD83.

10.4   Along the divide to the west are two smaller domes. Follow the divide northwest then southwest until you are in the saddle between them. The digression rejoins the route here. 0540943 E, 4322669 N Z12 NAD83.

10.5   Go south-southwest from the saddle to the rim of Sulphur Canyon at its head. You will join Hike #6 here. 0540888 E, 4322510 N Z12 NAD83.

10.9   Descend into Sulphur Canyon by going southeast down the head of the canyon toward a large detached flake. Climb down a short chute behind the flake [difficult Class 4, 20']. A rope or webbing is a must here for lowering packs. Beginners may want a belay. Now scramble 750 feet down a steep rubble slope [Class 3], following occasional cairns, to a wonderful flat area. The 175-foot-tall Thin Man Pinnacle is to the right (S). If there is pothole water here, this is a delightful camping area. 0541289 E, 4322218 N Z12 NAD83.

11.1   Head southeast across the pinyon and juniper covered plaza, following the wash to the top of the next descent. 0541653 E, 4321981 N Z12 NAD83.

11.6   Go southeast down a cool little stone stairway [Class 4, 15'], followed by 950 feet of arduous [Class 4] boulder-hopping to reach the canyon floor. 0542133 E, 4321514 N Z12 NAD83.

14.6   The going is easy as you hike southeast down Sulphur Canyon the rest of the way. Just before you exit the mouth of the canyon you will intersect the old, closed portion of the Mexican Mountain Road. (You will also be intersecting Hike #13 here.) 0545765 E, 4319242 N Z12 NAD83.

15.9   Now simply follow the old road generally southwest back to the trailhead. 0544129 E, 4318477 N Z12 NAD83.

EM332/Cottonwood Wash Road Section

Access to Hikes #15, #16 and #19 through #21.

Access is from EM332/Buckhorn Draw Road and Interstate 70 Exit 131.
Provides access to TR643/Dexter Mine Road, B6757/Sinkhole Flat Road, B6755/
Jackass Bench Road, B7183/Oil Well Flat Road and EM332/Buckhorn Draw Road.
1:100,000 map: Huntington. San Rafael Desert.

The section of County Road 332 (Lawrence-to-Tan-Seeps Road) that goes
generally south from the San Rafael River bridge to Interstate 70 is known
as the Cottonwood Wash Road. North of the bridge it is called the Buckhorn
Draw Road and south of I-70 the Heart of Sinbad Road. It divides the Mexican Mountain area from the Sids Mountain area. The road is suitable for
most vehicles unless wet or snowy and there are many side roads that can be
used for camping.

0.0   Mileage begins at the San Rafael River bridge. 0528860 E, 4325828
N Z12 NAD83.

0.1   The San Rafael River campground is to the left (SE). The road goes
generally south up Road Draw. 0528775 E, 4325641 N Z12 NAD83.

0.4   The junction with the dirt road that goes to San Rafael River and
Cane Wash Hike #19 and Virgin Springs Canyon Hike #20 is on the
right (W). 0528352 E, 4325419 N Z12 NAD83.

> **Side road to Hikes #19 and #20**
>
> **0.0**   Mileage begins at the junction with the Cottonwood
> Wash Road. Go generally west on this good double track.
> 0528343 E, 4325499 N Z12 NAD83.
>
> **1.0**   Parking area near an information kiosk at the edge of a
> wash. This wash comes from Moore Canyon. The Johansen
> corral is to the northeast. The start of San Rafael River and
> Cane Wash Hike #19 and Virgin Springs Canyon Hike #20

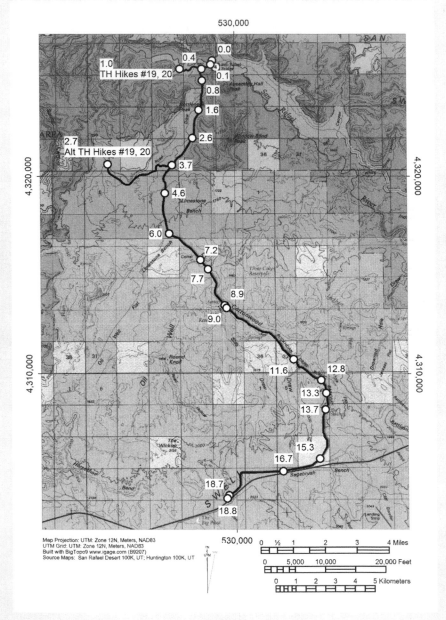

530,000

1.0
TH Hikes #19, 20

0.4

0.0

0.1

0.8

1.6

2.6

2.7
Alt TH Hikes #19, 20

3.7

4,320,000

4.6

6.0

7.2

7.7

8.9

9.0

4,310,000

11.6

12.8

13.3

13.7

15.3

16.7

18.7

18.8

530,000

Map Projection: UTM: Zone 12N, Meters, NAD83
UTM Grid: UTM: Zone 12N, Meters, NAD83
Built with BigTopo9 www.igage.com (B9207)
Source Maps: San Rafael Desert 100K, UT; Huntington 100K, UT

0   ½   1   2   3   4 Miles

0   5,000   10,000   20,000 Feet

0   1   2   3   4   5 Kilometers

1:100,000

(these hikes are described in detail in the Sids Mountain chapter). 0527202 E, 4325414 N Z12 NAD83.

0.8   Continue heading south on the Cottonwood Wash Road. Bottleneck Peak and sign are on the right (W). 0528334 E, 4324824 N Z12 NAD83.

1.6   Window Blind Peak, an important landmark, is to the left (E). 0528172 E, 4323339 N Z12 NAD83.

2.6   The road crosses a small wash. You will be able to see Pinnacle #1 (Hike #21) straight ahead. It is the larger tower to the left of a smaller tower. 0527824 E, 4321930 N Z12 NAD83.

3.7   Once you have passed Window Blind Peak, you will come to the junction with a dirt road on the right (W). This track is TR643/ Cane Wash Road and goes to the Dexter Mine and the alternate trailhead for Hikes #19 and #20 in Cane Wash. 0526753 E, 4320486 N Z12 NAD83.

4.6   A fence starts on the right. 0526333 E, 4319147 N Z12 NAD83.

6.0   The junction with B7183/Oil Well Flat Road will be on the right (S) atop Limestone Bench. This dirt road provides access to the Pinnacle #1 Ascent Hike #21 (see the Sids Mountain chapter for details on this road section and hike). 0526569 E, 4317106 N Z12 NAD83.

7.2   The road leaves Road Draw and begins trending southeast. A track on the right (SW) leads to a corral. 0528241 E, 4315775 N Z12 NAD83.

7.7   After the road crosses the wash of Oil Well Draw you will reach the junction with a dirt road leading to Three Coves Reservoir on the left (NW). 0528621 E, 4315308 N Z12 NAD83.

8.9   The road now heads up Sids Draw. The junction with a dirt road on the right (W) leads to Sids Holes. 0529458 E, 4313486 N Z12 NAD83.

9.0   You will quickly reach a junction with another dirt road on the right (W). This one leads to Sids Reservoir. 0529568 E, 4313329 N Z12 NAD83.

11.6   The road is now going up Cottonwood Draw. On the left (NE) is a junction with a dirt road. This track is B650 and goes generally north to the boundary of the Mexican Mountain Wilderness Study Area near Lockhart Box. 0532859 E, 4310799 N Z12 NAD83.

13.3   The road exits Cottonwood Draw and begins to head south just before the marked junction with B6757/Sinkhole Flat Road on the left (E). This road goes to B6755/Jackass Bench Road leading to Drowned Hole Draw Hike #15 and Lower Black Box Hike #16 (see the Sinkhole Flat/Jackass Bench Road Section in this chapter for details). 0534564 E, 4309017 N Z12 NAD83.

13.7   You will pass the Sinkhole, surrounded by a fence, on the left (E). 0534558 E, 4308189 N Z12 NAD83.

15.3   The road continues south then begins going southwest. The second marked junction with B6757/Sinkhole Flat Road is on the left (SSE). This is the southern end of the Sinkhole Flat Road and can be used to access B6755/Jackass Bench Road to the northeast or you can go south through the Interstate 70 underpass to B7192/Red Draw Road and B6756/Cliff Dweller Flat Road (see volume 2 for details). 0534234 E, 4305694 N Z12 NAD83.

16.7   Now the road swings to the west and parallels Interstate 70. You will cross a cattle guard and see a sagebrush test area to the right (N). This is definitely worth looking at to see the dramatic effects that grazing has had on this region. 0532369 E, 4305077 N Z12 NAD83.

18.7   Just before reaching the junction with Interstate 70 you will come to the junction with a dirt road on the right (N). 0529636 E, 4303841 N Z12 NAD83.

This is BLM Trail #642 and is the start of a good, 25-mile-long, mountain bike ride. Follow the track north-northwest for a mile to a junction. TR646 goes right (N) and TR645 goes left (W). Go west for 7.4 miles on TR645 as it goes by the south side of the Wickiup, then swings north to rejoin TR646 and intersect the Oil Well Flat Road near the base of Pinnacle #1. You can either take TR646 southeast then south for 7.9 miles back to the start, or go northeast on the Oil Well Flat Road for four miles. It will take you back to the Cottonwood Wash Road at mile 6.0. Now follow the Cottonwood Wash Road generally south for thirteen miles back to the start.

18.8   Junction with Interstate 70 at Exit 131. 0529524 E, 4303701 N Z12 NAD83.

EM332 continues south under the interstate and becomes the Heart of Sinbad Road (see volume 2 for details).

B6757/Sinkhole Flat and B6755/Jackass Bench Road Section

Access to Hikes #15 and #16.

Access is from EM332/Cottonwood Wash Road.

1:100,000 map: Huntington. San Rafael Desert.

The Sinkhole Flat Road heads southeast from EM332/Cottonwood Wash Road. The sandy track soon hooks up with the Jackass Bench Road that goes northeast and makes a loop across the Jackass Benches. Several 4WD spur roads that radiate from the loop lead to Drowned Hole Draw, the Swaseys Leap and Sulphur Springs Road trailheads for the Lower Black Box, and Black Dragon Wash. The network of roads would make for decent mountain biking. There is plenty of camping throughout the area.

0.0 Mileage begins at mile 13.3 on EM332/Cottonwood Wash Road. 0534564 E, 4309017 N Z12 NAD83.

1.7 Go east then southeast on the Sinkhole Flat Road to the junction with a dirt road on the left (NE). This is the beginning of B6755/ Jackass Bench Road. It has a sign saying, "Rattlesnake Flat, Jackass Benches, Swazys Leap." Swaseys Leap is misspelled "Swazys" in many places, including on the Spotted Wolf Canyon map. 0536834 E, 4307608 N Z12 NAD83.

4.4 Turn left (NE) onto this medium-clearance double track and follow it generally northeast across Rattlesnake Flat to a junction. This is the beginning of the loop. 0539028 E, 4310343 N Z12 NAD83.

Turn right (E) to go to the Black Dragon Road and the Sulphur Springs Road trailhead. This is the standard way to access the Lower Black Box. Or turn left (W) to go to Drowned Hole Draw and the alternate, Swaseys Leap trailhead for the Lower Black Box.

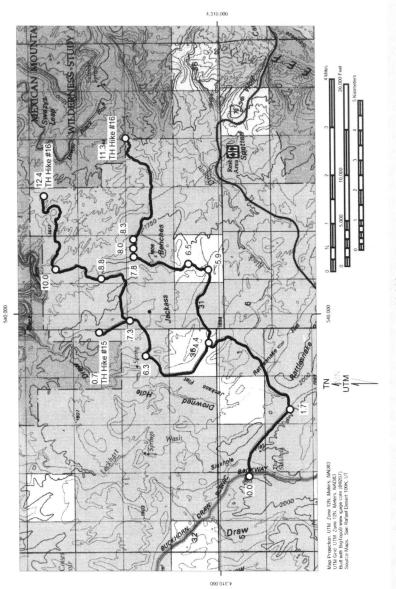

1:100,000

Left on loop

Mileage resumes from the junction at mile 4.4.

6.3   The road heads to the northwest then north across Jackass Flat. It then turns northeast and goes over a pass between two small buttes. 0538610 E, 4312472 N Z12 NAD83.

7.3   Keep going northeast over the pass. The track becomes rocky before turning north and meeting a faint double track coming in from the left (NNW). 0539798 E, 4313011 N Z12 NAD83.

    This track is TR651. Down this high-clearance side road is the start of Drowned Hole Draw Hike #15. Follow the track north-northwest for 0.7 mile until it comes to the edge of a drainage on the left (W) that runs to the northwest. This is a side-drainage of Drowned Hole Draw. Park anywhere alongside the road. 0539396 E, 4314045 N Z12 NAD83.

8.8   Continue on the main road (NNE) to go to the Swaseys Leap trailhead for Hike #16. Just past the junction with the double track the road turns to the east then swings to the north before coming to a fork. The road to the right (NE) is the continuation of the Jackass Bench Road. It goes to the Sulphur Springs Road and eventually returns to the junction at mile 4.4. To the left (NW) is TR652. 0541200 E, 4313958 N Z12 NAD83.

10.0   Go left (NW). A sign says, "Lower Black Box, Swazys Leap 6.5. Road Closed 4." Follow the track generally north. Just past a flat area the road gets very rough. High-clearance 4WDs only beyond this point. Many people will park here and ride a mountain bike the remaining 2.4 miles to the trailhead. 0541508 E, 4315482 N Z12 NAD83.

12.4   The road turns and goes generally east to the Mexican Mountain Wilderness Study Area boundary and the Swazys Leap trailhead for Hike #16. 0543969 E, 4315856 N Z12 NAD83.

    The closed road continues generally east for another 2.6 miles to Swazys Leap at the top of the Lower Black Box (0546145 E, 4315874 N Z12 NAD83), but is closed to vehicles.

Right on loop

Mileage resumes from the junction at mile 4.4.

Be prepared for much swimming in the Lower Black Box.

5.9   Follow the road generally east. A faint dirt track comes in on the right (E). 0541504 E, 4310359 N Z12 NAD83.

6.5   The road turns to the north. You will come to the junction with a dirt road on the right (E). This high-clearance 4WD track, TR647, is called the Black Dragon Wash Road and heads east down Black Dragon Wash (Hike #18) to Interstate 70 (see the Black Dragon Wash Road Section for details). Though it's a popular ORV route, it is a fun mountain bike ride as well. 0541709 E, 4311024 N Z12 NAD83.

7.8   Keep heading north on the main road to the junction with another dirt road on the right (E). This is TR653, also called the Sulphur Springs Road. (Continue north on the main track to get to the Swaseys Leap trailhead for Hike #16.) 0541937 E, 4312860 N Z12 NAD83.

8.0   Turn right (E) onto this track and follow it east into the head of a drainage. The road gets very rough as it crosses the wash. High-clearance 4WDs and mountain bikes only beyond this point. 0542216 E, 4312874 N Z12 NAD83.

8.3   On the far side of the drainage is a sign stating, "San Rafael River 5.4, Sulphur Springs 5.6." 0542515 E, 4312872 N Z12 NAD83.

11.3 The road climbs a rocky draw and continues going generally east to the Mexican Mountain Wilderness Study Area boundary and the Sulphur Springs trailhead. Start of Lower Black Box Hike #16. 0545910 E, 4313111 N Z12 NAD83.

The track is closed beyond the trailhead but continues going generally east for another 2.1 miles to the San Rafael River just below the Lower Black Box (0548126 E, 4313807 N Z12 NAD83).

Hike #15: Drowned Hole Draw

SEASON:	Any. No recent rain or snow.
TIME AND DISTANCE:	Two to three hours (3.6 miles).
WATER:	Seasonal pools. Bring your own water.
MAPS:	Drowned Hole Draw. (San Rafael Desert).
LOOP HIKE:	No.
SKILL LEVEL:	(2A). Easy route finding. [Class 5.1] climbing, with exposure. Rock climbers only. A rope will be helpful for those less skilled.

Drowned Hole Draw, when seen from the start, is the type of canyon no one in their right mind would think of hiking. Even the map shows it as barely being a wash. Rock climbers, though, will find a pristine and pretty little canyon that presents several vertical challenges.

The route goes down Drowned Hole Draw, past several obstacles, to a pothole on the edge of an impassable drop overlooking the San Rafael River as it winds its way through the upper section of the Upper Black Box.

0.0 Mileage begins at the track on the rim of the side-drainage. 0539396 E, 4314045 N Z12 NAD83.

0.8 Hike generally northwest down the drainage to the confluence with Drowned Hole Draw. You will be entering the Mexican Mountain Wilderness Study Area. 0538912 E, 4314976 N Z12 NAD83.

1.6 Now work your way generally north down the ever-deepening canyon. There are several fun challenges on the way. The first obstacle is a fall that is passed on the right (E) down a striped friction slab [5.0, 30']. At some large boulders there are several ways down. The easiest is to cross a log onto a large boulder and climb down a chimney to the left [5.0, 30']. At the double drop, traverse a ledge that is

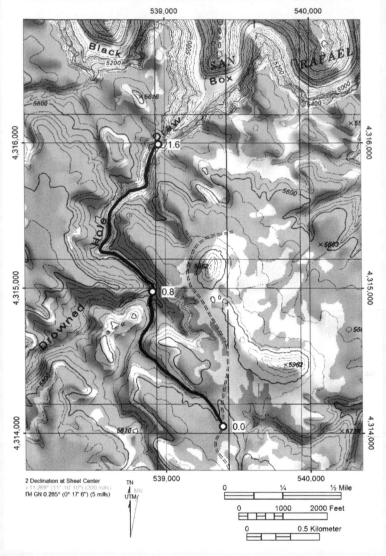

2 Declination at Sheet Center
< 11.269° (11° 16' 10") (200 mils)
TM GN 0.285° (0° 17' 6") (5 mils)

1:24,000

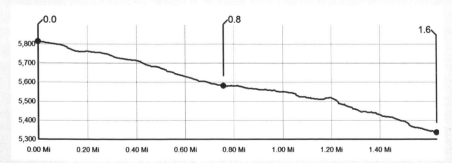

Elev Loss −486 Ft; Climb 77 Ft; Drop −563 Ft; Max Elev 5813 Ft; Min Elev 5328 Ft; Map Dist 1.634 Mi; Ground Dist 1.641 Mi

up ten feet and to the right (E). There is one tricky move [5.1, 40']. A rope is advisable for less confident climbers. 0538960 E, 4315991 N Z12 NAD83.

3.2   After you reach the pool on the lip of the massive dry-fall at the end of the canyon, return to the trailhead the way you came. Or at a number of points along the way, exit the canyon to the east, up steep slopes or gullies. Walk the rim or the track back to the start. 0539396 E, 4314045 N Z12 NAD83.

Hike #16: Lower Black Box

SEASON:	Best in late April to mid-May and August, September, or October. Early spring and late fall can be too cold. Skip the summer monsoon season altogether. Extreme flash flood danger. River level must be very low.
TIME AND DISTANCE:	Sulphur Springs Road trailhead: Eight to ten hours (10.8 miles). Swaseys Leap trailhead: Nine to eleven hours (11.8 miles). Times and distances will be greater if you can't drive all the way to the trailheads. Some people like to do this as an overnight hike, camping near the Sulphur Springs or Swaseys Leap, but you'd want to carry enough water for your whole trip.
WATER:	San Rafael River. You will be in the river most of the time, but only drink from it if you must (it is known to have a laxative effect on some people). The Sulphur Springs are not potable. Bring your own drinking water.
MAPS:	Mexican Mountain, Spotted Wolf Canyon. (San Rafael Desert, Huntington.)
LOOP HIKE:	No.
SKILL LEVEL:	(2 B/C). Easy route finding. [Class 3] scrambling. You must be willing to spend a long day that includes hiking and swimming in the river. Shoes you can wade with are essential. Carefully read the additional material below.

The Lower Black Box is a little brother to the Upper Black Box (Hike #11). But like all little brothers, it should be taken seriously. A sign posted by the BLM states, "WARNING! EXTREME FLASH FLOODING AND HYPOTHERMIA DANGER DURING THE SPRING, SUMMER, FALL

AND WINTER MONTHS. ENTER AT YOUR OWN RISK!! TWO DEATHS OCCURRED IN THE BLACK BOXES IN 1999. DON'T LET THE NEXT ONE BE YOU!". Although it is the Upper Black Box that has the dangerous reputation, it was in the Lower Black Box where these tragedies took place.

Before reading about the hike, realize that, though a bit less daunting than the Upper Black Box, it is nonetheless a hike for which you must be properly prepared.

1. Water flow in the river should be below 30 cubic feet per second (cfs). The flow rate can be checked on the Daily Recreational River Report at 801-539-1311 or online at waterdata.usgs.gov.
2. You will be swimming and wading almost continuously.
3. A short rope may be handy for lowering packs over boulders.
4. A walking stick for probing pools will prove invaluable.
5. Everybody needs something that floats well to aid in swimming. Some people use inner tubes, but they can be cumbersome when not being used. The best method is to line your day-pack with doubled plastic bags, fill the bags with your gear, and tie them off. Not only will this keep the things inside your pack dry, but now it will float like a cork. Wear a life jacket under the pack for the watery sections and you will be both mobile and buoyant.
6. Dogs will have problems on some boulder-hopping sections.
7. On a cold day hypothermia, which is life threatening, is a real possibility. Even on an 80-degree day you willed be chilled inside the box. Sunlight doesn't reach the bottom of the canyon very often. Some people wear wetsuits when the water temperature is not optimal (you can check at the bridge on the Buckhorn Draw Road).
8. With a long day, cold water, and large boulders to negotiate, leave children behind. A well-prepared group of teens, with competent leadership, could have a lot of fun doing this hike.
9. Sturdy shoes you can hike, wade, and swim with are a must. No sandals or flip-flops. It would be wise to pack dry shoes and socks for the walk out.

    The Lower Black Box is a real treasure. The Coconino Sandstone walls are up to 400 feet high and in places only ten yards apart. Unlike the Upper Black Box, you do not have three hours of boulder-hopping and bushwhacking before getting to the good stuff. Instead, access is easy on retired jeep trails.

There are two trailheads for the Lower Black Box, one near Swaseys Leap at the top of the box and one near Sulphur Springs at the bottom (see the Sinkhole Flat and Jackass Bench Road Section for details). Both trailheads are at the end of rough, high-clearance 4WD roads. Those who can't make it all the way to the trailheads, and are doing the hike in one day, will often use a mountain bike to get there. This turns the hike into a fun triathlon of sorts. The Sulphur Springs access is shorter and more popular so will be described as the standard route.

0.0   Mileage begins at the trailhead at the end of the open portion of TR653/Sulphur Springs Road. 0545910 E, 4313111 N Z12 NAD83.

1.3   Beyond the trailhead the Sulphur Springs Road enters the Mexican Mountain Wilderness Study Area and is closed to all vehicles. Follow the old track generally east. You will be heading out onto a flat-topped peninsula between the San Rafael River to the north and a drainage to the south. As you near the eastern end of the peninsula, the road splits. 0547699 E, 4313432 N Z12 NAD83.

1.4   Turn right (E) and follow the road east down to the floor of the drainage that you have been paralleling. You will be intersecting Hike #18 which comes over a pass from Black Dragon Wash. 0547919 E, 4313358 N Z12 NAD83.

1.9   Head east then north down the drainage until it joins the San Rafael River. Hike #18 diverges here and goes down the river to Thompson Hole and Tidwell Bottoms. Wade across to the north side of the river. Now is the time to take a real look at the river level. It should be about knee deep. If it is much higher than that, or it is difficult to cross the river here, turn back now. 0548126 E, 4313807 N Z12 NAD83.

2.6   Now work your way west alongside the river on a maze of cattle trails. After passing the Sulphur Springs near the mouth of the box, the cattle trails begin to consolidate into one path and climb up onto the bench above. Cairns show the way. 0547135 E, 4313997 N Z12 NAD83.

4.9   Follow the trail along the bench, generally northwest then northeast, until it returns you to river level just upstream (NE) from the

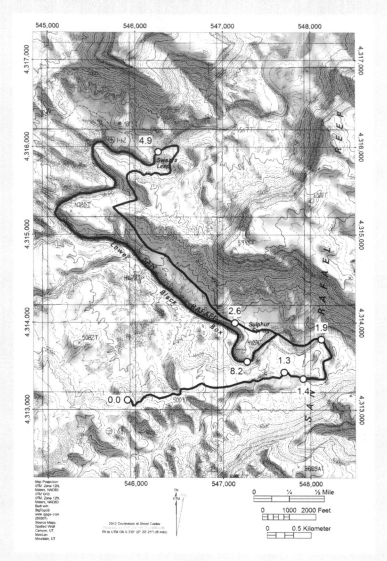

1:24,000.

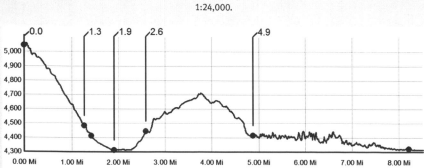

Elev Loss −730 Ft; Climb 2318 Ft; Drop −3048 Ft; Max Elev 5059 Ft; Min Elev 4309 Ft; Map Dist 8.520 Mi; Ground Dist 8.657 Mi

top of the Box and Swaseys Leap (misspelled "Swazys" on the Spotted Wolf Canyon map). 0546265 E, 4315943 N Z12 NAD83.

> *Digression:* This is where the route from the alternate Swaseys Leap trailhead (0543969 E, 4315856 N Z12 NAD83) on TR652 comes in. To do the hike from there, follow the closed track generally east from the trailhead for 2.6 miles until you reach Swaseys Leap. Access the river by descending one of the draws to the east. Go down the box first, then take the trail along the east bench back. Round trip is 11.8 miles.

> *Historical note:* Swaseys Leap (also called Sids Leap) is named after Sid Swasey. Sid bet his brother, Joe, that he could jump the gap over the river gorge on his saddle horse. According to the legend, he did. Later, sheepherder, Paul Hansen, built a makeshift bridge over the leap with cottonwood logs and an old wagon box to move his stock across the river. The bridge finally collapsed in the late 1990s.

8.2   Go southwest down the river and enter the Lower Black Box. You will immediately go under Swaseys Leap. The canyon walls rise as the river winds its way generally south. You will be in the water most of the time, either wading or swimming (there is much swimming at any water level). When not in the water, there is plenty of [Class 3] boulder-hopping. As you near the end of the box the swimming becomes more sporadic. There are quite a few escape routes out of the canyon. Most are [Class 3], but should be thoroughly checked before bringing up tired or cold swimmers. Plan on three to four hours of actual hiking and swimming time to negotiate the box. With picture taking and other diversions this could take substantially longer. 0547274 E, 4313554 N Z12 NAD83.

8.9   Now follow the river east, past the Sulphur Springs on the right (S), back to the mouth of the drainage at mile 2.1. 0548126 E, 4313807 N Z12 NAD83.

10.8   Head south up the drainage and retrace your steps along the old Sulphur Springs Road back to the trailhead. 0545910 E, 4313111 N Z12 NAD83.

Historical note: While you are scrambling, wading, and swimming through the Lower Black Box, it is interesting to note that perhaps the first traverse of the canyon was by the John C. Fremont Expedition of 1853–54. They came up the San Rafael River from its confluence with the Green River and pushed up through the Lower Black Box into Mexican Bend. From there they tried to ascend the Upper Black Box, but turned around in failure. What is noteworthy is that they were riding horses!

In 1909 H. L. A. Culmer presaged the naming of the canyon: "As for going up the San Rafael Canyon, that is considered quite an achievement on foot or horseback at the lowest stage of the stream, and it is quite impossible in the Spring time. It involves leaping your horse from rocky ledges into deep water and many a quick pitapat over quicksand down in the dark boxes of the canyon. The trip is said to contain more thrills to the mile than any other trail in the universe."

TR647/Black Dragon Wash Road Section

Access to Hikes #17 and #18.

Access is from Interstate 70.

1:100,000 map: San Rafael Desert.

This good dirt road heads north from Interstate 70 just before it cuts through the eastern San Rafael Reef as one drives west from Green River. It is also at the northern end of EM1028/The Squeeze Road. The road goes past Box Spring and Double Arch Canyons and then up Black Dragon Wash. It is suitable for most medium-clearance vehicles to the Black Dragon Wash junction unless wet or snowy. High-clearance vehicles only to the pictograph parking area and then the track quickly becomes a high-clearance 4WD trail after that. This would make for good mountain biking. There are some good campsites in the area but camping is prohibited in Black Dragon Wash.

The road was built in 1918 to service mining activity that never paid off. Before Interstate 70 was forced through Spotted Wolf Canyon, this was the only road through the northern part of the Swell.

If coming from Green River, go west on Interstate 70 for 13 miles to a dirt road on the right (N) between mile markers 144 and 145 (0550547 E, 4308636 N Z12 NAD83). With no signs, this road is easy to miss. Go through a wire gate and follow the road northwest a short way down into a wash. To the left (S) is a dirt road coming north from the 4WD underpass and The Squeeze Road. If you are coming east on I-70, exit onto a dirt road on the south side of the interstate just after crossing over the 4WD underpass (0550402 E, 4308536 N Z12 NAD83). This will be fifteen miles east of Exit 131. Go south through a wire gate and then follow the dirt road as it swings north into the wash. Go through another wire gate then through the I-70 underpass to the north side of the interstate where the dirt roads converge. This is the start of TR647/Black Dragon Wash Road (0550495 E, 4308706 N Z12 NAD83). Be sure to close the gates that lead to the interstate, leave the

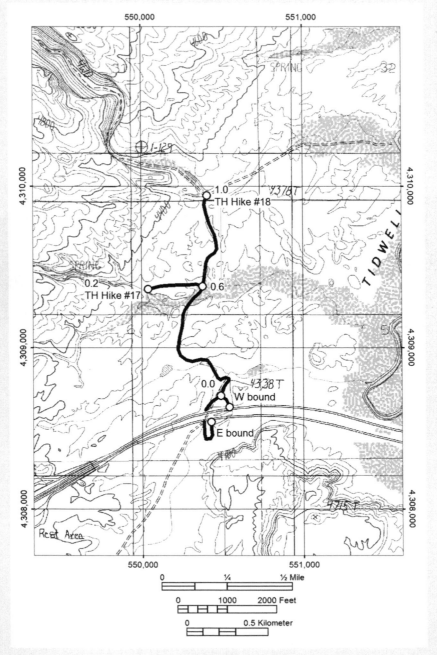

Black Dragon Canyon.

other one the way you found it, and note that the underpass is for 4WD vehicles only and is too low for campers to fit through.

0.0   Mileage begins at the junction in the wash just north of I-70. 0550495 E, 4308706 N Z12 NAD83.

0.6   Follow the Black Dragon Wash Road generally north. Soon you will come to the junction with a dirt road on the left (W). It leads to the trailhead for Hike #17. 0550376 E, 4309380 N Z12 NAD83.

Side road to Hike #17

0.0   Mileage begins at the junction. 0550376 E, 4309380 N Z12 NAD83.

0.2   Head west on this medium-clearance track to a parking area beneath some tall cottonwoods. This is the trailhead for Box Spring, Double Arch, and Petroglyph Fork Canyons Hike #17. 0550043 E, 4309357 N Z12 NAD83.

1.0 Continue heading north to a road junction in Black Dragon Wash. Go left (NW) on the Black Dragon Wash Road to a parking area on the left (W) near the junction. This is the trailhead for Black Dragon Wash and the San Rafael River Hike #18. 0550411 E, 4309942 N Z12 NAD83.

The road to the right (NE) goes east to the edge of the San Rafael River at Tidwell Bottoms (0551547 E, 4310269 N Z12 NAD83). This road can be used to set up a car or mountain bike shuttle for Part 2 of Hike #18, saving you some road walking.

If you are in a high-clearance vehicle, you can continue northwest up the Black Dragon Wash Road another 0.7 mile to a parking area on the right (NE) for the pictographs and alternate start of Hike #18 (0549873 E, 4310577 N Z12 NAD83). The road deteriorates quickly after this but continues for another six miles to the junction with B6755/Jackass Bench Road. Only serious 4WDs and off-road vehicles will make it that far. Note that overnight parking is not allowed in Black Dragon Wash.

Hike #17: Box Spring, Double Arch, and Petroglyph Fork Canyons

SEASON:	Any. Spring or fall are best.
TIME AND DISTANCE:	Part 1: Thirty minutes to one hour (1 mile). Part 2: Two to three hours (1.8 miles).
WATER:	Potholes. Seasonal springs. Box Spring Canyon has a reasonably reliable spring. Bring your own water.
MAPS:	Spotted Wolf Canyon. (San Rafael Desert).
LOOP HIKE:	No.
SKILL LEVEL:	(1A). Easy route finding. [Class 2] walking. This is an easy but rewarding hike especially suited for youngsters and seniors.

Exceptional and rare, this short hike exemplifies variety. The route goes along the face of the Northern Reef, with side trips into three unique box canyons. Box Spring Canyon is noteworthy for its springs and lush riparian habitat. Double Arch Canyon has two sets of arches, one large and one small, and its Petroglyph Fork has two small panels of petroglyphs, one faded and vandalized, the other as crisp and detailed as any in the Swell.

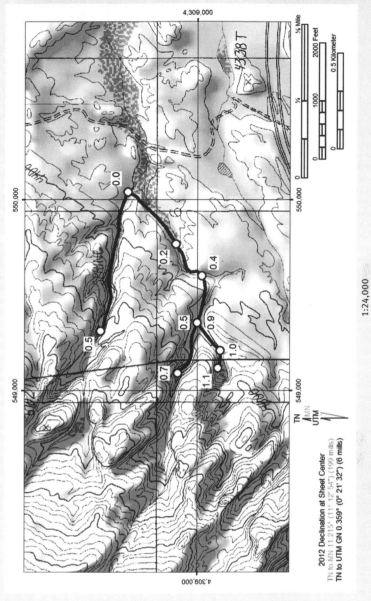

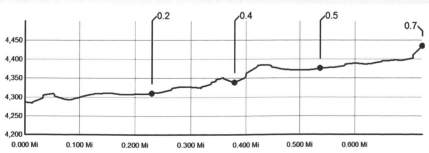

Elev Gain 153 Ft; Climb 227 Ft; Drop −74 Ft; Max Elev 4441 Ft; Min Elev 4284 Ft; Map Dist 0.723 Mi; Ground Dist 0.728 Mi

Petroglyph Fork.

Part 1

0.0 Mileage begins at the trailhead parking area. 0550043 E, 4309357 N Z12 NAD83.

0.5 Go west into Box Spring Canyon on a good trail to the plunge pool at the head of the canyon. You'll have to do a little bushwhacking and some stream hopping but the trail is easy to follow. There are several seasonal springs along the way. This is a perfect place for lunch. 0549317 E, 4309496 N Z12 NAD83.

1.0 Go east, back out of the canyon the way you came, and return to the trailhead. 0550043 E, 4309357 N Z12 NAD83.

Part 2

0.0 Mileage begins at the trailhead parking area. 0550043 E, 4309357 N Z12 NAD83.

0.2 The wash to the south comes from Double Arch Canyon. Go south on a good trail to the edge of the wash. Follow the trail just above the wash a short way as it swings to the southwest then goes into the wash at a slickrock area. 0549773 E, 4309109 N Z12 NAD83.

0.4 A cairn marks a trail on the left side of the wash (S). Take this trail southwest as it traverses above the south side of the wash and bypasses a small pour-off. The trail returns to the wash just above the pour-off. 0549606 E, 4308975 N Z12 NAD83.

0.5   Follow the trail as it swings west-northwest into the mouth of Double Arch Canyon and the route divides. The trail to the left (SW) goes into Petroglyph Fork. 0549359 E, 4308999 N Z12 NAD83.

0.7   Turn right (WNW) and go up Double Arch Canyon to its end to visit the arches, dry-fall, and plunge pool. 0549094 E, 4309100 N Z12 NAD83.

0.9   Now go back down Double Arch Canyon the way you came and return to the Petroglyph Fork trail junction. 0549359 E, 4308999 N Z12 NAD83.

1.0   Go southwest at the junction and take the trail southwest into Petroglyph Fork. You will quickly come to another trail junction. 0549214 E, 4308878 N Z12 NAD83.

The trail to the left (S) goes southwest up the left side of a small draw and exits the canyon by going south, over a small pass and down a purple ramp into the drainage below. This wash can then be followed back around to the northwest then north to rejoin the trail at mile 0.4.

1.1   Turn right (W) at the junction and continue up the canyon to the petroglyphs. They are at the bottom of a well-varnished wall on the right (N). This pretty little canyon ends shortly past the petroglyphs. 0549120 E, 4308888 N Z12 NAD83.

1.8   Now follow the trail back the way you came, generally east then northeast, to the trailhead parking area. 0550043 E, 4309357 N Z12 NAD83.

Hike #18: Black Dragon Wash and the San Rafael River

SEASON:	Part 1: Any. Part 2: Spring through fall, except during runoff (mid-May to July).
TIME AND DISTANCE:	Part 1: Five to six hours (8.2 miles). Part 2: Ten to twelve hours or two days (13.9 miles). With digressions and explorations this could be made into a trip of several days.
WATER:	Part 1: None. Bring your own water. Part 2: San Rafael River if you must. Bring your own water.

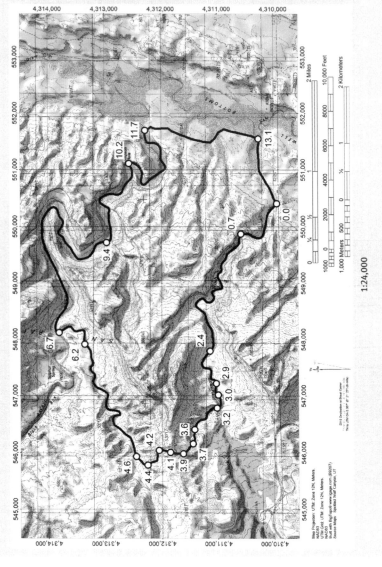

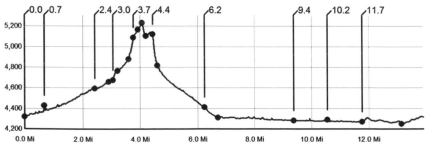

Elev Gain 0 Ft; Climb 1764 Ft; Drop −1764 Ft; Max Elev 5228 Ft; Min Elev 4247 Ft; Map Dist 13.900 Mi; Ground Dist 13.951 Mi

MAPS:	Spotted Wolf Canyon. (San Rafael Desert).
LOOP HIKE:	Part 1: No. Part 2: Yes.
SKILL LEVEL:	Part 1: (1A). Easy route finding. [Class 2] scrambling. Part 2: (1A). Moderate route finding. [Class 2+] scrambling. This is a long day hike. For those doing the hike in two days, low-impact camping skills are essential. Bring a pair of wading shoes.

Black Dragon Wash is one of the most frequently visited canyons in the San Rafael Swell. It contains a large, well known Barrier Canyon style pictograph site. It is not unusual to find groups of people visiting the panels, though they rarely continue up the canyon. It is pleasant to hike, with easy walking along an old dirt road.

The hike is divided into two parts. Part 1 goes to the rock art panels, proceeds up Black Dragon Wash, and ascends a steep hillside to a pass and marvelous overlook. Part 2 continues over the pass, intersects the San Rafael River right below the Lower Black Box, and follows the river as it cuts through the Northern Reef.

Part 1

0.0   Mileage begins at the parking area at mile 1.0 on TR647/Black Dragon Wash Road. 0550411 E, 4309942 N Z12 NAD83.

0.7   Follow the track northwest into the deepening canyon. In a giant, fenced-off alcove on the right (NE) is the Black Dragon Wash rock art site. A parking area is at its base. If you can drive this far up the rocky, high-clearance track, park here. This pictograph panel was listed on the National Register of Historic Places in 1980. 0549873 E, 4310577 N Z12 NAD83.

2.4   Continue following the track northwest up the wash. The track is not shown past the pictographs on the Spotted Wolf Canyon map, but it intermingles with the wash. The canyon turns to the west and begins to open up. At a junction a track enters from the left (ESE). 0547798 E, 4311136 N Z12 NAD83.

This rough track goes southeast for a half-mile onto a promontory and to an old mining shack (0547328 E, 4310786 N Z12 NAD83). The track is not shown on the Spotted Wolf Canyon map, but the shack is marked northwest of elevation 5830.

2.9   Stay with the main dirt road generally west up the wash. Another track enters from the left (SE). 0547223 E, 4311025 N Z12 NAD83.

3.0   Keep going straight (W) on the Black Dragon Wash Road. Soon the track leaves the wash and starts heading up onto a bench layer. 0547021 E, 4310992 N Z12 NAD83.

3.2   Follow the track west onto the bench then north as it meets a wash coming in from the right (N). 0546789 E, 4311015 N Z12 NAD83.

3.6   Leave the track and head generally northwest up the wash. You will see a sixty-foot-high pinnacle ahead. Just before you reach the pinnacle, you will intersect a use-trail coming down a steep slope on the left (SW) marked by a cairn. 0546408 E, 4311413 N Z12 NAD83.

3.7   Head southwest then west on this cairned trail as it angles up and traverses to the head of a draw. 0546158 E, 4311444 N Z12 NAD83.

3.9   Continue following the trail generally northwest out of the draw and across the flat top of a divide between two shallow washes. The trail crosses the wash on the right (N) and turns north up a gully. Cairns show the way. You will be entering the Mexican Mountain Wilderness Study Area. 0545983 E, 4311618 N Z12 NAD83.

4.1   Go north up this gully and climb out its head onto a saddle with a large cairn. You will be due west of elevation 5309 on the Spotted Wolf Canyon map. 0546007 E, 4311850 N Z12 NAD83.

8.2   After enjoying the splendid view, if you are just doing Part 1, retrace your steps back to the start. 0550411 E, 4309942 N Z12 NAD83.

Part 2

Resume from mile 4.1.

4.2   From the saddle head north into the head of the drainage to the north. Scramble your way down the steep ridge that divides the drainage into two [Class 2]. Go right (E) to bypass some small cliffs. Keep following the drainage north a short way to the top of a wide, gray cliff band. 0546041 E, 4312052 N Z12 NAD83.

4.4   Traverse northwest along the top of the cliffs and out onto a prominent prow. On the northeast corner of the prow is a large cairn marking the top of a descent route through the gray cliff band. 0545782 E, 4312251 N Z12 NAD83.

4.6   Scramble north down the cliffs to the top of a big talus apron. Carefully work your way northeast down this [Class 2+] rubble to the floor of the large drainage below. 0545932 E, 4312451 N Z12 NAD83.

6.2   Now follow the floor of the drainage generally northeast. Just before the canyon swings to the north, notice the old dirt track coming into the wash from the west. This is where Lower Black Box Hike #16 intersects the route. 0547919 E, 4313358 N Z12 NAD83.

6.7   Continue down the canyon until you intersect the San Rafael River. There is good camping by the river. Hike #16 diverges here and heads upstream. 0548126 E, 4313807 N Z12 NAD83.

Digression: A day hike through the Lower Black Box (7.5 miles round trip) can easily be done from here, as long as you are taking several days to complete Hike #18 (see Lower Black Box Hike #16 for details).

9.4   Turn right (NE) and follow the river downstream. It cuts generally southeast through the San Rafael Reef, but flows in every conceivable direction as it winds its way along through this spectacular canyon. It is possible to avoid wading in the river for a couple of miles by thrashing through tamarisk forests and traversing along ledges. Eventually though, unless the water is very low, you will have to wade. It is easiest to just wade the whole way. The water rarely gets above knee deep and the bottom of the river is smooth and sandy. Campsites can be found all along the river, usually behind the walls of tamarisks. After three miles an interesting side canyon comes in on the right (SW). 0549721 E, 4312968 N Z12 NAD83.

10.2   Continue on down the river. In another 0.8 mile you will reach a large abandoned meander (Thompson Hole) on the left (E). 0551115 E, 4312566 N Z12 NAD83.

Digression: An old dirt track heads east out of Thompson Hole and joins the Tidwell Draw Track—South on the other side of the Reef. This can be used to access the many rarely seen canyons running east out of the Reef into Tidwell Draw.

11.7   As you follow the river past Thompson Hole, the canyon walls start to get lower and you will begin to exit the reef. You will come to a point where the river runs along the south side of the corridor and you can easily access the low bench to the south. You will be leaving the Mexican Mountain WSA. 0551703 E, 4312283 N Z12 NAD83.

> *Historical note:* Depending on the source, Thompson Hole was named for either Alt Thompson or Wynn Thompson. They were pioneer ranchers. In the early 1900s a dam was proposed for the San Rafael River near Thompson Hole. It would have flooded the Lower Black Box. Some survey work was done.

13.1   Head generally south across benches and in and out of shallow washes. Use old dirt roads and cattle trails to find your way along the base of the Reef. You will intercept a graded dirt road near the river. 0551554 E, 4310266 N Z12 NAD83.

13.9   Follow this road generally west until you reach the trailhead at the junction with the Black Dragon Wash Road. 0550411 E, 4309942 N Z12 NAD83.

3 | SIDS MOUNTAIN

Sids Mountain, named for pioneer rancher Sid Swasey, is located in the northwestern part of the San Rafael Swell. It is bounded by the Cottonwood Wash Road on the east, the Green River Cutoff Road on the north, Highway 10 on the west, and Interstate 70 on the south. It is an area of wide, deep canyons that all eventually run into the San Rafael River as it slices through an area called the Little Grand Canyon. The dominant feature is Sids Mountain, a mesa at the center of the area. Without roads or tracks, it is accessible only to hikers and horse packers.

Sids Mountain is an area rich in history, starting with the Desert Archaic Culture. These people left their indelible mark of Barrier Canyon style pictograph panels in Cane Wash, Virgin Springs Canyon, along the San Rafael River, and in other scattered locations. The Fremont Indians left a remarkable set of petroglyph panels at Rochester Creek. The early Mormon pioneers used the canyon bottoms for grazing cattle and horses. Their signs, too, are scattered about. There was little mining in the area, though there was extensive exploration. Many glory holes and access roads were left behind. The San Rafael River, between Fuller Bottom and the San Rafael River bridge, is a favorite area for river-runners when there is enough water. Sids Mountain is in the Sids Mountain Wilderness Study Area.

The next two hikes, #19 and #20, are accessed by the Cottonwood Wash Road. For directions to the trailhead, please see the Cottonwood Wash Road Section in the Northern Reef and Mexican Mountain chapter.

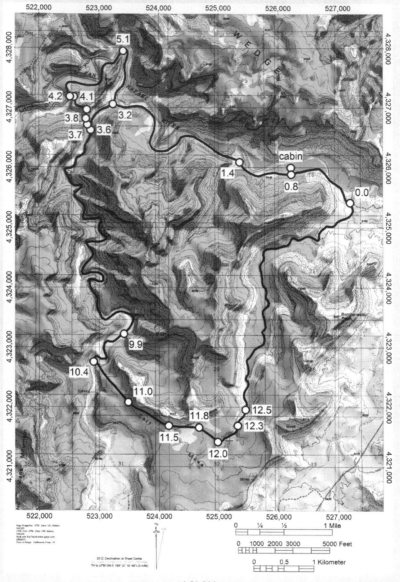

1:24,000

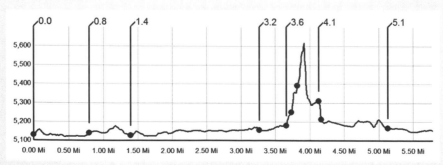

Elev Gain 27 Ft; Climb 933 Ft; Drop −906 Ft; Max Elev 5621 Ft; Min Elev 5120 Ft; Map Dist 5.779 Mi; Ground Dist 5.843 Mi

Hike #19: San Rafael River and Cane Wash

SEASON:	Any. After rain or snow the old mining road you follow along the San Rafael River to Cane Wash could be muddy. The Good Water Canyon digression can only be done during times when the San Rafael River is low enough to cross safely.
TIME AND DISTANCE:	Part 1: Three to four hours to Cane Wash and back (6.4 miles). Four to six hours if you go to the second set of pictographs and back (9 miles). Part 2: Eight to ten hours. This is best done as an overnight hike, but all of your drinking water will have to be carried (15.6 miles).
WATER:	San Rafael River if you must; it is known to have a laxative effect. Good Water Canyon has nice springs. Seasonal in Cane Wash and Moore Canyon. Bring your own water.
MAPS:	Bottleneck Peak. (Huntington.)
LOOP HIKE:	Part 1: No. Part 2: Yes.
SKILL LEVEL:	Part 1: San Rafael River Gorge to Cane Wash (1A). Easy route finding. This is a good hike for everyone. Good Water Canyon (1A). Easy route finding. [Class 2+] walking. The route through the notch has some [Class 3] scrambling. Part 2: Cane Wash (1A), Moore Canyon (1A). Moderate route finding. [Class 4] scrambling. This is a long day hike. If you do this as an overnight hike, low impact camping skills are essential.

This is the premier short hike in the Sids Mountain area. Its enjoyment is threefold. You walk along the San Rafael River for most of Part 1 of the hike. You hike in the Little Grand Canyon, an area that many look into from the Wedge Overlook, but few enjoy from a river-level perspective. You also gain a sense of history by seeing pioneer cabins and viewing prehistoric pictograph and petroglyph panels.

The hike comes in two parts. Part 1 goes along the San Rafael River on a mining track and then a use-trail to the confluence with Cane Wash and its pictograph panel, and then along a prehistoric trail to another fabulous pictograph panel an hour away. A digression takes you into the rarely visited and pristine Good Water Canyon. Part 2 goes up Cane Wash with its towers, spires, and pinnacles. Since the route overlaps part of Hike #20 in Cane Wash (and they share the same trailhead), the two hikes can be combined into longer trips with many variations. The route exits Cane Wash and crosses Calf Mesa to Moore Canyon, which is then descended back to the start.

Part 1

0.0   Mileage begins at the information kiosk near the parking area. The Johansen corral is visible to the northeast. 0527202 E, 4325414 N Z12 NAD83.

0.8   Cross the wash on the closed track and follow it northwest then west into the mouth of the San Rafael River gorge. Look to the right (N) in the cottonwood bottoms for the tumbled-down remains of two hand-hewn log cabins. 0526215 E, 4325998 N Z12 NAD83.

1.4   Continue up the canyon on the old track. The track climbs a short hill and then descends again to near river level and crosses a small wash. After this the track dissipates into a use-trail. You will be crossing into the Sids Mountain Wilderness Study Area. 0525358 E, 4326087 N Z12 NAD83.

3.2   Follow the trail generally west-northwest alongside the river. The trail forks at the mouth of Cane Wash. The right fork continues up the river gorge and is the return for the end of Part 1. Go left (SW) into Cane Wash. 0523230 E, 4327052 N Z12 NAD83.

> *Historical note:* Just inside the mouth of the canyon is a shelter cave on the left (SE). In the ceiling of the cave are several red and ochre pictographs of geometric designs. There are also some red handprints. You have to wonder how many people have taken shelter here over the centuries. In modern times the cave has become a place where backpackers, equestrians, and river-runners will occasionally camp. Be aware that the entire cave, not just the pictograph panel, is an archeological site and is protected under the Antiquities Act. Please don't damage this unique site by building fires inside the cave as other careless visitors have done. The smoke will cause irreversible harm to the paintings and the heat from a big fire could cause the already crumbling rock surface to peel away. If you must have a fire, please build it in the wash where the next rains will wipe away the evidence.

From the cave look to the west. Dominating the view is the large Wingate cliff that forms the western wall of Cane Wash. This is actually a massive fin that juts northwest out into the river gorge (elevation 5723). The final pictograph panel is on the far side of the fin. You could easily follow the river to the rock art site, as it winds its way around to the back side of the fin. But there is a far more interesting, albeit more strenuous, way to get there. Visually follow the wall south. The wall drops and forms a notch with a talus slope leading up to it. This will be your route. It appears to be a prehistoric trail, as is evi-

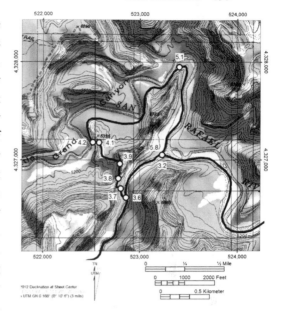

Hike #19. Detail from Mile 3.2 to 5.1. 1:24,000.

denced by a pictograph on one side of the notch and some petro-glyphs on the other. The route short-cuts the big meander as the river goes around the fin. If scrambling 250 feet to the top of the talus and through the notch looks to be too daunting, take the river route instead.

3.6 To get to the notch, head southwest up Cane Wash. The canyon turns to the south. There is a cairn here at the bottom of a break in the low cliffs on the right (W) (see map above). 0522863 E, 4326618 N Z12 NAD83.

3.7 Follow the cairned route up small ledges and onto the bench above [Class 3]. Once on top of the bench turn toward the notch. Take the cairned use-trail leading to the northwest across the bench and to the bottom of a switchback trail at the base of the talus slope. 0522810 E, 4326709 N Z12 NAD83.

3.8 Take the switchback trail up the talus slope following cairns until you are on the ledge running along the base of the tall cliffs. Tra-verse right (NNE) to the base of the notch. A short scramble up [Class 3] will put you at the apex. 0522787 E, 4326812 N Z12 NAD83.

3.9 After enjoying the view, pass through the notch and follow a use-trail north along the base of the western side of the fin. If you stay right up against the bottom of the cliff you will end up under a huge, detached boulder that is leaning against the cliff, creating a perfect shelter from sun or rain. Just after you come out the other side of the boulder, look for some faint petroglyphs at knee level on the base of the wall. 0522801 E, 4326961 N Z12 NAD83.

4.1   Follow the trail northwest past a circular arrangement of stones and then west-northwest out onto a red and gray peninsula. Continue on the trail as it swings north and follows the top of this ridge to the monolith at its end. The pictographs are on the western side of it. The similarity to the setting of the Rochester rock art site (Hike #24) is pretty uncanny. 0522586 E, 4327175 N Z12 NAD83.

> *Historical note:* To find the pictographs, follow a use-trail that contours around the western side of the monolith. At times the way is bouldery and loose. Under an overhanging part of the cliffs forming the monolith is a nice panel of Fremont style pictographs depicting several large anthropomorphs and geometric designs in red and ochre. There are zigzags and a row of triangles reminiscent of the shelter cave glyphs in Cane Wash. Look closely for the faint images of bighorn sheep in white. This panel is remarkably well preserved. Please help it to remain that way by not adding your own marks and by not touching the paintings. If you are coming up from the river, a cairned trail switchbacks up the talus slope from the river to the southern end of the monolith. Follow the use-trail to traverse to the site.

After viewing the rock art and surroundings, return to Cane Wash by either retracing your steps over the notch or by following the river back. The river route offers the chance to visit Good Water Canyon, a seldom explored box canyon that can only be visited from its mouth, and so will be described here.

4.2   From the ridge at the southern end of the monolith, go west down the talus slope on a cairned switchback trail. At the bottom you will intersect the use-trail that follows the river. This is where this hike diverges from Hike #20. 0522520 E, 4327179 N Z12 NAD83.

5.1   Follow the use-trail east then northeast down the river. As you near the northern end of the giant fin, the mouth of Good Water Canyon will be directly across the river to the northwest. 0523354 E, 4328013 N Z12 NAD83.

> *Historical note:* There is some nice rock art beneath an overhang on the north side of the river just west of the mouth of Good Water Canyon. Look for several petroglyphs on the boulders as you work your up to the pictograph panel.

> *Digression:* It is 3.4 miles to the end of this box canyon and back. Cross the river and enter the mouth of Good Water Canyon. In 0.3 mile you will come to a dry fall. Pass this on the right (N). It would appear that this dry fall is impassable to cattle. Because there is no way to enter the canyon from above, and no way for the cows to get in from below, the rest of the canyon beyond the fall is pretty much pristine. Please help keep it this way and treat it with care. You are more likely to see the tracks of bighorn sheep and cougars here than you are those of other people. From the fall it is 1.4 miles up the canyon to its impassable headwall. Aptly named, Good Water Canyon has many nice seasonal springs and pools. Return to the river and trail the way you came.

5.8   Continue following the trail alongside the river as it swings to the south around the fin. You will reach the mouth of Cane Wash on the right 0523230 E, 4327052 N Z12 NAD83.

9.0   If you are just doing Part 1, it is 3.2 miles downriver along the trail back to the trailhead. 0527202 E, 4325414 N Z12 NAD83.

Part 2

Mileage resumes at mile 5.8 at the mouth of Cane Wash. If you are planning to camp somewhere up Cane Wash or beyond, you will want to have enough water to see you all the way to the end. You may be a little sorry for lugging all that water if the springs up ahead are flowing, but you'll be so glad you did if they aren't!

9.9   Go generally south up Cane Wash. The going is easy along the floor of the canyon. The canyon opens up and you will intersect a

Where Cane Wash meets the San Rafael River.

small wash coming in from the left (SSE). 0523412 E, 4323223 N Z12 NAD83.

The low bench to the south is the northwestern end of Calf Mesa. There are two ways to access Calf Mesa from here. You can work your way up onto the low bench to the south and pick up the old mining track that crosses Calf Mesa. After acquiring the bench, the track goes south-southwest then south along the western side of the prominent ridge to the south. Continue south-southeast along the track to rejoin the standard route at mile 11.7. This first route is a little more direct and skips the [Class 4] move found on the second route. Because of the desire to connect this hike with Hike #20 at an important junction, the second access will be described as the standard route instead.

10.4   To find the standard route, continue going southwest up Cane Wash for another 0.5 mile until you intersect a small wash coming in from the right (W). You will be going around the inside of a cove formed by a bend in the wash with a sloping horn of land forming the cove's western side. This junction is where this hike diverges from Hike #20. 0522910 E, 4322756 N Z12 NAD83.

Digression: If you continue going south for 1.7 miles up Cane Wash you will intersect the double track, TR643/Cane Wash-Dexter Mine Road. This high-clearance, rough dirt road makes a good alternate trailhead for Hikes #19 and #20. It is 2.7 miles on TR643 from Cane Wash to the EM332/Cottonwood Wash Road and you'll pass some interesting mine relics along the way (see the Cottonwood Wash Road Section for details on finding the start of this road).

11.0 Due east of the wash junction is the tip of the horn of land that forms the western side of the walled cove in the wash. On the eastern side of the tip is an angled break in the short cliffs. Follow this break south onto the top of Calf Mesa, at one point making a [Class 4] move up a small ledge. Once on top, head southeast across the gradually rising mesa. You will intersect the old mining track at the base of the talus that is to the east. 0523486 E, 4322079 N Z12 NAD83.

11.5 Follow the sometimes faint track southeast then east until you are on a flat divide due south of elevation 6025 on the Bottleneck Peak map. The track seems to peter out here near some discarded core samples. 0524163 E, 4321685 N Z12 NAD83.

11.8 Head east from the divide until you intersect a southeast trending gully. 0524673 E, 4321657 N Z12 NAD83.

12.0 Go generally southeast down the gully until you come to the main wash leading down Moore Canyon. 0524986 E, 4321416 N Z12 NAD83.

12.3 Now follow the sandy wash generally northeast. You will come to the top of the steep, rocky head of Moore Canyon. 0525321 E, 4321688 N Z12 NAD83.

12.5 Continue down the drainage, carefully picking your way through the boulders, until you reach the hard-packed wash in the floor of the canyon. 0525454 E, 4321954 N Z12 NAD83.

15.6 Follow the wash generally north then northeast for 3.3 miles of easy walking back to the parking area. 0527202 E, 4325414 N Z12 NAD83.

Hike #20: Virgin Springs Canyon

SEASON:	Any. No snow for the pass between Virgin Springs Canyon and Cane Wash.
TIME AND DISTANCE:	Two or three days (13.5 miles with the Moore Canyon end; 19.6 miles with the Cane Wash end); three or four days if you do the Swazy digression.
WATER:	San Rafael River if you must. There is always spring water in the box of Virgin Springs Canyon. There are seasonal springs farther up the canyon and seasonal potholes in the West Fork of Virgin Springs Canyon. Cane Wash also has seasonal springs, but they are not very reliable.
MAPS:	Bottleneck Peak, Sids Mountain. (Huntington.)
LOOP HIKE:	Yes.
SKILL LEVEL:	San Rafael River Gorge (1A), Virgin Springs Canyon (1A), Cane Wash (1A), Moore Canyon (1A). Moderate route finding. [Class 3 and 4] scrambling getting between Virgin Springs Canyon and Cane Wash. A long last day. Familiarity with low-impact camping techniques is essential.

No humorous riposte, no pedantic diatribe, no scintillating verse. Virgin Springs Canyon is the best darn canyon in the Sids Mountain area. It is one of the few canyons that cannot be entered and trashed by cattle. It is truly virgin.

This hike is an extension of Hike #19 and shares the same trailhead. From Cane Wash it continues up the San Rafael River to Virgin Springs Canyon, with its box, a perennial spring, and a Barrier Canyon style pictograph panel. After camping near the box the route goes up Virgin Springs Canyon. It exits the canyon by crossing a steep ridge and dropping back into Cane Wash. You can finish the hike by either going down Cane Wash to the San Rafael River, crossing Calf Mesa to Moore Canyon, or going up Cane Wash to the alternate trailhead on TR 643. See the Cottonwood Wash Road Section in the Northern Reef and Mexican Mountain chapter for details on finding the trailhead to this hike.

0.0 Mileage begins at the information kiosk near the parking area. The Johansen corral is visible to the northeast. 0527202 E, 4325414 N Z12 NAD83.

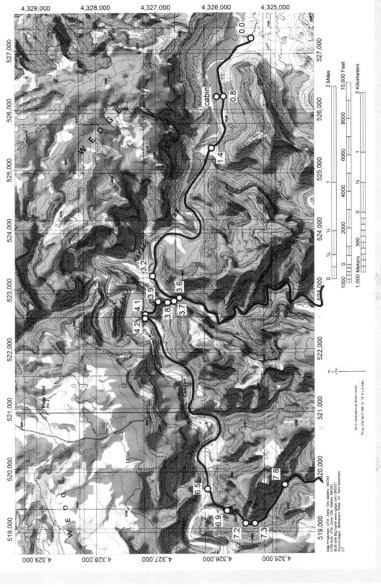

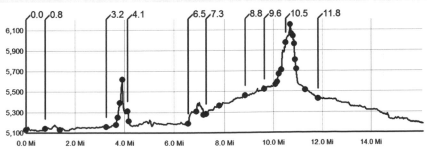

Elev Gain 52 Ft; Climb 2893 Ft; Drop −2841 Ft; Max Elev 6149 Ft; Min Elev 5120 Ft; Map Dist 16.106 Mi; Ground Dist 16.256 Mi

0.8   Cross the wash on the closed track and follow it northwest then west into the mouth of the San Rafael River gorge. Look to the right (N) in the cottonwood bottoms for the tumbled-down remains of two hand-hewn log cabins. 0526215 E, 4325998 N Z12 NAD83.

1.4   Continue up the canyon on the old track. The track climbs a short hill and then descends again to near river level and crosses a small wash. After this the track dissipates into a use-trail. 0525358 E, 4326087 N Z12 NAD83.

3.2   Follow the trail generally west-northwest alongside the river. The trail forks at the mouth of Cane Wash. The right fork continues up the river gorge. Go left (SW) into Cane Wash. 0523230 E, 4327052 N Z12 NAD83.

> *Historical note:* Just inside the mouth of the canyon is a shelter cave on the left (SE). In the ceiling of the cave are several red and ochre pictographs of geometric designs. There are also some red handprints. You have to wonder how many people have taken shelter here over the centuries. In modern times the cave has become a place where backpackers, equestrians, and river-runners will occasionally camp. Be aware that the entire cave, not just the pictograph panel, is an archeological site and is protected under the Antiquities Act. Please don't damage this unique site by building fires inside the cave as other careless visitors have done. The smoke will cause irreversible harm to the paintings and the heat from a big fire could cause the already crumbling rock surface to peel away. If you must have a fire, please build it in the wash where the next rains will wipe away the evidence.

From the cave look to the west. Dominating the view is the large Wingate cliff that forms the western wall of Cane Wash. This is actually a massive fin that juts northwest out into the river gorge (elevation 5723). The final pictograph panel is on the far side of the fin. You could easily follow the river to the rock art site, as it winds its way around to the back side of the fin. But there is a far more interesting, albeit more strenuous, way to get there. Visually follow the wall south. The wall drops and forms a notch with a talus slope leading up to it. This will be your route. It appears to be a prehistoric trail, as is evidenced by a pictograph on one side of the notch and some petroglyphs on the other. The route short-cuts the big meander as the river goes around the fin. If scrambling 250 feet to the top of the talus and through the notch looks to be too daunting, take the river route instead.

3.6   To get to the notch, head southwest up Cane Wash. The canyon turns to the south. There is a cairn here at the bottom of a break in the low cliffs on the right (W). 0522863 E, 4326618 N Z12 NAD83.

3.7   Follow the cairned route up small ledges and onto the bench above [Class 3]. Once on top turn toward the notch. Take the cairned use-trail leading to the northwest across the bench and to the bottom of a switchback trail at the base of the talus slope. 0522810 E, 4326709 N Z12 NAD83.

3.8   Take the switchback trail up the talus slope following cairns until you are on the ledge running along the base of the tall cliffs. Traverse right (NNE) to the base of the notch. A short scramble up [Class 3] will put you at the apex. 0522787 E, 4326812 N Z12 NAD83.

3.9   After enjoying the view, pass through the notch and follow a use-trail north along the base of the western side of the fin. If you stay right up against the bottom of the cliff you will end up under a huge, detached boulder that is leaning against the cliff, creating a perfect shelter from sun or rain. Just after you come out the other side of the boulder, look for some faint petroglyphs at knee level on the base of the wall. 0522801 E, 4326961 N Z12 NAD83.

4.1   Follow the trail northwest past a circular arrangement of stones and then west-northwest out onto a red and gray peninsula. Continue on the trail as it swings north and follows the top of this ridge to the monolith at its end. The pictographs are on the western side of it. The similarity to the setting of the Rochester rock art site (Hike #24) is pretty uncanny. 0522586 E, 4327175 N Z12 NAD83.

> *Historical note:* To find the pictographs, follow a use-trail that contours around the western side of the monolith. At times the way is bouldery and loose. Under an overhanging part of the cliffs forming the monolith is a nice panel of Fremont style pictographs depicting several large anthropomorphs and geometric designs in red and ochre. There are zigzags and a row of triangles reminiscent of the shelter cave glyphs in Cane Wash.

Look closely for the faint images of bighorn sheep in white. This panel is remarkably well preserved. Please help it to remain that way by not adding your own marks and by not touching the paintings. If you are coming up from the river, a cairned trail switchbacks up the talus slope from the river to the southern end of the monolith. Follow the use-trail to traverse to the site.

4.2   From the ridge at the southern end of the monolith, go west down the talus slope on a cairned switchback trail. At the bottom you will intersect the use-trail that follows the river. This is where this hike diverges from Hike #19. 0522520 E, 4327179 N Z12 NAD83.

6.5   Follow the trail generally west up the river gorge. There is much bushwhacking and long pants are recommended. You will pass three small side canyons on the left (S). After 2.5 miles start looking for a route on the left (S) that accesses the bench above. It is a cairned stock trail so is pretty easy to find. If you miss the stock trail at first, you will soon come to the mouth of Virgin Springs Canyon. 0519660 E, 4326161 N Z12 NAD83.

> *Note:* This old stock trail bypasses the box of Virgin Springs Canyon, but also provides access to it without getting your feet wet. The San Rafael River sweeps across the mouth of Virgin Springs Canyon. To enter the canyon from river level one must wade through the river during low water or climbers can carefully traverse around and into the box. You'll need to hook up with the stock trail to continue up Virgin Springs Canyon past the box. Most will find it more efficient to drop heavy packs along the stock trail on the rim of the box and explore the box without them.

6.9   Go up the stock trail and follow it southwest across the bench. You'll come to the rim of the box of Virgin Springs Canyon. Continue following the cairned trail along the rim of the box. Just before reaching a slickrock bowl the route divides. To the right (NW) is the descent into the box. To the left (SE) is the continuation of the stock trail. This junction is where this hike joins Hike #23. 0519298 E, 4325830 N Z12 NAD83.

Barrier Canyon style pictographs in Virgin Springs Canyon.

Digression: Though there is camping in the box, the area has become impacted by backpackers and river-runners. Try not to camp in the box itself. If you do, low-impact camping techniques are essential. It is best to drop packs at this junction, explore the box, take water from the spring if needed, and then camp farther up the canyon. From the junction follow the cairned descent [Class 3] generally north as it angles down ledges and to the floor of the box (0519309 E, 4325896 N Z12 NAD83). The box is about a half mile long. Go up it to the south to find the spring and pour-off. Head down it to the north to visit the pictographs and the river. The pictographs are on the western wall of the box and are identified with a small BLM marker.

7.2	Now follow the stock trail generally southwest around the sandstone bowl and across a talus slope, until you rejoin the floor of Virgin Springs Canyon a short way above the box. There are numerous cairns along the way. 0519087 E, 4325516 N Z12 NAD83.
7.3	Go south up the floor of the canyon. You will soon come to a small pour-off. This can be easily passed on the left (E). 0519085 E, 4325359 N Z12 NAD83.
7.8	Just beyond this pour-off the canyon begins to turn to the southeast. Continue up the canyon. You will encounter a big, semipermanent pothole. 0519727 E, 4324850 N Z12 NAD83.
8.8	Another 1.1 miles up the canyon and you will reach the junction with the West Fork of Virgin Springs Canyon on the right (SW) and its seasonal springs. There is good camping in the area. Should the

springs near the junction be dry, try the potholes a little way up the West Fork. 0519961 E, 4323463 N Z12 NAD83.

> **Digression:** Hike #23 diverges here and goes up the West Fork. The route leads to Swazy, the highest point on Sids Mountain, and to a unique line cabin that is worth seeing (see Hike #23 for details). Plan on four to six hours round trip, 1,100 feet of elevation gain, easy route finding, and [Class 3] scrambling.

9.6   Go southeast up Virgin Springs Canyon. A short side canyon enters from the left (NE). 0520661 E, 4322707 N Z12 NAD83.

10.1   Continue heading southeast up Virgin Springs Canyon for another 0.5 mile. A small drainage enters from the left once again. This will be your exit route and is shown between elevations 5952 and 6419 on the Sids Mountain map. You'll know it's the right one because the main canyon turns and runs to the south-southwest just past it. However, don't enter the drainage yet because it is blocked after 150 yards by a fall (see map on page 206). 0520973 E, 4322066 N Z12 NAD83.

10.15   Go southeast just a short way past the mouth of the drainage and find the small cleft that runs to the northeast. This bypasses the fall in the side drainage. There is a cairned use-trail leading up the cleft. 0521024 E, 4321975 N Z12 NAD83.

10.2   Follow the use-trail northeast up the cleft until you reach the bench layer above the fall. 0521090 E, 4322048 N Z12 NAD83.

10.3   Now head east-northeast back into the side drainage and look for the cairned use-trail on the left (N) side at the base of a pretty obvious rubble ramp. 0521211 E, 4322143 N Z12 NAD83.

10.5   Follow the use-trail northeast up the rubble to a ledge below the last cliff band. Circle right (SE) under an overhang to an easy break in the cliff and scramble up. 0521432 E, 4322076 N Z12 NAD83.

10.7   Now head east-southeast up the watercourse and then up a steep slope to a saddle high between Virgin Springs Canyon and Cane Wash. The view from the saddle is sublime. 0521749 E, 4322011 N Z12 NAD83.

10.75   Look far down to the northeast and you will see Cane Wash. Head east off the saddle and go down 100 feet onto a white, discontinuous ledge system. Decision time. The quickest way into Cane Wash is

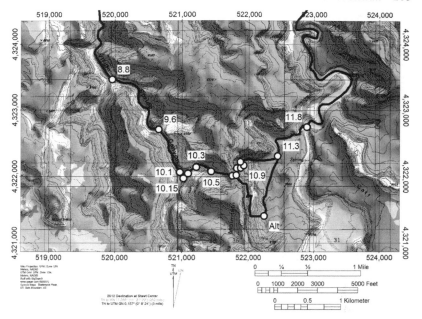

Hike #20. Detail from Mile 8.8 to 11.8. 1:24,000.

to the northeast but the [Class 4] route has some challenging exposure and a friction section that might not work when wet. An easier,
but longer, [Class 3] route heads off to the southeast from here. The
more direct route to the northeast is far more efficient and so will be
described in detail. 0521812 E, 4322020 N Z12 NAD83.

> *Digression:* The alternate route traverses right (SE), around a
> point, and then continues on the ledge for another five minutes.
> There are occasional cairns along the way. Go down a broken
> area (NE). For several hundred feet go diagonally left toward a
> wide, yellow ledge system. Once there go right and follow the
> ledge system south for 0.25 mile until a slide/gully is reached.
> Descend this on a cairned use-trail to a slickrock plain (0522245
> E, 4321407 N Z12 NAD83). Follow the watercourse north-
> northeast until you intersect the route at mile 11.3 (0522450 E,
> 4322310 N Z12 NAD83).

10.8 Go north on the white ledge and find the route that goes north off
the ledge, marked by a cairn. 0521821 E, 4322126 N Z12 NAD83.

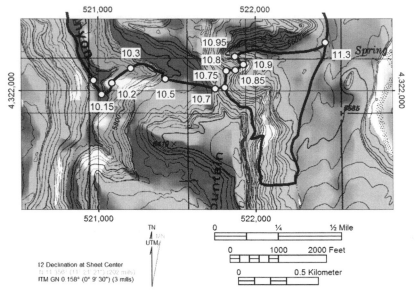

Hike #20. Detail from Mile 10.15 to 11.3. 1:24,000.

10.85 Drop through the first hard layer and then traverse left (W) on a ledge until you can descend to the next ledge below. Now traverse right (E) on this bench until you come around a point. You'll have to step over a small void along the way. Be careful to not let your pack knock you off this one. Drop down a ramp to the top of a banded sandstone nose and a cairn. 0521880 E, 4322131 N Z12 NAD83.

10.9 Follow cairns northeast down sandstone ledges, at one point sticking to a rather severe friction slab, to the top of a sandstone platform and a large cairn. 0521930 E, 4322167 N Z12 NAD83.

10.95 Now head northwest and contour into the back of the drainage. You will be beneath a large alcove and at the top of a large rubble slope leading to the floor of the drainage below. 0521876 E, 4322220 N Z12 NAD83.

11.3 Head northeast down this rubble then east down the drainage, going right to bypass a pour-off. You will intersect a larger wash coming in from the right (S). The two different routes reunite at this junction. 0522450 E, 4322310 N Z12 NAD83.

11.8 Go down the wash, first north then west-northwest for 0.5 mile until you reach Cane Wash. You will be linking up with Hike #19 here. 0522898 E, 4322748 N Z12 NAD83.

Digression: Most will want to head north down Cane Wash and then follow the San Rafael River back to the trailhead, but you do have some options. You could follow the Calf Mesa and Moore Canyon part of Hike #19 for 5.2 miles back to the trailhead. This is shorter but not as scenic. Or you can go 1.7 miles south up Cane Wash to the alternate trailhead on TR 643. See Hike #19 for details.

16.4   Follow Cane Wash generally north until you reach the San Rafael River. The going is easy along the mostly flat canyon floor. 0523230 E, 4327052 N Z12 NAD83.

19.6   Now turn right (SE) and follow the trail alongside the river for 3.4 miles back to the trailhead. 0527202 E, 4325414 N Z12 NAD83.

B7183/Oil Well Flat/Saddle Horse Canyon Road Section

Access to Hike #21.

Access is from EM332/Cottonwood Wash Road.

1:100,000 map: San Rafael Desert. Huntington.

This road goes southwest from mile 6 on the Cottonwood Wash Road (detailed in the Northern Reef and Mexican Mountain chapter) to the upper reaches of Cane Wash and the junctions with TR643/Cane Wash Road and TR638/North Fork Coal Wash Road. The Oil Well Flat Road is suitable for most medium-clearance vehicles and mountain bikes. TR643 and TR638 are high-clearance 4WD tracks. They are fine mountain bike routes, but are used heavily by ORVs and there are several long pushes. There is good camping throughout the area.

0.0	Mileage starts at the Oil Well Flat Road junction on EM332/Cottonwood Wash Road. 0526569 E, 4317106 N Z12 NAD83.
1.0	Go southwest on the Oil Well Flat Road. After a mile you will come to a marked fork. The right fork (SW) goes to TR643/Cane Wash Road and the left fork (SSW) is B7183/Oil Well Flat Road. Note that there is a dirt road shown on the Wickiup 1:24,000 and San Rafael Desert 1:100,000 maps heading off to the right (NW) just before this junction. This track no longer exists. 0525460 E, 4315939 N Z12 NAD83.

> *Digression:* The track on the right goes generally west as a high-clearance 4WD track to TR643 in Cane Wash. From there one can head north down Cane Wash to the alternate trailhead for Hikes #19 and #20, and then return to the Cottonwood Wash Road via the Dexter Mine Road. Or you can head south up Cane

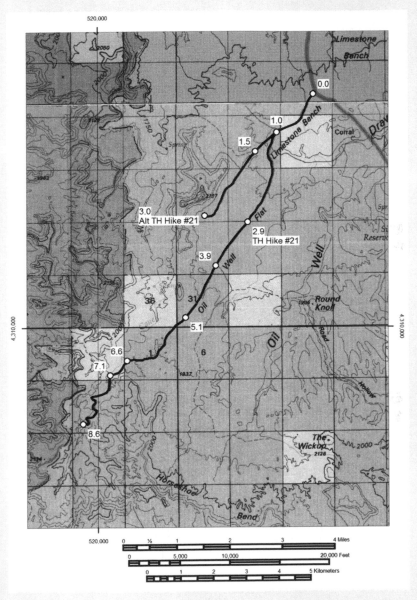

520,000

2080

1750

1125

Limestone Bench

0.0

1.0

Limestone Bench

Corral

Draw

1.5

Spring

1942

2187

3.0
Alt TH Hike #21

Flat

2.9
TH Hike #21

Spr

Well

Reservo

3.9

2135

36

31

Oil

Well

Round
Knoll

1906

4,310,000

4,310,000

5.1

2000

6.6

1

6

Oil

Road

7.1

1837

Hollow

8.6

Horseshoe

The
Wickup
2128

2000

2000

Bend

520,000

| 0 | ½ | 1 | 2 | 3 | 4 Miles |

| 0 | | 5,000 | 10,000 | | 20,000 Feet |

| 0 | 1 | 2 | 3 | 4 | 5 Kilometers |

1:100,000

Wash past Mexican Seep and eventually reconnect with the Oil Well Flat Road at its southern end. The route is very sandy and should not be attempted when wet.

There are two options for accessing Hike #21. One for medium-clearance vehicles and the other for high-clearance vehicles or mountain bikes. The route for medium-clearance vehicles will be described first as the standard. The second route will be described as the digression.

2.9   Go left (SSW) at the fork and follow the Oil Well Flat Road. Several tracks branch off of it. Stay with the main road. You will cross various washes, then the road climbs onto a flat plain (Oil Well Flat). You will see Pinnacle #1 to the right (NW). You will be roughly between elevations 6072 and 6024 on the Wickiup map. This is the start of Pinnacle #1 Ascent Hike #21. There is no established parking area, just park completely off the road in a logical place. 0524588 E, 4313217 N Z12 NAD83.

> *Digression:* If you are in a high-clearance 4WD or on a mountain bike, you can get about a mile closer to Pinnacle #1. From the fork at mile 1.0 on the Oil Well Flat Road, go right (SW) on this track for 0.5 mile to another fork (0524836 E, 4315367 N Z12 NAD83). If you go right (W) at the fork you will reach Cane Wash. Go left (SW) and follow this track southwest along the base of Pinnacle #1. The track gets quite rough and crosses numerous small washes. As you approach the southern end of the pinnacle the road leads to a large, yellow, triangular-shaped rubble slide that is an obvious route up through the first cliffs. Park completely off the track wherever you can (0523243 E, 4313420 N Z12 NAD83).

3.9   Continue heading southwest on the Oil Well Flat Road. After a mile there will be a track on the left (SE). This is TR646 and is where the described mountain bike loop from mile 18.7 on the Cottonwood Wash Road intersects the Oil Well Flat Road (see the Cottonwood Wash Road Section for details). 0523603 E, 4311895 N Z12 NAD83.

5.1   Keep going southwest on the Oil Well Flat Road. Though not shown on the San Rafael Desert or Wickiup maps, the junction with TR645 will be on the left (E). 0522674 E, 4310300 N Z12 NAD83.

6.6   The Oil Well Flat Road continues southwest then turns to the west and crosses a wash. 0520899 E, 4308981 N Z12 NAD83.

7.1   The road turns to the southwest again and you will come to the signed junction with TR643 in Cane Wash. This is the end of B7183/ Oil Well Flat Road. 0520400 E, 4308550 N Z12 NAD83.

8.6   Head generally southwest up Cane Wash on TR643. You will come to the end of TR643 at the junction with TR638, also known as the North Fork Coal Wash Road. Just before the junction is a series of small overhangs known locally as the Indian Caves. 0519570 E, 4307073 N Z12 NAD83.

   If you were to go left (S) on TR638 this high-clearance 4WD track leads to the Head of Sinbad area. If you go right the track exits Cane Wash and goes over Fix It Pass into the Sids Mountain Wilderness Study Area and down to Saddle Horse Canyon. It is a rough, high-clearance 4WD road to that point. The old track that leads down Saddle Horse Canyon is presently closed to all vehicles (this includes mountain bikes). TR638 continues on to the North Fork of Coal Wash and is currently cherry-stemmed through the WSA. Please stay on the designated route and obey all road closures or this route may become closed in the future.

Hike #21: Pinnacle #1 Ascent

SEASON:	Any. Rain or snow could cause trouble on the final push to the summit.
TIME AND DISTANCE:	Three to four hours (3.4 miles).
WATER:	None. Bring your own water.
MAPS:	The Wickiup, Bottleneck Peak. (San Rafael Desert, Huntington.)
LOOP HIKE:	No.
SKILL LEVEL:	Easy/moderate route finding. [Class 4+] climbing. Much uphill scrambling. A rope may be useful for beginners.

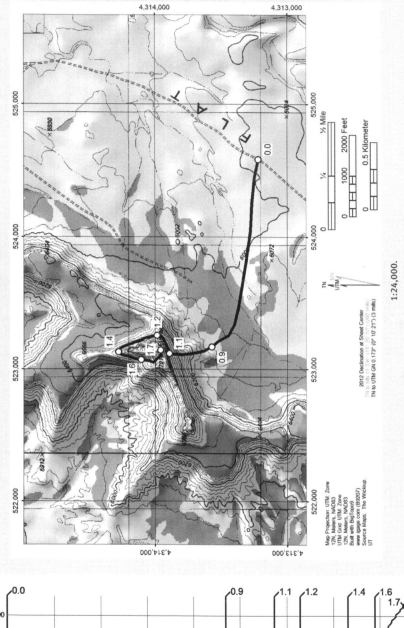

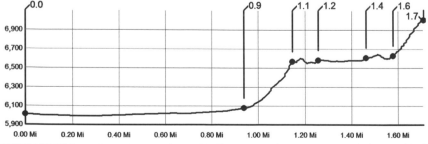

Elev Gain 996 Ft; Climb 1177 Ft; Drop −181 Ft; Max Elev 7008 Ft; Min Elev 5991 Ft; Map Dist 1.711 Mi; Ground Dist 1.767 Mi

Pinnacle #1.

This hike/climb has it all. It is for the person who has seen the great desert spires—the Totem Pole, Castleton Tower, the Fisher Towers—and has wanted to climb one of them. However, they can take an immense amount of skill, training, and equipment to surmount. A hike up Pinnacle #1 (also called Dille Butte) will give you a similar thrill, but you can scramble up it! There is never an exposure problem if you stick to the route. You are always safe, secure, and away from big drops. This is an adventure any fit person, with competent leadership, can handle. It is well worth the effort.

0.0   Mileage begins at mile 2.9 on B7183/Oil Well Flat Road. 0524588 E, 4313217 N Z12 NAD83.

0.9   Look northwest toward Pinnacle #1. At its base, on the southern side, is a large, yellow, triangular-shaped rubble slide that is an obvious route up through the first cliffs. Hike west-northwest across the plain to the base of the slide. 0523173 E, 4313568 N Z12 NAD83.

1.1   Scramble north on a cairned use-trail up the slide to the base of the big cliff that makes up the summit tower. The route to the top is on the opposite side (NW) of this cliff. 0523121 E, 4313891 N Z12 NAD83.

1.2   Traverse northeast along the base of the cliff to the eastern side of the summit tower. 0523261 E, 4313985 N Z12 NAD83.

1.4   Continue traversing along the base of the cliffs, now north, until you are on the northern end of the summit tower. 0523132 E, 4314278 N Z12 NAD83.

1.6   Now head south along the base of the cliffs until you reach the bottom of a steep ramp that leads to the summit. 0523074 E, 4314105 N Z12 NAD83.

1.7   Work your way up this ramp, zigzagging south-southeast up ledges and slabs. There is one moderate section [Class 4, 12'] at the bottom behind a boulder. A harder section [Class 4+, 15'] is about halfway up. When you reach the final ridge the summit is just to the left (E). It is labeled Pinnacle #1 (7010) on a USGS bench mark from 1937. Hats off to those men! 0523148 E, 4313959 N Z12 NAD83.

3.4   Plan on spending a little time on the marvelous summit platform. Return the way you came. 0524588 E, 4313217 N Z12 NAD83.

Dutch Flat Road to
Fuller Bottom Road Section

Access to Hikes #22 and #23.

Access is from Highway 10 in Ferron and B6767/Fuller Bottom Road.

Provides access to B6767/Fuller Bottom Road.

1:100,000 maps: Manti, Huntington.

County Road EM705, also called the Dutch Flat Road, is the best way to access the western side of the Sids Mountain area of the San Rafael Swell. This well-maintained dirt road goes generally east from the town of Ferron and is suitable for most vehicles to its end at an information kiosk in Horn Silver Gulch. If wet or snowy this road may be impossible to negotiate. Numerous other dirt roads branch off of it providing access to Coal Canyon, North Salt Wash, and the San Rafael River at Fuller Bottom. From Horn Silver Gulch to Fuller Bottom the road is for medium-clearance vehicles only. Though quite scenic, the road is heavily used by ORV enthusiasts towing trailers, so mountain bikers may find it dusty and busy with traffic. There is plenty of at-large camping in the area, especially on the smaller side roads.

0.0 Mileage begins at the junction of 100 South Street and Highway 10 in Ferron. 0488610 E, 4326578 N Z12 NAD83.

3.0 Go east on the paved 100 South Street (also called the Molen Road) to the intersection with 2400 East Street. A sign here says "Molen, Dutch Flat Desert." 0493510 E, 4326593 N Z12 NAD83.

4.2 Turn right (S) on 2400 East. This road is also called EM608/Molen Cutoff. The pavement soon ends and the road turns to dirt. This road goes south past some farms, crosses Ferron Creek, then turns to the southeast just before you come to the intersection with EM705/Dutch Flat Road on top of a hill. 0493678 E, 04324615 N Z12 NAD83.

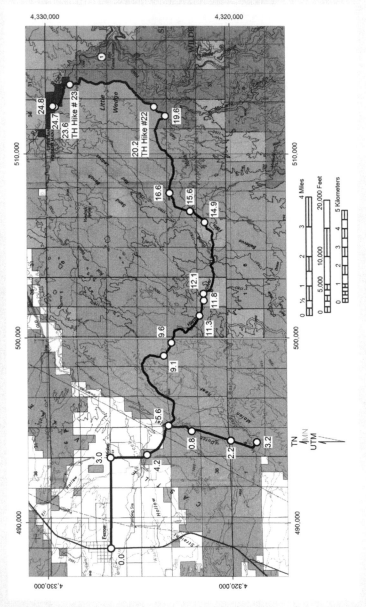

5.6   Go straight (SE) through the intersection and follow the Dutch Flat Road southeast, across Dutch Flat, to the junction with two dirt roads on the right (S) on the edge of Shearing Corral Draw. The first road is EM706 and the second is EM707. EM706 leads to a wonderful rock art site in Molen Seep Wash. 0495232 E, 4323443 N Z12 NAD83.

EM706/Molen Seep Road

0.0   Mileage begins at the junction with the Dutch Flat Road. 0495232 E, 4323443 N Z12 NAD83.

0.8   Head generally south on EM706. The road is suitable for most vehicles unless wet or snowy. You will pass the junction with EM722 on the right (W). 0494959 E, 4322201 N Z12 NAD83.

2.2   Continue heading south on the main road. The road then begins to head south-southwest. On the left (E) will be the junction with EM707. 0494431 E, 4320076 N Z12 NAD83.

3.2   Keep following EM706 south-southwest. There are side roads branching off. Stay with the main, graded road. The road will turn left (SE) and end at a turnaround on the edge of Molen Seep Wash. 0494344 E, 4318623 N Z12 NAD83.

Historical note: The Molen Seep rock art site is well worth visiting. There are Barrier Canyon style pictographs as well as some interesting Fremont style petroglyphs depicting what would appear to be numerous sandals with different patterns on them. From the turnaround at the end of EM706 simply follow the use-trail down into the shallow canyon that is Molen Seep Wash and then follow the trail to the rock art. Please be very careful not to harm this important site. Even touching the rock art is enough to cause irreversible harm.

9.1   Continue heading southeast on the Dutch Flat Road. The road soon turns to the northeast, exits the Molen Reef, and then swings around to the south. Look for the large, spherical concretions eroding from the steep slopes. Just as the road begins heading southeast again you will reach the junction with EM708/South Sand Bench Loop on the left (E). 0499017 E, 4323661 N Z12 NAD83.

9.6 Follow the Dutch Flat Road southeast. You will soon reach the junction with B6792 on the right (S). This high-clearance dirt road heads generally southwest to the paved Moore Cutoff Road. 0499732 E, 4323231 N Z12 NAD83.

11.3 Continue heading southeast. On the left (NE) will be the junction with the other end of EM708/South Sand Bench Loop. 0501207 E, 4321695 N Z12 NAD83.

11.8 The road is now following Horn Silver Gulch. On the right (S) is the junction with TR633. This high-clearance 4WD track is not shown on the Huntington map but heads generally southwest to the Moore Cutoff Road. 0502055 E, 4321453 N Z12 NAD83.

12.1 A short way farther down the Dutch Flat Road you will see the junction with TR630 on the left (N). Also not shown on the Huntington map, this high-clearance 4WD track heads northeast to South Red Wash. 0502436 E, 4321476 N Z12 NAD83.

14.9 The road continues following Horn Silver Gulch, generally east, as it cuts through the Red Ledges. You will come to a major junction with an information kiosk. On the left (N) is B6770. EM705 continues straight (E) through the junction and soon ends at the intersection with B6768 and TR638. 0506312 E, 4321414 N Z12 NAD83.

15.6 Go left on B6770 and follow this medium-clearance dirt road northeast. You will cross the wash of Horn Silver Gulch just above its confluence with North Salt Wash. This crossing may be impassable when wet. 0506883 E, 4322202 N Z12 NAD83.

16.6 Continue following B6770 northeast. You will come to the junction with TR629 on the right (E). 0507867 E, 4323296 N Z12 NAD83.

B6770 continues heading northeast for another 5.2 miles to the ford at Fuller Bottom. This can be an option for accessing Hike #23. Just before reaching the ford you will come to the junction with the other end of TR629 on the right (SE) (0512552 E, 4329486 N Z12 NAD83). You can then hike, bike, or drive southeast on TR629 to the trailhead (0513709 E, 4328658 N Z12 NAD83).

19.6 Head east on TR629. This track is for medium-clearance vehicles and only 4WDs if it is wet. You will begin paralleling the rim of North Salt Wash. The road turns to the northeast for a while then heads southeast. On the right side of the road, just before it turns northeast again, will be a wooden fence. Beyond the fence is the Sids Mountain Wilderness Study Area and all vehicles are forbidden. A closed track, the McCarty Canyon Trail, heads south from here into North Salt Wash. As this is an equestrian trailhead, if you park here please do so in a manner that will allow those towing horse trailers to be able to do the same. 0512073 E, 4323544 N Z12 NAD83.

> *Digression:* A somewhat popular trail for horseback riders, the trail goes down into North Salt Wash. From there the trail heads south up McCarty Canyon and exits the canyon via Still Canyon. It crosses a narrow divide between McCarty Canyon and Saddle Horse Canyon then heads west onto Cactus Flat. The trail then descends into Mesquite Wash and follows it north back down into North Salt Wash and back to the start. This 18-mile loop can make for some decent hiking, but be prepared for encountering plenty of cattle and their associated biting insects and excrement.

20.2   Follow TR629 northeast. From here to the trailhead for Hike #23, the land on the right (E) side of the road is within the Sids Mountain WSA. You will see another wooden fence across a closed track on the right (SE). At the fence are a small parking area and the trailhead for Sids Mountain and Saddle Horse Canyon Hike #22. This can also be used as an alternate trailhead for Hike #23. 0512541 E, 4324152 N Z12 NAD83.

23.6   Keep heading northeast along the road. You will pass several more closed tracks on the right and the road will leave the rim of North Salt Wash and begin heading generally north. You will come onto an open plain and see an information kiosk, a small parking area, and a closed track on the right (E) beside the corner of a wire fence. This is the trailhead for San Rafael River, Virgin Springs Canyon, Sids Mountain, and North Salt Wash Hike #23. 0513709 E, 4328658 N Z12 NAD83.

24.7   The road heads north then northwest and descends into Fuller Bottom. Just as it turns north again will be the junction with B6770 on the left (W). 0512552 E, 4329486 N Z12 NAD83.

24.8   A short way north down the road is the ford across the San Rafael River. 0512601 E, 4329625 N Z12 NAD83.

The ford is for high-clearance 4WD vehicles only and should not be attempted unless the river is very low. It would be wise to wade across it first to check the depth and condition of the stream bed. On the north side of the river is B6767/Fuller Bottom Road. It is 5.8 miles up this medium-clearance dirt road to the junction with the Green River Cutoff Road at the Buckhorn Well Intersection (see the Green River Cutoff Road Section in the Northern Reef and Mexican Mountain chapter for details).

Hike #22: Sids Mountain and Saddle Horse Canyon

SEASON:	Spring and fall are best. Snow could make the stock trail difficult to follow.
TIME AND DISTANCE:	Part 1: Six to eight hours (11.2 miles). Part 2: Ten to twelve hours, should be done in two days (15.8 miles).
WATER:	North Salt Wash always has water. Saddle Horse Canyon has some nice, reliable springs. There is no dependable source of water on Sids Mountain. Bring your own water.
MAPS:	Sids Mountain. (Huntington.)
LOOP HIKE:	Part 1: No. Part 2: Yes.
SKILL LEVEL:	Part 1: North Salt Wash (1A/B). Moderate route finding. [Class 2] walking, mostly on a stock trail. Part 2: Saddle Horse Canyon (1A), North Salt Wash (1A/B). Moderate route finding. [Class 3] scrambling. Low-impact camping skills are essential.

Fantasyland is an apt description of Sids Mountain. It is a flat-topped mesa strewn with large Navajo domes. There is much to see and do. The goal of the hike is to get atop Sids Mountain and among its many domes. On the way you will encounter a unique line cabin tucked between two of the domes. Keep your eyes peeled for bighorn sheep as you travel through this part of the Swell.

The hike comes in two parts. Part 2 is an extension of Part 1. Both start on the rim of North Salt Wash near the confluence with Saddle Horse Canyon and follow a stock trail to the top of Sids Mountain. Part 1 returns the same way. Part 2 crosses Sids Mountain, descends into Saddle Horse Canyon, and heads down it to the confluence with North Salt Wash.

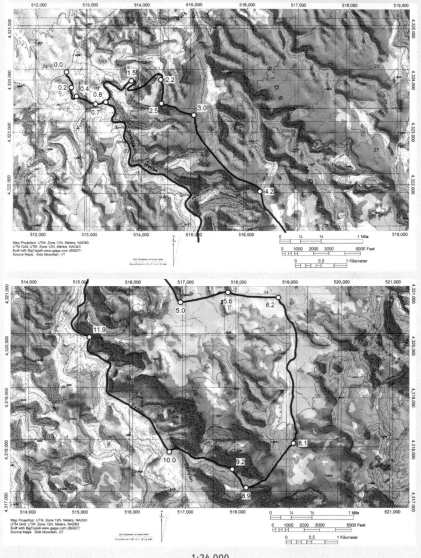

1:24,000

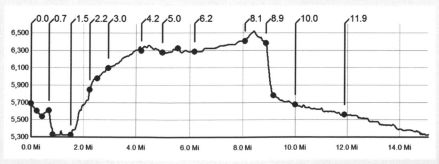

Elev Loss −358 Ft; Climb 1999 Ft; Drop −181 Ft; Max Elev 7008 Ft; Min Elev 5991 Ft; Map Dist 1.711 Mi; Ground Dist 1.767 Mi

Part 1

0.0   Mileage begins at the trailhead parking area at mile 20.2 on TR629/ Dutch Flat to Fuller Bottom Road. 0512541 E, 4324152 N Z12 NAD83.

0.2   Beyond the wooden fence is a now-closed track that descends part of the way into North Salt Wash. Follow the track south-southwest down from the rim. You will be entering the Sids Mountain Wilderness Study Area. The track leads to the head of a small draw. 0512637 E, 4323855 N Z12 NAD83.

0.4   Take the track generally south down the draw. After a small wash enters from the right (S) the track swings to the northeast and exits the floor of the shallow wash and goes up onto a bench layer to the north. 0512740 E, 4323687 N Z12 NAD83.

0.7   Follow the track generally east along this bench. It will lead you out to the end of a prow overlooking the floor of North Salt Wash. On the north side of the point of the prow is a cairn marking the top of the route into the canyon. 0513111 E, 4323538 N Z12 NAD83.

0.8   Head east down the steep trail to the bottom of the canyon. The [Class 2] route is easy to follow and numerous cairns lead the way. You will be across from the mouth of Saddle Horse Canyon. 0513309 E, 4323576 N Z12 NAD83.

1.5   Now go generally northeast down North Salt Wash, following a well-defined stock trail. You will have to cross the perennial stream running along the floor of the canyon several times. If the stream is low you should be able to step across it and keep your feet dry. The canyon winds through here. Just before the stream bends to the northwest start searching for the beginning of the stock trail that leads to the top of Sids Mountain. It goes up onto the low bench to the east. It may be hard to locate at first as it is hidden behind tall streamside growth. You will be joining Hike #23 here. 0513802 E, 4323982 N Z12 NAD83.

> *Note:* If you will be doing Parts 1 and 2 as an overnight trip you will want to have enough water to see you from this point all the way to the springs in Saddle Horse Canyon, a distance of 10.4 miles. There is no reliable water anywhere on Sids Mountain.

2.2 Head east up the trail onto the low bench. Follow the trail southwest as it traverses the bench then east as it begins to climb up ledges and rubble. It will start angling to the northeast as it gradually contours up. The [Class 2] trail is easy to follow with cairns showing the way. The trail swings to the south and ascends the edge of a draw onto a large bench. 0514364 E, 4324004 N Z12 NAD83.

2.5 From the bench follow the trail southeast then south as it climbs up to a flat area. When you reach the edge of a small drainage flowing west into Saddle Horse Canyon, the trail turns to the east-southeast. 0514378 E, 4323548 N Z12 NAD83.

3.0 Follow the trail east-southeast along the rim of this drainage. It turns south at the head of the wash. 0514998 E, 4323325 N Z12 NAD83.

4.2 Take the trail south then generally southeast through sparse pinyon and juniper. The terrain is flat as you are now atop Sids Mountain. You will come to a narrow divide between two large drainages to the east and west. Just before reaching the divide you will cross over the remnants of an old log fence. 0516262 E, 4321871 N Z12 NAD83.

5.0 Continue following the trail southeast. It will swing around to the east on the southern side of the large Navajo ridge marked 6449 on the Sids Mountain map. 0516907 E, 4320841 N Z12 NAD83.

5.6 To the east are two large Navajo domes. Follow the trail east-northeast between the domes and on to the Kofford cabins. 0517798 E, 4321032 N Z12 NAD83.

Historical note: Sids Mountain is named after Sid Swasey who, according to legend, followed a bighorn sheep up the mountain's steep flanks and so discovered the mesa. For a number of years Swasey ran stock here in the winter. The unique cabin on stilts was built by Rex Kofford in the 1940s. He had a 440-acre homestead here. The land was later sold to Loren Beach, Monte Swasey, and Clyde Baillings. The BLM acquired the land in 1985. Please do not disturb the cabin.

Digression: You can easily visit some interesting petroglyph panels and summit the Swazy landform (elevation 6610 on the

North Salt Wash near the confluence with Saddle Horse Canyon.

Sids Mountain map) from the cabins. Total round trip will be 2.8 miles (see Hike #23 for details).

11.2 After visiting the cabins, and if you are just doing Part 1, retrace your steps back to the trailhead on the rim of North Salt Wash. 0512541 E, 4324152 N Z12 NAD83.

Part 2

Mileage resumes from the cabins.

6.2 You will be diverging from Hike #23 here. From the cabins head east across an open plain until you intersect a wash that is running to the northwest. 0518777 E, 4320931 N Z12 NAD83.

8.1 Now follow this wash generally south. The wash goes up the middle of a large, sage-studded open area. You will be paralleling a long Navajo ridge that will be to the west. As you near the end of the open area you will see the southern end of this ridge. The end of the ridge has a dome marked 6693 on the Sids Mountain map. The wash, still trending south, leaves the open area and enters sparse pinyon and juniper. Soon the wash turns abruptly to the southwest. 0519078 E, 4318125 N Z12 NAD83.

8.9   Leave the wash here and start heading southwest. You will be passing to the south of the dome marked 6693 and will come to the rim
of a small side canyon of Saddle Horse Canyon. A narrow ridge
heads west along the south rim of this side canyon. It separates this
side canyon from a larger one to the south. Go west along this ridge
until you find a cairn marking the top of the route that goes north-
northwest, down 600 feet of rubble, to the floor of the side canyon.
0518122 E, 4317261 N Z12 NAD83.

9.2   Head north-northwest down through steep [Class 3] rubble to the
floor of the side canyon. 0517894 E, 4317626 N Z12 NAD83.

10.0   Follow the floor of the side canyon west-northwest to the confluence
with Saddle Horse Canyon. Look to the southeast up Saddle Horse
Canyon and you will see a large natural arch perched high on the
eastern wall of the canyon. 0516704 E, 4317962 N Z12 NAD83.

11.9   Now head generally northwest down Saddle Horse Canyon. An easy
to follow stock trail goes down the canyon and cuts off the many
meanders, saving a lot of steps. In 2 miles you will reach the first of
four reliable springs. 0515174 E, 4320172 N Z12 NAD83.

15.0   Continue following Saddle Horse Canyon, generally north then
northwest, to the confluence with North Salt Wash. You will pass
a large freestanding pinnacle and the remaining springs along the
way. As you near the mouth of the canyon you will likely have to step
across running water several times. Cross to the northwest side of
the stream running down North Salt Wash and rejoin the stock trail
that comes down from the rim. 0513309 E, 4323576 N Z12 NAD83.

15.8   Now retrace your steps generally northwest up the stock trail back
to the trailhead on the rim of the canyon. 0512541 E, 4324152 N Z12
NAD83.

Hike #23: San Rafael River, Virgin Springs Canyon, Sids Mountain, and North Salt Wash

SEASON: Early spring or fall. Because of numerous river crossings, this
hike would be difficult during the high flows of late spring
and early summer. Snow could make the stock trail difficult to
follow.

TIME AND DISTANCE: Two to three days. Two days would be difficult and leave little time for exploring. Three days should be taken if possible. This could take longer if day hikes are added (21.6 miles).

WATER: San Rafael River if you must. There is an excellent spring in Virgin Springs Canyon that is always flowing. Upper Virgin Springs has seasonal springs. There is no reliable water on Sids Mountain. Saddle Horse Canyon and North Salt Wash have small perennial springs that you can depend on.

MAPS: Sids Mountain. (Huntington.)

LOOP HIKE: Yes.

SKILL LEVEL: San Rafael River Gorge (1B/C), Virgin Springs Canyon and Saddle Horse Canyon (1A), North Salt Wash (1B). Moderate route-finding. [Class 3 and 4] scrambling. The long uphill section to exit Virgin Springs Canyon can be jading with a pack. Low-impact camping techniques are essential. Wading shoes are helpful for the San Rafael River portion.

Backpacking trips are generally swell. Camping high on a mesa top or deep in a sand-floored canyon are unforgettable experiences. This hike provides the opportunity to do both. The route not only goes through several outstanding canyons, but also goes to the top of Sids Mountain, a mesa dotted with Navajo domes, and accesses numerous Native American rock art sites along the way.

The route goes down the San Rafael River into the Little Grand Canyon, past the mouth of North Salt Wash then up Virgin Springs Canyon and onto Sids Mountain. After visiting the Kofford cabins and crossing the mountain, the route drops down into North Salt Wash, which is descended back to the San Rafael River.

Enough information is given in this section to allow you to tie into Hikes #20 and #22. The steadfast adventurer could easily spend a week hiking the maze of canyons in and around Sids Mountain.

0.0 Mileage begins at the information kiosk and trailhead parking at mile 23.6 on TR629. Or you could start at the ford at Fuller Bottom (0512601 E, 4329625 N), but it would add an additional mile on both ends of your hike. You could also start this hike at the trailhead for Hike #22 (0512541 E, 4324152 N Z12 NAD83) at mile 20.2 on TR629. 0513709 E, 4328658 N Z12 NAD83.

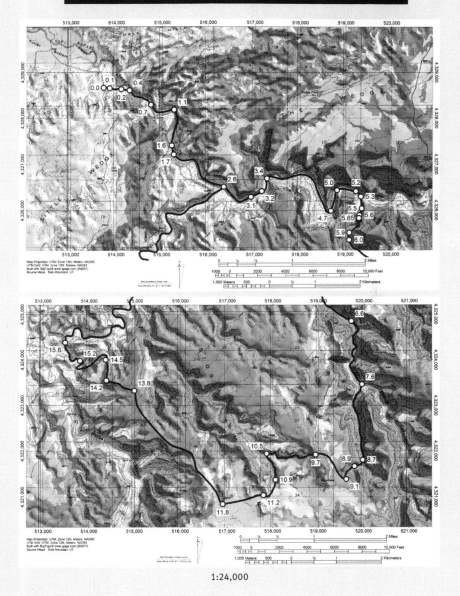

1:24,000

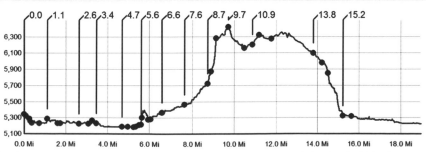

Elev Loss −118 Ft; Climb 2835 Ft; Drop −2954 Ft; Max Elev 6418 Ft; Min Elev 5181 Ft; Map Dist 18.945 Mi; Ground Dist 19.045 Mi

0.1   Beginning at the trailhead parking area is a now-closed track heading east. Walk east on this track a short way until you reach the rim of a shallow draw. The track turns into a use-trail here. 0513854 E, 4328654 N Z12 NAD83.

0.2   Follow the trail east as it descends into the draw, follows the floor of the draw a short way, then climbs back out of it and onto a bench above the river. 0514108 E, 4328630 N Z12 NAD83.

0.4   Continue east on the trail as it crosses the bench and then descends to the cottonwood bottoms next to the San Rafael River. 0514286 E, 4328606 N Z12 NAD83.

0.7   Now follow the trail generally southeast alongside the river, then wade across to the north side. Plan on crossing the river a total of ten times between here and Virgin Springs Canyon. The river gorge gets deeper and narrower from here on as you enter the Little Grand Canyon. 0514755 E, 4328291 N Z12 NAD83.

1.1   The trail continues southeast then turns east. After 0.4 mile you will come to a very nice petroglyph panel on the left (N). The panel is located at the base of the cliffs where the river and trail bend to the south. 0515264 E, 4328183 N Z12 NAD83.

1.6   From the petroglyphs, take the trail south along a bench paralleling the river and then follow it as it crosses to the south side of the river. 0515212 E, 4327408 N Z12 NAD83.

1.7   The trail only stays on the south side of the river for a short time before crossing to the north side again. 0515257 E, 4327213 N Z12 NAD83.

> *Digression:* While on the south side of the river, the trail crosses a wash coming out of a small side canyon on the right (SW). Past the mouth of the canyon you will see the light-colored slag from a mine. This is the Sorrel Mule Mine, a copper mine that was excavated in 1898. It goes 2,000 feet into the cliffs. The narrow side canyon next to the mine is worth a short side trip. There are some interesting miners' inscriptions etched on a wall.

2.6   Continue following the trail generally southeast alongside the north bank of the river. After a mile you will pass the mouth of North Salt Wash. 0516330 E, 4326518 N Z12 NAD83.

3.1   In another half-mile the trail crosses to the south side of the river once again. 0516921 E, 4326295 N Z12 NAD83.

3.2   The trail follows the south side of the river for a short way before crossing again to the north. 0517159 E, 4326419 N Z12 NAD83.

3.4   Here the trail and river swing to the north. Soon the trail crosses to the south side of the river again just before reaching the mouth of a short but very interesting side canyon on the left (N). 0517270 E, 4326692 N Z12 NAD83.

4.7   Take the trail east then southeast to the next crossing. 0518678 E, 4325988 N Z12 NAD83.

5.0   Now go north on the trail and cross to the south side of the river once again. 0518810 E, 4326435 N Z12 NAD83.

5.2   Follow the trail east. The trail crosses back to the north side of the river a short way before reaching the mouth of Virgin Springs Canyon. 0519230 E, 4326410 N Z12 NAD83.

5.3   Go east on the trail a short way until you reach Virgin Springs Canyon on the right (S). Leave the trail here and cross the river into the mouth of the canyon. Although there are some great campsites in the box portion of the canyon, the area has become heavily impacted by backpackers and river-runners. Low-impact camping techniques are essential if you decide to camp here. There are seasonal springs 2.3 miles farther up the canyon at the junction with the West Fork of Virgin Springs Canyon. They are usually running well in the spring and fall and there is camping in the vicinity. 0519340 E, 4326295 N Z12 NAD83.

5.5   Go south up the canyon on a use-trail to where the wash runs along the western side of the canyon. About 12 feet above the ground on the overhanging canyon wall on the right (W) are three outstanding groups of Barrier Canyon style pictographs. They are much smaller than the ones at Buckhorn Draw, but share many similar characteristics and show no signs of vandalism. 0519358 E, 4326038 N Z12 NAD83.

5.6   Continue south up the canyon. Soon you will come to the junction with another use-trail on the left (SE). This is the exit route out of the box and could be easy to miss. The springs are a little farther up the canyon near the end of the box. If you reach the end of the box before finding the exit, simply backtrack until you do. 0519309 E, 4325896 N Z12 NAD83.

Cabin on Sids Mountain.

5.65 Follow the [Class 3] exit trail south as it angles up small ledges. You may have to scramble up a couple of them. When you reach the edge of a slickrock bowl you will intersect a stock trail that comes in from the northeast. This junction is where this hike joins Hike #20. 0519298 E, 4325830 N Z12 NAD83.

5.9 Now follow the stock trail generally southwest around the sandstone bowl and across a talus slope, until you rejoin the floor of Virgin Springs Canyon a short way above the pour-off. There are numerous cairns along the way. 0519087 E, 4325516 N Z12 NAD83.

6.0 Go south up the floor of the canyon. You will soon come to a small pour-off. This can be easily passed on the left (E). 0519085 E, 4325359 N Z12 NAD83.

6.6 Just beyond this pour-off the canyon begins to turn to the southeast. Continue up the canyon. You will encounter a big, semipermanent pothole. 0519727 E, 4324850 N Z12 NAD83.

7.6 Another mile farther up the canyon and you will reach the junction with the West Fork of Virgin Springs Canyon on the right (SW) and its seasonal springs. Should the springs near the junction be dry, try the potholes a little way up the West Fork. If you are planning on doing the hike in three days or more, you can camp near here. If you plan to camp on Sids Mountain, you will need to take enough water to see you all the way to North Salt Wash, 7.6 miles away. 0519961 E, 4323463 N Z12 NAD83.

8.7 Hike #20 continues southeast up Virgin Springs Canyon. Go southwest then south up the West Fork. The canyon becomes bouldery with several easy-to-negotiate pour-offs. In 1.1 miles you will come to a major fork at the base of a buttress near the end of the canyon. 0519980 E, 4321803 N Z12 NAD83.

8.9 You will want to follow the right (SW) fork but there is a large pour-off to be negotiated a short way up. At the junction of the forks, take a faint use-trail south-southwest onto a peninsula between the forks. The trail goes up the talus, angles behind a huge boulder, and then goes up onto a ledge [Class 4, 15']. Follow the ledge southwest. Soon you will reach the bottom of the wash above the pour-off. 0519800 E, 4321665 N Z12 NAD83.

9.1 Look to the south-southwest. The low point on the ridge above is the top of the exit out of the canyon and is 0.3 mile away. To get there, continue up the wash for a short distance until it divides. Take the right (SW) drainage until you can go up the [Class 3] talus on a faint use-trail toward the low spot on the rim. Just before reaching the rim you will come to the base of a cliff. Angle left (SSE) up a fault and over small ledges to the rim. There is a cairn marking the top of the exit. 0519624 E, 4321382 N Z12 NAD83.

9.7 From the rim go generally northwest then east, contouring around to the slickrock saddle on the north-northwest side of the elongated dome marked Swazy 6610. (Swazy is misspelled on the map) 0518941 E, 4321918 N Z12 NAD83.

Digression: You can easily summit the Swazy landform by going southeast up its northwest ramp then south the rest of the way to the top. It will be a 1 mile round trip. From the summit you will see many large Navajo domes around you. It is especially gratifying not to see roads or tracks anywhere! To find the Kofford cabins look to the west-southwest. There is a large, steep-sided, flat-topped dome sitting by itself in a sizeable meadow.

The cabin is between the dome and a slickrock ridge to the north.

10.5   Go west from the saddle down into the wash below. Follow the floor of the wash generally west. As you do, look for two interesting panels of petroglyphs on the right (N). You will come to the junction with a wash coming in on the left (S). 0517869 E, 4321941 N Z12 NAD83.

10.9   Turn left at the junction and follow this wash generally south up to the junction with another wash coming in from the left (SE). 0518063 E, 4321370 N Z12 NAD83.

11.2   From this junction contour south out of the wash, then head south-southwest around the base of a sandstone ridge to the Kofford cabins. The cabins are between the southern end of the ridge and the large Navajo dome to the south-southeast. You will be joining Hike #22 here. 0517798 E, 4321032 N Z12 NAD83.

> *Historical note:* Sids Mountain is named after Sid Swasey who, according to legend, followed a bighorn sheep up its steep flanks and so discovered the mesa. For a number of years Swasey ran stock here in the winter. The unique cabin on stilts was built by Rex Kofford in the 1940s. He had a 440-acre homestead here. The land was later sold to Loren Beach, Monte Swasey, and Clyde Baillings. The BLM acquired the land in 1985. Please do not disturb the cabin.

11.8   From the cabin go generally west-southwest on a stock trail, passing north of the large Navajo dome to the south, until you are south of the third dome to the north marked 6449 on the Sids Mountain map. 0516907 E, 4320841 N Z12 NAD83.

13.8   The trail swings around this dome and heads off to the northwest. Follow the trail generally northwest for 2 miles. 0514998 E, 4323325 N Z12 NAD83.

14.2   The trail parallels a small drainage to the southwest. Then the trail swings to the north and becomes easier to follow. 0514379 E, 4323549 N Z12 NAD83.

14.5   Follow the trail generally north as it angles off of the flat-top and down onto a broad bench that is suspended between the lower end of North Salt Wash and the lower end of Saddle Horse Canyon. 0514364 E, 4324004 N Z12 NAD83.

15.2   The well-cairned trail goes north off the northeast side of the bench at the head of a small draw, then wraps around under the short cliffs on the north side of the bench. The trail then angles generally west-southwest down through talus and small ledges onto the final bench just above the floor of North Salt Wash. Here the trail turns to the northeast and follows the bench back to the head of a small dirt gully. Now follow the trail west down the gully to the floor of North Salt Wash. You will be diverging from Hike #22 here. 0513802 E, 4323982 N Z12 NAD83.

> *Digression:* If you go up North Salt Wash for 0.7 mile you will reach the junction with Saddle Horse Canyon (0513320 E, 4323525 N Z12 NAD83). This wonderful canyon with several springs is a worthy side hike and can be used to create varied loop hikes in the Sids Mountain area (see Hike #22 for details).

15.6   Go down North Salt Wash, first west-northwest then northwest. The canyon turns north here and goes through a narrow break. The big open area to the west is one end of a large abandoned meander, the other end of which is on the other side of the break. There is good camping in the area. 0513477 E, 4324383 N Z12 NAD83.

> *Historical note:* On the northwest wall of the abandoned meander, or rincon, is a small panel of petroglyphs of uncertain origin of a couple of elongated bighorn sheep. On the northern wall is a nice petroglyph panel depicting a probable hunting scene with bison, bighorn sheep, and an armed anthropomorph riding a horse.

19.0   Continue going down North Salt Wash, generally northeast, until you intersect the San Rafael River. 0516330 E, 4326518 N Z12 NAD83.

21.6   Cross to the north side of the river and return the remaining 2.6 miles northwest up the river to the trailhead by retracing your previous steps from here. 0513720 E, 4328664 N Z12 NAD83.

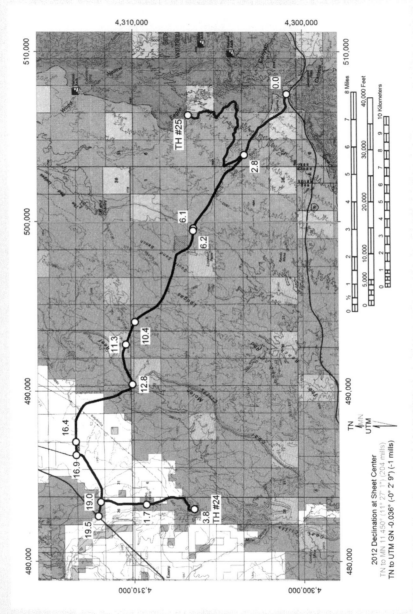

EM803/Moore Cutoff Road Section

Provides access to Hikes #24 and #25.

Access is from Interstate 70 and Highway 10.

1:100,000 maps: Manti, San Rafael Desert.

This paved road goes from Exit 116 on Interstate 70 to the small town of Moore then on to Highway 10. It saves many miles of travel if you are going from Interstate 70 to the upper Castle Valley area (Price and Castle Dale). This road was recently paved and realigned and in many places is not shown on the San Rafael Desert or Salina maps correctly. Its course is accurately shown on the map in this guide. There is decent camping along the many dirt tracks that branch off of the paved road, but be prepared to share the area with cattle and ORV enthusiasts.

0.0 Mileage starts at the sign on the north side of Interstate 70 at Exit 116. From the four-way stop at the end of the exit ramp, turn north to reach the junction with EM803/Moore Cutoff Road. Note that the Interstate and Exit 116 have been realigned since the San Rafael Desert map was last updated, therefore the exit is not shown accurately. 0507503 E, 4300915 N Z12 NAD83.

2.8 Turn left (W) onto the Moore Cutoff Road. (If you go east you will soon come to a turnaround and parking area with great views of Eagle Canyon and beyond.) The road heads generally northwest. You will begin to descend into the South Salt Wash Valley. On the right (NE) will be the junction with a dirt road that goes through a gate. This high-clearance track is TR637 and goes to the start of Eagle Canyon—North and Forgotten Canyon Hike #25 (see map on page 236). 0503929 E, 4303440 N Z12 NAD83.

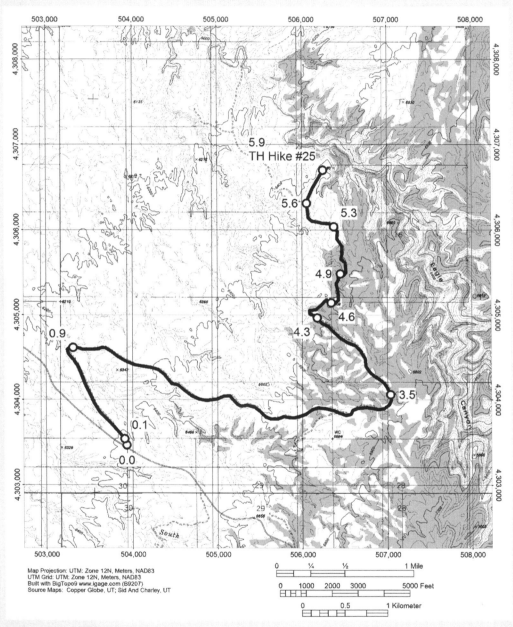

503,000 504,000 505,000 506,000 507,000 508,000

4,308,000

4,307,000

5.9
TH Hike #25

5.6
5.3

4.9

4.6
4.3

0.9

3.5

0.1

0.0

4,306,000

4,305,000

4,304,000

4,303,000

Map Projection: UTM: Zone 12N, Meters, NAD83
UTM Grid: UTM: Zone 12N, Meters, NAD83
Built with BigTopo9 www.igage.com (B9207)
Source Maps: Copper Globe, UT; Sid And Charley, UT

0   ¼   ½   1 Mile

0   1000   2000   3000   5000 Feet

0   0.5   1 Kilometer

1:24,000

TR637

0.0   Mileage begins at the junction with the Moore Cutoff Road. 0503929 E, 4303440 N Z12 NAD83.

0.1   After going northeast through the gate (please close the gate behind you to keep cattle off the road) the road turns to the northwest and you will quickly come to a junction. 0503917 E, 4303533 N Z12 NAD83.

0.9   Go left (NW) and follow the road northwest. The road turns to the east and you will cross a small wash. 0503302 E, 4304647 N Z12 NAD83.

3.5   Follow the road southeast then east as you gradually go uphill. You will cross a couple of small washes, then the road turns to the north and you will come to the top of a rocky, gray hill. The land on the right (S and E) side of the road is within the Sids Mountain Wilderness Study Area and all vehicles are prohibited.

There is a faint, closed track and a cairn on the right. This is the start of the Bighorn Sheep route into Eagle Canyon and will be described in Hike #25 as a digression. It is a far more direct access into the canyon but requires a sketchy, exposed [Class 4] friction traverse that some will find unnerving. 0507042 E, 4304058 N Z12 NAD83.

4.3   The terrain flattens out and the road heads northwest. You will come to the junction with a dirt road on the left. 0506186 E, 4304961 N Z12 NAD83.

4.6   Go straight (NW) through the junction. The road soon turns northeast then briefly southeast. On the right is a USGS benchmark (6608) and a WSA boundary sign. 0506351 E, 4305161 N Z12 NAD83.

4.9   The road turns and heads north. You will cross a rocky wash that may stop some vehicles. If you can't make it across, park near here. The trailhead is about a mile away. 0506351 E, 4305161 N Z12 NAD83.

5.3   Continue heading north. Just as the road begins to turn to the northwest you will come to the junction with a track on the right (N). This track heads north and ends shortly at a turnaround. 0506404 E, 4306036 N Z12 NAD83.

5.6   Go left (NW) and follow the road west then north. You will come to another junction with a track on the right. 0506056 E, 4306335 N Z12 NAD83.

5.9   Turn right onto this track and follow it north. It ends at a turnaround at the end of a peninsula above Eagle Canyon. This is the trailhead for Eagle Canyon—North and Forgotten Canyon Hike #25. 0506307 E, 4306778 N Z12 NAD83.

6.1   Continue following the Moore Cutoff Road northwest. Just as the road turns west will be the junction with TR635 on the left (S). This dirt track heads southwest down South Salt Wash and eventually reaches Interstate 70 at Exit 108. 0499622 E, 4306442 N Z12 NAD83.

6.2   Immediately after the junction with TR635 is the junction with B7696 on the right (N). This high-clearance 4WD track makes for good mountain biking. It heads north to North Salt Wash and the Sid and Charley pinnacle (0500269 E, 4311647 N Z12 NAD83). This is a freestanding pinnacle formed from Entrada Sandstone that sits in the middle of a barren plain. Near the pinnacle are several rock art panels and the remnants of a granary. 0499459 E, 4306465 N Z12 NAD83.

10.4   The road continues generally northwest. This section of the road has been greatly realigned and is not shown accurately on the Salina map. On the right (NE) is the junction with TR633. This high-clearance dirt road goes northeast and joins EM705/Dutch Flat Road. 0494107 E, 4309911 N Z12 NAD83.

11.3   Just before you reach the large cliffs of the Molen Reef will be the junction with B6792 on the right (NE). This high-clearance dirt road also heads northeast to EM705/Dutch Flat Road. 0492741 E, 4310460 N Z12 NAD83.

12.8   The road begins to head to the southwest. As it bends again to the northwest there is a parking area on the right (N). There are several petroglyphs and a small dinosaur trackway located on the scattered boulders here. This is a worthy stop. 0490408 E, 4310099 N Z12 NAD83.

16.4   Follow the road northwest as it climbs up through the Molen Reef. It then turns east and comes to the junction with the paved EM802 on the right (N). EM802 goes north for 3.8 miles and joins Highway 10 south of Ferron. 0487022 E, 4313429 N Z12 NAD83.

16.9   Go straight (W) through the junction. You will come to a stop sign in Moore at the junction with EM801. 0486200 E, 4313416 N Z12 NAD83.

19.0   Go left (S) onto EM801 and follow this paved road south then southwest. After the road turns west you will reach the junction with EM805 on the left (S). This dirt road leads to the Rochester Rock Art Site and has a sign saying so. 0483486 E, 4311972 N Z12 NAD83.

EM805

0.0   Mileage begins at the junction of EM801 and EM805. 0483486 E, 4311972 N Z12 NAD83.

1.7   Head south on EM805. This good dirt road is suitable for most vehicles unless wet or snowy. The road passes through private land. Be sure to stay on the main road. You will pass a radio tower on the left (E). 0483337 E, 4309274 N Z12 NAD83.

3.8   Continue heading generally south on the main dirt road until you reach its end at a turnaround. This is the trailhead for the Rochester Petroglyphs Hike #24. There is a sign and trail register. 0483086 E, 4306440 N Z12 NAD83.

19.5   Continue heading west on EM801 to reach the junction with Highway 10. This signed junction is just north of Emery. 0482562 E, 4312062 N Z12 NAD83.

Hike #24: Rochester Petroglyphs

Season:	Any.
Time and distance:	One to two hours to view the rock art. Actual hiking time is twenty minutes (0.8 mile round trip).
Water:	None. Bring your own.
Maps:	Emery East. (Salina.)
Loop hike:	No.
Skill level:	(1A) Easy route finding. [Class 1] walking. This is an easy hike for all, from kids to seniors.

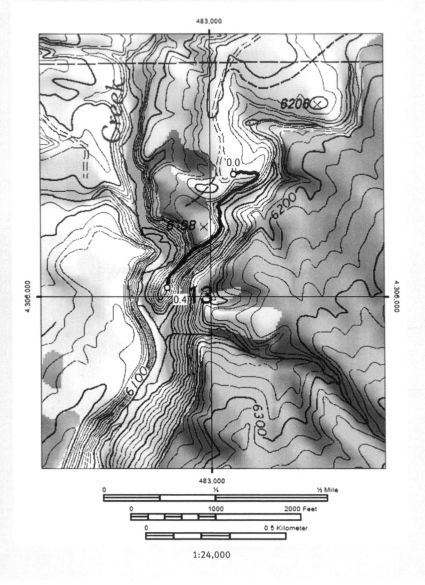

1:24,000

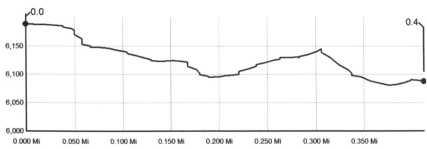

Elev Loss −101 Ft; Climb 75 Ft; Drop −177 Ft; Max Elev 6188 Ft; Min Elev 6078 Ft; Map Dist 0.413 Mi; Ground Dist 0.418 Mi

It may be out of character to have such a short hike listed in this guide, but the quality of this excursion deserves more than just a sidebar in a road section. The route follows a short trail to an extraordinary set of Southern San Rafael Fremont style petroglyph panels. This is perhaps the finest and most prolific site in the Swell. There are more than 100 figures in one panel alone. Some of these unusual looking images, especially the zoomorphs, have led to some pretty "fantastical" interpretations. The panels are located at the end of a peninsula of rock overlooking Muddy Creek on big stone blocks, resembling monumental monoliths, adding to the mystique. Luckily, there has been very little vandalism here. Please do your part to help preserve this important cultural site.

0.0	Mileage begins at the trailhead parking area at the sign and trail register. 0483086 E, 4306440 N Z12 NAD83.
0.4	Take the trail as it switchbacks down an open slope into the canyon that's to the southeast, then follow it generally southwest down the canyon. The trail gradually traverses to the top of the talus above the wash to a ridge separating the canyon from Muddy Creek. Just before you reach the ridge is a small group of petroglyphs on the right (NW). Follow the top of the ridge southwest to the main panels on the "standing stones" at its end. Look carefully as there are petroglyphs all around the end of the ridge. 0482844 E, 4306031 N Z12 NAD83.
0.8	After viewing the rock art, return to the trailhead the way you came. 0483086 E, 4306440 N Z12 NAD83.

> *Rock climber's note:* There is a cliff band of exceptionally solid rock running through the area. It is from fifteen to sixty feet high and provides many crack climbs, from on-widths to chimneys.

Hike #25: Eagle Canyon—North and Forgotten Canyon

SEASON:	Any. Spring and fall are best. No snow. After recent rains the pools in Forgotten Canyon may prove daunting. There is the potential for flash floods in both canyons.

Rochester petroglyphs detail.

TIME AND DISTANCE:	Part 1: Four to five hours (7.6 miles). Part 2: Five or six hours (9 miles).
WATER:	There is always water below the fall in Eagle Canyon. Forgotten Canyon has seasonal potholes. Bring your own water.
MAPS:	Sid and Charley. (San Rafael Desert.)
LOOP HIKE:	No.
SKILL LEVEL:	Part 1: Eagle Canyon (1A) Easy route finding. [Class 2] walking. Part 2: Forgotten Canyon (2A) Easy route finding. [Class 3] scrambling, [Class 5] climbing. A short length of rope or webbing may prove useful in aiding less adept climbers.

Eagle Canyon, as it drops from south to north, from the Swasey cabin area at the Head of Sinbad to North Salt Wash, is divided at its northern end by an impassable fall. Because of its easy access, the midsection of the canyon from Interstate 70 north to the fall is popular with ORV users and can be quite busy. Unbeknownst to most, though, is that the north part of Eagle Canyon, the section below the fall, is as peaceful as they come and contains one of the premier canyons in the northern part of the Swell (Forgotten Canyon).

The hike starts at the western edge of the Swell and goes up Eagle Canyon to the impassable fall. Part 1 returns the same way and makes for an easy day hike. Part 2 ascends Forgotten Canyon. With its [Class 5] boulder problems and muddy potholes, this route is for competent, experienced canyoneers. The rewards are splendid. Tight narrows and the spectacular Raptor Arch await the capable explorer. An alternate start to this hike follows a bighorn sheep route into the canyon and saves some miles. But it requires [Class 3] scrambling and an exposed, [Class 4] friction traverse that would prove impossible if the route was wet.

Part 1

0.0 Mileage begins at the turnaround and small parking area. 0506307 E, 4306778 N Z12 NAD83.

0.1 To the east of the parking area is a side canyon heading generally north into Eagle Canyon.

Head southeast along the top of the ridge above the side canyon and find the USGS benchmark shown as elevation 6396 on the Sid and Charley map (0506372 E, 4306721 N Z12 NAD83). From the benchmark follow a faint trail east down through the rubble toward the side canyon. The trail angles down to a cairn on the inner rim of the canyon. 0506438 E, 4306724 N Z12 NAD83.

0.3 Scramble east down into the floor of the side canyon. Several cairns mark the bottom of this descent. These will be useful on the return trip. Go north then northwest down the bouldery floor of the canyon. Bypass a fall by following a cairned route on the right (NNE). Just beyond the fall you will reach the junction with Eagle Canyon. 0506336 E, 4306988 N Z12 NAD83.

1.3 Now head generally southeast up Eagle Canyon. The canyon winds a bit and the going is easy along the sandy floor. You will pass a short side canyon on the left (SE). The main canyon goes south here. 0507305 E, 4306177 N Z12 NAD83.

2.5 The canyon heads generally southeast again. Another short side canyon enters from the left (SE) where the canyon turns southwest. 0507718 E, 4304961 N Z12 NAD83.

2.7 The canyon quickly turns southeast. Just before it turns to the southwest again is the bottom of the bighorn sheep route on the right (W). 0507830 E, 4304672 N Z12 NAD83.

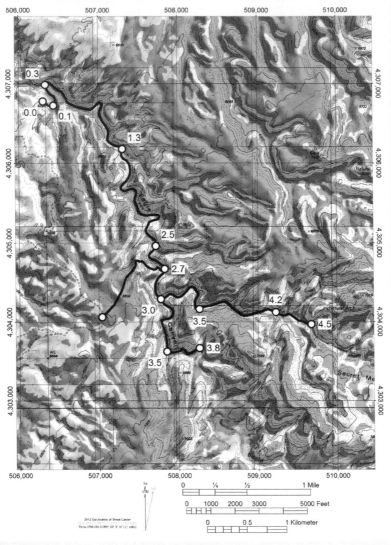

1:24,000

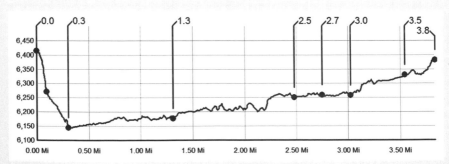

Elev Loss −34 Ft; Climb 877 Ft; Drop −911 Ft; Max Elev 6416 Ft; Min Elev 6143 Ft; Map Dist 3.839 Mi; Ground Dist 3.869 Mi

Digression: The bighorn sheep route [Class 4] coupled with Part 2 of this hike makes a challenging, but very rewarding, day hike for experienced canyoneers. From mile 3.5 on TR637 (0507042 E, 4304058 N Z12 NAD83) follow a north-northeast bearing through the pinyons and junipers and cross a shallow wash. Use elevation 6802 as a handrail and head out onto a peninsula between forming washes. Follow the top of the peninsula north-northeast to a cairn near its end (0507464 E, 4304739 N Z12 NAD83). A faint trail and cairns show the way from here. Drop down toward the detached pinnacle at the very end of the peninsula. In the saddle just before you reach the pinnacle is another cairn (0507471 E, 4304771 N Z12 NAD83). Go east off the saddle to the next cairn (0507487 E, 4304776 N Z12 NAD83). Now zigzag southeast down steep, loose dirt to another cairn at the top of a break in a cliff band (0507514 E, 4304762 N Z12 NAD83). Go down through the cliff and begin zigzagging east down the large talus apron. About halfway down it the trail begins to angle toward a white sandstone shoulder to the southeast. Follow it out onto the end of the shoulder (0507695 E, 4304659 N Z12 NAD83). From there the trail goes northeast down a series of ledges and onto a sandy shoulder (0507740 E, 4304694 N Z12 NAD83). Head southeast down a small gully to its end at a 40-foot drop above the canyon floor (0507787 E, 4304644 N Z12 NAD83). There is a thin, dark band imbedded in the sandstone creating a sloping ledge. Traverse left (NE) [Class 4] along the ledge and around the corner. The traverse is a little intimidating since you won't be able to see what's on the other side. Once around the bend the route mellows out for the last little scramble east down to the canyon floor (0507830 E, 4304672 N Z12 NAD83). From TR637 to the floor of the canyon is just under a mile.

3.0   Follow the canyon generally south. The next side canyon on the left (ENE) is Forgotten Canyon and the beginning of Part 2 of this hike. 0507779 E, 4304288 N Z12 NAD83.

3.5   Continue going generally south up Eagle Canyon. After 0.5 mile the canyon turns abruptly to the east. This is the beginning of a short narrows. This can be fun to negotiate but if it is wet there is a bypass

Forgotten Canyon.

route on the right (SW) that follows ledges east. 0507855 E, 4303622 N Z12 NAD83.

3.8 Head east through or around the narrows. Just beyond the narrows the canyon ends at a perennial pool, and a large Douglas fir beneath an impassable fall. 0508266 E, 4303667 N Z12 NAD83.

7.6 Return the way you came. 0506307 E, 4306778 N Z12 NAD83.

Part 2

Mileage resumes from mile 3.0 at the mouth of Forgotten Canyon.

3.5 Head east-northeast up Forgotten Canyon. You will immediately enter the narrows and quickly come to the first of three [Class 5] chockstones. These boulder problems are exacerbated by muddy pools at their bases that must first be negotiated. Climbing these obstacles can be especially challenging when you are dripping with mud. After the boulders the canyon turns to the south then makes a hard turn to the east and you will come to a large fall. 0508264 E, 4304162 N Z12 NAD83.

4.2 Pass the fall by ascending a friction slab on the right (S) and traversing back to the floor of the canyon above the fall [Class 4]. Another small pour-off is easily bypassed on the left (N). Once through the narrow section the canyon opens and enters a park-like area. 0509225 E, 4304123 N Z12 NAD83.

4.5 To find Raptor Arch follow the main wash east-southeast. You will pass two side canyons on the left (N). The third side canyon on the left (NE) contains the arch. It is easy to miss. Look for it perched at the head of this short, narrow canyon. It is shown as "Natural Arch" on the Sid and Charley map. 0509678 E, 4303970 N Z12 NAD83.

9.0 Retrace your steps back to the start. 0506307 E, 4306778 N Z12 NAD83.

Bibliography

Abbey, Edward and Philip Hyde. *Slickrock: The Canyon Country of Southeast Utah*. San Francisco: Sierra Club Books, 1971.

Aitchison, Stewart. *Utah Wildlands*. Salt Lake City: Utah Geographic Series, Inc., 1987.

Baars, Donald L. *Canyonlands Country*. Lawrence, Kans.: Cañon Publishers Ltd., 1989.

———. *Red Rock Country: The Geologic History of the Colorado Plateau*. Garden City, N.Y.: Doubleday, 1972.

———. *The Colorado Plateau: A Geologic History*. Albuquerque: University of New Mexico Press, 1983.

Baker, Pearl. *The Wild Bunch at Robbers Roost*. New York: Abelard-Schuman, 1965.

Baker, Pearl and Fern Farmon. Interviewed by Dee Anne Finken, Green River, Utah, July 12, 1977. San Rafael Swell Oral History Project. MSS 7752. L. Tom Perry Special Collections Library, Brigham Young University, Provo, Utah.

Barnes, F. A. *Canyon Country*. Salt Lake City: Wasatch Publishers, Inc., 1986.

———. *Canyon Country Prehistoric Rock Art*. Salt Lake City: Wasatch Publishers, Inc., 1978.

Barnes, F. A. and Michaelene Pendleton. *Canyon Country Prehistoric Indians*. Salt Lake City: Wasatch Publishers, Inc., 1979.

Bauman, Joseph. *Stone House Lands*. Salt Lake City: University of Utah Press, 1987.

Biddlecome, Millie and Hazel B. Ekker. *To Only the Fittest*. Cedar City: Privately printed by Gaye Ekker Thurston, 1974.

Bjornstad, Eric. *Desert Rock*. Denver: Chockstone Press, 1988.

Brower, David. *The Meaning of Wilderness to Science*. San Francisco: Sierra Club, 1960.

Castleton, Kenneth Bitner. *Petroglyphs and Pictographs of Utah.* Vol. 1. Salt Lake City: Utah Museum of Natural History, 1978.

Chronic, Halka. *Pages of Stone: Geology of the Western National Parks.* Seattle: The Mountaineers, 1986.

———. *Roadside Geology of Utah.* Missoula: Mountain Press Publishing, 1990.

Crampton, Gregory C. *Standing Up Country: The Canyon Lands of Utah and Arizona.* New York: Alfred A. Knopf, 1964.

Culmer, H. L. A. "Diary, 1909." MSS A 79-3. Utah State Historical Society, Salt Lake City.

———. "The San Rafael Swell." *Salt Lake Herald,* May 9, 1909.

Doolittle, Jerome. *Canyons and Mesas.* New York City: Time-Life Books, 1974.

Durrant, Jeffrey O. *Struggle Over Utah's San Rafael Swell: Wilderness, National Conservation Areas, and National Monuments.* Tucson: University of Arizona Press, 2007.

Ekker, Barbara. Miscellaneous Papers. Papers in the possession of Barbara Ekker and Steve Allen.

Ekker, Sylvia Harris. "Grand County (Utah) Historical Preservation Human History Program Collection, 1997." MSS B 1007. Interviewed by Bette L. Stanton, September 3–5, 1996, and July 1997. Utah State Historical Society, Salt Lake City, Utah.

Ekker, Ted. Interviewed by Steve Allen, Green River, Utah, March 22, 2000. Transcribed by Ellen Meehan.

Elmore, Francis H. *Shrubs and Trees of the Southwest Uplands.* Tucson: Southwest Parks and Monuments Association, 1976.

Emery County Archives. No title. Mountain West Digital Archives. Southern Utah University, Sherratt Library, Cedar City.

Farrer, William. "William Farrer Diary." In *Journals of Forty-niners: Salt Lake City to Los Angeles,* edited by Leroy R. Hafen. Glendale, Calif.: Arthur H. Clark, 1954.

Finken, Dee Anne. *A History of the San Rafael Swell.* Price, Utah: Western Interstate Commission for Higher Education, 1977.

Forgey, William. *Wilderness Medicine.* Merrillville, Ind.: ICS Books, 1987.

Geary, Edward A. *A History of Emery County.* Salt Lake City: Utah State Historical Society, 1996.

Hite, Ben R. "One of the Hites: Ben R., a Brother of Cass, Arrives in This City from the San Juan District." *Rocky Mountain News,* January 13, 1898.

Jennings, Jesse David. *Prehistory of Utah and the Eastern Great Basin.* Salt Lake City: University of Utah Press, 1978.

Kirk, Ruth. *Desert: The American Southwest.* Boston: Houghton Mifflin Co., 1973.

Larsen, Valera Fillmore. "Biography of Alma Staker, Pioneer." In the Alma Staker file. History Department, Daughters of Utah Pioneers, Salt Lake City.

Lister, Florence C. and Robert H. Lister. *Earl Morris and Southwestern Archaeology*. Albuquerque: University of New Mexico Press, 1968.

MacMahon, James A. *Deserts*. New York: Alfred A. Knopf, Inc., 1985.

May, Dean L. *Utah: A People's History*. Salt Lake City: University of Utah Press, 1987.

McClenahan, Owen. *Utah's Scenic San Rafael*. Castle Dale, Utah: Privately printed, 1986.

McElprang, Stella. *Castle Valley: A History of Emery County*: Emery County Company of the Daughters of Utah Pioneers, 1949.

McKern, Sharon S. *Living Prehistory: An Introduction to Physical Anthropology and Archaeology*. Menlo Park, Calif.: Cummings Publishing Company, 1974.

Pratt, Orville C. "The Journal of Orville C. Pratt." In *Old Spanish Trail*, edited by Leroy R. and Ann W. Hafen. Glendale, Calif: Arthur H. Clark, 1954.

Rigby, J. Keith. *Northern Colorado Plateau*. Dubuque, Iowa: Kendall/Hunt Publishing Co., 1976.

The Roads Less Traveled: Self Guided Driving Tours in the Northern San Rafael Swell. Vol. 1 of *Emory County, Utah*. Moab: Way Out Ideas and Emery County Travel Bureau, 2004.

Schaafsma, Polly. *Indian Rock Art of the Southwest*. Santa Fe: School of American Research, 1980.

Seely, Montell. *Emery County, 1880–1980*. Castle Dale, Utah: Emery County Historical Society, 1981.

Silliman, Bert J. Bert J. Silliman Papers. MSS B 202 Box 1. Utah State Historical Society, Salt Lake City.

Skinner, Brian J. *Physical Geology*. New York: Wiley, 1987.

Smith, Betty. Interview with Steve Allen, Green River, Utah, April 18, 2000. Transcribed by Ellen Meehan.

Smith, Muriel W. *They Were Here: Stories and Statistics of the People of Elgin, Utah and Green River, Utah*. Valley City, Utah: M.W. Smith, 2003.

Stokes, William Lee. *Geology of Utah*. Salt Lake City: Utah Museum of Natural History, 1986.

———. *Scenes of the Plateau Lands and How They Came To Be*. Salt Lake City: Publishers Press, 1971.

Strong, Emory. *Stone Age in the Great Basin*. Portland, Oreg.: Binford and Mort, 1969.

Swasey, Lee Mont. Interview with Steve Allen, Ferron, Utah, February 12, 2005. Transcribed by Ellen Meehan.

Welsh, Stanley L. and Bill Ratcliffe. *Flowers of the Canyon Country*. Moab, Utah: Canyonlands Natural History Association, 1971.

U.S. Department of the Interior. *Geology and Oil and Gas Prospects of Part of the San Rafael Swell, Utah*, by James Gilluly. U.S. Geological Survey Bulletin Number 806. Washington, DC: Government Printing Office, 1928.

U.S. Department of the Interior. *The Green River and its Utilization*, by Ralf R. Woolley. U.S. Geological Survey Water Supply Paper Number 618. Washington, DC: Government Printing Office, 1930.

Works Progress Administration. Utah Geographical Place Names Committee Records, 1938–1943. MSS.B. 721. Works Progress Administration Collection. Utah State Historical Society, Salt Lake City.

Works Progress Administration Writers' Program. *Utah: A Guide to the State*. Salt Lake City: Utah State Institute of Fine Arts, 1941.